# LIVING LITURGY™

## SUNDAY MISSAL

## 2017

## CELEBRATING THE EUCHARIST

℔

**LITURGICAL PRESS**
Collegeville, Minnesota

www.litpress.org

# Contents

The Order of Mass   **1**

Celebration of the Liturgy of the Word
[with Holy Communion]   **27**

# The Order of Mass

## THE INTRODUCTORY RITES

### ENTRANCE CHANT                                              STAND

### SIGN OF THE CROSS

Priest:   In the name of the Father, and of the Son, and of
the Holy Spirit.

People:   **Amen.**

### GREETING

**A**   Priest:   The grace of our Lord Jesus Christ,
and the love of God,
and the communion of the Holy Spirit
be with you all.

People:   **And with your spirit.**

**B**   Priest:   Grace to you and peace from God our Father
and the Lord Jesus Christ.

People:   **And with your spirit.**

**C**   Priest:   The Lord be with you.

People:   **And with your spirit.**

### PENITENTIAL ACT

**A**   Priest:   Brethren (brothers and sisters), let us acknowledge our sins,
and so prepare ourselves to celebrate the sacred
mysteries. (Pause)

All:   **I confess to almighty God**
**and to you, my brothers and sisters,**
**that I have greatly sinned,**
**in my thoughts and in my words,**
**in what I have done and in what I have failed**
**to do,**

And, striking their breast, they say:

**through my fault, through my fault,**
**through my most grievous fault;**

Then they continue:

> **therefore I ask blessed Mary ever-Virgin,**
> **all the Angels and Saints,**
> **and you, my brothers and sisters,**
> **to pray for me to the Lord our God.**

Priest:  May almighty God have mercy on us,
forgive us our sins,
and bring us to everlasting life.

People:  **Amen.**

**B**  Priest:  Brethren (brothers and sisters), let us
acknowledge our sins,
and so prepare ourselves to celebrate the sacred
mysteries. (Pause)

Priest:  Have mercy on us, O Lord.
People:  **For we have sinned against you.**

Priest:  Show us, O Lord, your mercy.
People:  **And grant us your salvation.**

Priest:  May almighty God have mercy on us,
forgive us our sins,
and bring us to everlasting life.

People:  **Amen.**

**C**  These or other invocations may be used:

Priest:  Brethren (brothers and sisters), let us
acknowledge our sins,
and so prepare ourselves to celebrate the sacred
mysteries. (Pause)

Priest (Deacon or another minister):
You were sent to heal the contrite of heart:
Lord, have mercy.    Or:  Kyrie, eleison.

People:  **Lord, have mercy.**    Or:  **Kyrie, eleison.**

Priest:  You came to call sinners:
Christ, have mercy.    Or:  Christe, eleison.

People:  **Christ, have mercy.**    Or:  **Christe, eleison.**

Priest: You are seated at the right hand of the Father to
intercede for us:
Lord, have mercy.   Or:  Kyrie, eleison.

People: **Lord, have mercy.**   Or:  **Kyrie, eleison.**

Priest: May almighty God have mercy on us,
forgive us our sins,
and bring us to everlasting life.

People: **Amen.**

## KYRIE

The **Kyrie, eleison** (Lord, have mercy) invocations follow, unless they have just occurred in a formula of the Penitential Act.

℣. Lord, have mercy.        ℟. **Lord, have mercy.**
℣. Christ, have mercy.      ℟. **Christ, have mercy.**
℣. Lord, have mercy.        ℟. **Lord, have mercy.**

Or:

℣. Kyrie, eleison.          ℟. **Kyrie, eleison.**
℣. Christe, eleison.        ℟. **Christe, eleison.**
℣. Kyrie, eleison.          ℟. **Kyrie, eleison.**

## GLORIA

All:  **Glory to God in the highest,
and on earth peace to people of good will.**

**We praise you,
we bless you,
we adore you,
we glorify you,
we give you thanks for your great glory,
Lord God, heavenly King,
O God, almighty Father.**

**Lord Jesus Christ, Only Begotten Son,
Lord God, Lamb of God, Son of the Father,
you take away the sins of the world,
    have mercy on us;
you take away the sins of the world,
    receive our prayer;
you are seated at the right hand of the Father,
    have mercy on us.**

**For you alone are the Holy One,**
**you alone are the Lord,**
**you alone are the Most High,**
**Jesus Christ,**
**with the Holy Spirit,**
**in the glory of God the Father.**
**Amen.**

## COLLECT (OPENING PRAYER)

Priest:  **Let us pray.**

All pray in silence with the Priest for a while.

Then the Priest, with hands extended, says the Collect prayer, at the end of which the people acclaim:

**Amen.**

# THE LITURGY OF THE WORD

## FIRST READING                                                    SIT

Then the reader goes to the ambo and reads the First Reading, while all sit and listen.

To indicate the end of the reading, the reader acclaims:

**The word of the Lord.**

All:  **Thanks be to God.**

## RESPONSORIAL PSALM

The psalmist or cantor sings or says the Psalm, with the people making the response.

## SECOND READING

After this, if there is to be a Second Reading, a reader reads it from the ambo, as above.

To indicate the end of the reading, the reader acclaims:

**The word of the Lord.**

All:  **Thanks be to God.**

## GOSPEL ACCLAMATION                                         STAND

There follows the **Alleluia** or another chant laid down by the rubrics, as the liturgical time requires.

GOSPEL DIALOGUE

Deacon or Priest: The Lord be with you.

People: **And with your spirit.**

Deacon or Priest: A reading from the holy Gospel according to N.

People: **Glory to you, O Lord.**

GOSPEL READING

At the end of the Gospel, the Deacon, or the Priest, acclaims:

The Gospel of the Lord.

All: **Praise to you, Lord Jesus Christ.**

HOMILY **SIT**

PROFESSION OF FAITH **STAND**

All: **I believe in one God,**
**the Father almighty,**
**maker of heaven and earth,**
**of all things visible and invisible.**

**I believe in one Lord Jesus Christ,**
**the Only Begotten Son of God,**
**born of the Father before all ages.**
**God from God, Light from Light,**
**true God from true God,**
**begotten, not made, consubstantial with the Father;**
**through him all things were made.**
**For us men and for our salvation**
**he came down from heaven,**

At the words that follow, up to and including **and became man**, all bow.

**and by the Holy Spirit was incarnate of the Virgin Mary,**
**and became man.**

**For our sake he was crucified under Pontius Pilate,**
**he suffered death and was buried,**
**and rose again on the third day**
**in accordance with the Scriptures.**

**He ascended into heaven**
**and is seated at the right hand of the Father.**
**He will come again in glory**
**to judge the living and the dead**
**and his kingdom will have no end.**

**I believe in the Holy Spirit, the Lord, the giver of life,**
**who proceeds from the Father and the Son,**
**who with the Father and the Son is adored and**
**glorified,**
**who has spoken through the prophets.**

**I believe in one, holy, catholic and apostolic Church.**
**I confess one Baptism for the forgiveness of sins**
**and I look forward to the resurrection of the dead**
**and the life of the world to come. Amen.**

Instead of the Niceno-Constantinopolitan Creed, especially during Lent and Easter Time, the baptismal Symbol of the Roman Church, known as the Apostles' Creed, may be used.

All:   **I believe in God,**
**the Father almighty,**
**Creator of heaven and earth,**
**and in Jesus Christ, his only Son, our Lord,**

At the words that follow, up to and including the Virgin Mary, all bow.

**who was conceived by the Holy Spirit,**
**born of the Virgin Mary,**
**suffered under Pontius Pilate,**
**was crucified, died and was buried;**
**he descended into hell;**
**on the third day he rose again from the dead;**
**he ascended into heaven,**
**and is seated at the right hand of God the Father**
**almighty;**
**from there he will come to judge the living and the**
**dead.**

**I believe in the Holy Spirit,**
**the holy catholic Church,**
**the communion of saints,**
**the forgiveness of sins,**
**the resurrection of the body,**
**and life everlasting. Amen.**

UNIVERSAL PRAYER
(*or* PRAYER OF THE FAITHFUL *or* BIDDING PRAYERS)

## THE LITURGY OF THE EUCHARIST

PRESENTATION AND PREPARATION OF THE GIFTS **SIT**

The Priest, standing at the altar, takes the paten with the bread and holds it slightly raised above the altar with both hands, saying in a low voice:

**Blessed are you, Lord God of all creation,**
**for through your goodness we have received**
**the bread we offer you:**
**fruit of the earth and work of human hands,**
**it will become for us the bread of life.**

If, however, the Offertory Chant is not sung, the Priest may speak these words aloud; at the end, the people may acclaim:

**Blessed be God for ever.**

The Deacon, or the Priest, pours wine and a little water into the chalice, saying quietly:

**By the mystery of this water and wine**
**may we come to share in the divinity of Christ**
**who humbled himself to share in our humanity.**

The Priest then takes the chalice and holds it slightly raised above the altar with both hands, saying in a low voice:

**Blessed are you, Lord God of all creation,**
**for through your goodness we have received**
**the wine we offer you:**
**fruit of the vine and work of human hands,**
**it will become our spiritual drink.**

If, however, the Offertory Chant is not sung, the Priest may speak these words aloud; at the end, the people may acclaim:

**Blessed be God for ever.**

After this, the Priest, bowing profoundly, says quietly:

**With humble spirit and contrite heart**
**may we be accepted by you, O Lord,**
**and may our sacrifice in your sight this day**
**be pleasing to you, Lord God.**

Then the Priest, standing at the side of the altar, washes his hands, saying quietly:

**Wash me, O Lord, from my iniquity**
**and cleanse me from my sin.**

Standing at the middle of the altar, facing the people, extending and then joining his hands, he says:

**Pray, brethren (brothers and sisters),**
**that my sacrifice and yours**
**may be acceptable to God,**
**the almighty Father.**

The people rise and reply:　　　　　　　　　　　　　　**STAND**

**May the Lord accept the sacrifice at your hands**
**for the praise and glory of his name,**
**for our good**
**and the good of all his holy Church.**

### PRAYER OVER THE OFFERINGS

Then the Priest, with hands extended, says the Prayer over the Offerings, at the end of which the people acclaim:

**Amen.**

## THE EUCHARISTIC PRAYER

Priest:　The Lord be with you.

People:　**And with your spirit.**

Priest:　Lift up your hearts.

People:　**We lift them up to the Lord.**

Priest:　Let us give thanks to the Lord our God.

People:　**It is right and just.**

### PREFACE

## PREFACE ACCLAMATION

At the end of the Preface he joins his hands and concludes the Preface with the people, singing or saying aloud:

**Holy, Holy, Holy Lord God of hosts.**
**Heaven and earth are full of your glory.**
**Hosanna in the highest.**
**Blessed is he who comes in the name of the Lord.**
**Hosanna in the highest.**

## EUCHARISTIC PRAYER I (The Roman Canon)          **KNEEL**

Priest:

To you, therefore, most merciful Father,
we make humble prayer and petition
through Jesus Christ, your Son, our Lord:
that you accept
and bless ✛ these gifts, these offerings,
these holy and unblemished sacrifices,
which we offer you firstly
for your holy catholic Church.
Be pleased to grant her peace,
to guard, unite and govern her
throughout the whole world,
together with your servant N. our Pope
and N. our Bishop,*
and all those who, holding to the truth,
hand on the catholic and apostolic faith.

Commemoration of the Living

Remember, Lord, your servants N. and N.
and all gathered here,
whose faith and devotion are known to you.
For them, we offer you this sacrifice of praise
or they offer it for themselves
and all who are dear to them:
for the redemption of their souls,
in hope of health and well-being,
and paying their homage to you,
the eternal God, living and true.

In communion with those whose memory we venerate,
especially the glorious ever-Virgin Mary,

---

*Mention may be made here of the Coadjutor Bishop, or Auxiliary Bishops,
as noted in the *General Instruction of the Roman Missal*, no. 149.

Mother of our God and Lord, Jesus Christ,
† and blessed Joseph, her Spouse,
your blessed Apostles and Martyrs,
Peter and Paul, Andrew,
(James, John,
Thomas, James, Philip,
Bartholomew, Matthew,
Simon and Jude;
Linus, Cletus, Clement, Sixtus,
Cornelius, Cyprian,
Lawrence, Chrysogonus,
John and Paul,
Cosmas and Damian)
and all your Saints;
we ask that through their merits and prayers,
in all things we may be defended
by your protecting help.
(Through Christ our Lord. Amen.)

On the Nativity of the Lord and throughout the Octave
Celebrating the most sacred night (day)
on which blessed Mary the immaculate Virgin
brought forth the Savior for this world,
and in communion with those whose memory we venerate,
especially the glorious ever-Virgin Mary,
Mother of our God and Lord, Jesus Christ, †

On the Epiphany of the Lord
Celebrating the most sacred day
on which your Only Begotten Son,
eternal with you in your glory,
appeared in a human body, truly sharing our flesh,
and in communion with those whose memory we venerate,
especially the glorious ever-Virgin Mary,
Mother of our God and Lord, Jesus Christ, †

From the Mass of the Easter Vigil until the Second Sunday of Easter
Celebrating the most sacred night (day)
of the Resurrection of our Lord Jesus Christ in the flesh,
and in communion with those whose memory we venerate,
especially the glorious ever-Virgin Mary,
Mother of our God and Lord, Jesus Christ, †

On the Ascension of the Lord
Celebrating the most sacred day
on which your Only Begotten Son, our Lord,
placed at the right hand of your glory

our weak human nature,
which he had united to himself,
and in communion with those whose memory we venerate,
especially the glorious ever-Virgin Mary,
Mother of our God and Lord, Jesus Christ, †

*On Pentecost Sunday*

Celebrating the most sacred day of Pentecost,
on which the Holy Spirit
appeared to the Apostles in tongues of fire,
and in communion with those whose memory we venerate,
especially the glorious ever-Virgin Mary,
Mother of our God and Lord, Jesus Christ, †

Therefore, Lord, we pray:
graciously accept this oblation of our service,
that of your whole family;
order our days in your peace,
and command that we be delivered from eternal damnation
and counted among the flock of those you have chosen.
(Through Christ our Lord. Amen.)

*From the Mass of the Easter Vigil until the Second Sunday of Easter*

Therefore, Lord, we pray:
graciously accept this oblation of our service,
that of your whole family,
which we make to you
also for those to whom you have been pleased to give
the new birth of water and the Holy Spirit,
granting them forgiveness of all their sins:
order our days in your peace,
and command that we be delivered from eternal damnation
and counted among the flock of those you have chosen.
(Through Christ our Lord. Amen.)

Be pleased, O God, we pray,
to bless, acknowledge,
and approve this offering in every respect;
make it spiritual and acceptable,
so that it may become for us
the Body and Blood of your most beloved Son,
our Lord Jesus Christ.

On the day before he was to suffer,
he took bread in his holy and venerable hands,
and with eyes raised to heaven

to you, O God, his almighty Father,
giving you thanks, he said the blessing,
broke the bread
and gave it to his disciples, saying:

TAKE THIS, ALL OF YOU, AND EAT OF IT,

FOR THIS IS MY BODY,

WHICH WILL BE GIVEN UP FOR YOU.

In a similar way, when supper was ended,
he took this precious chalice
in his holy and venerable hands,
and once more giving you thanks, he said the blessing
and gave the chalice to his disciples, saying:

TAKE THIS, ALL OF YOU, AND DRINK FROM IT,

FOR THIS IS THE CHALICE OF MY BLOOD,

THE BLOOD OF THE NEW AND ETERNAL COVENANT,

WHICH WILL BE POURED OUT FOR YOU AND FOR MANY

FOR THE FORGIVENESS OF SINS.

DO THIS IN MEMORY OF ME.

The mystery of faith.

And the people continue, acclaiming:

A We proclaim your Death, O Lord,
and profess your Resurrection
until you come again.

B When we eat this Bread and drink this Cup,
we proclaim your Death, O Lord,
until you come again.

C Save us, Savior of the world,
for by your Cross and Resurrection
you have set us free.

Priest:
Therefore, O Lord,
as we celebrate the memorial of the blessed Passion,
the Resurrection from the dead,
and the glorious Ascension into heaven
of Christ, your Son, our Lord,
we, your servants and your holy people,
offer to your glorious majesty
from the gifts that you have given us,
this pure victim,
this holy victim,

this spotless victim,
the holy Bread of eternal life
and the Chalice of everlasting salvation.

Be pleased to look upon these offerings
with a serene and kindly countenance,
and to accept them,
as once you were pleased to accept
the gifts of your servant Abel the just,
the sacrifice of Abraham, our father in faith,
and the offering of your high priest Melchizedek,
a holy sacrifice, a spotless victim.

In humble prayer we ask you, almighty God:
command that these gifts be borne
by the hands of your holy Angel
to your altar on high
in the sight of your divine majesty,
so that all of us, who through this participation at the altar
receive the most holy Body and Blood of your Son,
may be filled with every grace and heavenly blessing.
(Through Christ our Lord. Amen.)

Commemoration of the Dead

Remember also, Lord, your servants N. and N.,
who have gone before us with the sign of faith
and rest in the sleep of peace.

Grant them, O Lord, we pray,
and all who sleep in Christ,
a place of refreshment, light and peace.
(Through Christ our Lord. Amen.)

To us, also, your servants, who, though sinners,
hope in your abundant mercies,
graciously grant some share
and fellowship with your holy Apostles and Martyrs:
with John the Baptist, Stephen,
Matthias, Barnabas,
(Ignatius, Alexander,
Marcellinus, Peter,
Felicity, Perpetua,
Agatha, Lucy,
Agnes, Cecilia, Anastasia)
and all your Saints;
admit us, we beseech you,
into their company,
not weighing our merits,

but granting us your pardon,
through Christ our Lord.

Through whom
you continue to make all these good things, O Lord;
you sanctify them, fill them with life,
bless them, and bestow them upon us.

Through him, and with him, and in him,
O God, almighty Father,
in the unity of the Holy Spirit,
all glory and honor is yours,
for ever and ever.

People:   **Amen.**

Then follows the Communion Rite, p. 23.

## EUCHARISTIC PRAYER II

Preface

It is truly right and just, our duty and our salvation,
always and everywhere to give you thanks, Father most holy,
through your beloved Son, Jesus Christ,
your Word through whom you made all things,
whom you sent as our Savior and Redeemer,
incarnate by the Holy Spirit and born of the Virgin.

Fulfilling your will and gaining for you a holy people,
he stretched out his hands as he endured his Passion,
so as to break the bonds of death and manifest the resurrection.

And so, with the Angels and all the Saints
we declare your glory,
as with one voice we acclaim:

**Holy, Holy, Holy Lord God of hosts.**
**Heaven and earth are full of your glory.**
**Hosanna in the highest.**
**Blessed is he who comes in the name of the Lord.**
**Hosanna in the highest.**

Priest:

You are indeed Holy, O Lord,
the fount of all holiness.
Make holy, therefore, these gifts, we pray,
by sending down your Spirit upon them like the dewfall,
so that they may become for us
the Body and ✝ Blood of our Lord Jesus Christ.

At the time he was betrayed
and entered willingly into his Passion,

he took bread and, giving thanks, broke it,
and gave it to his disciples, saying:

TAKE THIS, ALL OF YOU, AND EAT OF IT,
FOR THIS IS MY BODY,
WHICH WILL BE GIVEN UP FOR YOU.

In a similar way, when supper was ended,
he took the chalice
and, once more giving thanks,
he gave it to his disciples, saying:

TAKE THIS, ALL OF YOU, AND DRINK FROM IT,
FOR THIS IS THE CHALICE OF MY BLOOD,
THE BLOOD OF THE NEW AND ETERNAL COVENANT,
WHICH WILL BE POURED OUT FOR YOU AND FOR MANY
FOR THE FORGIVENESS OF SINS.

DO THIS IN MEMORY OF ME.

The mystery of faith.

People:

**A** We proclaim your Death, O Lord,
and profess your Resurrection
until you come again.

**B** When we eat this Bread and drink this Cup,
we proclaim your Death, O Lord,
until you come again.

**C** Save us, Savior of the world,
for by your Cross and Resurrection
you have set us free.

Priest:

Therefore, as we celebrate
the memorial of his Death and Resurrection,
we offer you, Lord,
the Bread of life and the Chalice of salvation,
giving thanks that you have held us worthy
to be in your presence and minister to you.

Humbly we pray
that, partaking of the Body and Blood of Christ,
we may be gathered into one by the Holy Spirit.

Remember, Lord, your Church,
spread throughout the world,
and bring her to the fullness of charity,

EUCH II

together with N. our Pope and N. our Bishop*
and all the clergy.

> In Masses for the Dead, the following may be added:
>
> Remember your servant N.,
> whom you have called (today)
> from this world to yourself.
> Grant that he (she) who was united with your Son in a death like his,
> may also be one with him in his Resurrection.

Remember also our brothers and sisters
who have fallen asleep in the hope of the resurrection,
and all who have died in your mercy:
welcome them into the light of your face.
Have mercy on us all, we pray,
that with the Blessed Virgin Mary, Mother of God,
with blessed Joseph, her Spouse,
with the blessed Apostles,
and all the Saints who have pleased you throughout the ages,
we may merit to be coheirs to eternal life,
and may praise and glorify you
through your Son, Jesus Christ.

Through him, and with him, and in him,
O God, almighty Father,
in the unity of the Holy Spirit,
all glory and honor is yours,
for ever and ever.

People: **Amen.**

Then follows the Communion Rite, p. 23.

## EUCHARISTIC PRAYER III
Priest:

You are indeed Holy, O Lord,
and all you have created
rightly gives you praise,
for through your Son our Lord Jesus Christ,
by the power and working of the Holy Spirit,
you give life to all things and make them holy,
and you never cease to gather a people to yourself,
so that from the rising of the sun to its setting
a pure sacrifice may be offered to your name.

---

* Mention may be made here of the Coadjutor Bishop, or Auxiliary Bishops,
  as noted in the *General Instruction of the Roman Missal*, no. 149.

Therefore, O Lord, we humbly implore you:
by the same Spirit graciously make holy
these gifts we have brought to you for consecration,
that they may become the Body and ✠ Blood
of your Son our Lord Jesus Christ,
at whose command we celebrate these mysteries.

For on the night he was betrayed
he himself took bread,
and, giving you thanks, he said the blessing,
broke the bread and gave it to his disciples, saying:

TAKE THIS, ALL OF YOU, AND EAT OF IT,
FOR THIS IS MY BODY,
WHICH WILL BE GIVEN UP FOR YOU.

In a similar way, when supper was ended,
he took the chalice,
and, giving you thanks, he said the blessing,
and gave the chalice to his disciples, saying:

TAKE THIS, ALL OF YOU, AND DRINK FROM IT,
FOR THIS IS THE CHALICE OF MY BLOOD,
THE BLOOD OF THE NEW AND ETERNAL COVENANT,
WHICH WILL BE POURED OUT FOR YOU AND FOR MANY
FOR THE FORGIVENESS OF SINS.

DO THIS IN MEMORY OF ME.

The mystery of faith.

People:

**A** We proclaim your Death, O Lord,
and profess your Resurrection
until you come again.

**B** When we eat this Bread and drink this Cup,
we proclaim your Death, O Lord,
until you come again.

**C** Save us, Savior of the world,
for by your Cross and Resurrection
you have set us free.

Priest:
Therefore, O Lord, as we celebrate the memorial
of the saving Passion of your Son,
his wondrous Resurrection
and Ascension into heaven,
and as we look forward to his second coming,

EUCH III

we offer you in thanksgiving
this holy and living sacrifice.

Look, we pray, upon the oblation of your Church
and, recognizing the sacrificial Victim by whose death
you willed to reconcile us to yourself,
grant that we, who are nourished
by the Body and Blood of your Son
and filled with his Holy Spirit,
may become one body, one spirit in Christ.

May he make of us
an eternal offering to you,
so that we may obtain an inheritance with your elect,
especially with the most Blessed Virgin Mary, Mother of God,
with blessed Joseph, her Spouse,
with your blessed Apostles and glorious Martyrs
(with Saint N.: the Saint of the day or Patron Saint)
and with all the Saints,
on whose constant intercession in your presence
we rely for unfailing help.

May this Sacrifice of our reconciliation,
we pray, O Lord,
advance the peace and salvation of all the world.
Be pleased to confirm in faith and charity
your pilgrim Church on earth,
with your servant N. our Pope and N. our Bishop,*
the Order of Bishops, all the clergy,
and the entire people you have gained for your own.

Listen graciously to the prayers of this family,
whom you have summoned before you:
in your compassion, O merciful Father,
gather to yourself all your children
scattered throughout the world.

† To our departed brothers and sisters
and to all who were pleasing to you
at their passing from this life,
give kind admittance to your kingdom.
There we hope to enjoy for ever the fullness of your glory
through Christ our Lord,
through whom you bestow on the world all that is good. †

---

* Mention may be made here of the Coadjutor Bishop, or Auxiliary Bishops,
  as noted in the *General Instruction of the Roman Missal*, no. 149.

When this Eucharistic Prayer is used in Masses for the Dead, the following may be said:

† Remember your servant N.
whom you have called (today)
from this world to yourself.
Grant that he (she) who was united with your Son in a death like his,
may also be one with him in his Resurrection,
when from the earth
he will raise up in the flesh those who have died,
and transform our lowly body
after the pattern of his own glorious body.
To our departed brothers and sisters, too,
and to all who were pleasing to you
at their passing from this life,
give kind admittance to your kingdom.
There we hope to enjoy for ever the fullness of your glory,
when you will wipe away every tear from our eyes.
For seeing you, our God, as you are,
we shall be like you for all the ages
and praise you without end,
through Christ our Lord,
through whom you bestow on the world all that is good. †

Through him, and with him, and in him,
O God, almighty Father,
in the unity of the Holy Spirit,
all glory and honor is yours,
for ever and ever.

People: **Amen.**

Then follows the Communion Rite, p. 23.

## Eucharistic Prayer IV

### Preface

It is truly right to give you thanks,
truly just to give you glory, Father most holy,
for you are the one God living and true,
existing before all ages and abiding for all eternity,
dwelling in unapproachable light;
yet you, who alone are good, the source of life,
have made all that is,
so that you might fill your creatures with blessings
and bring joy to many of them by the glory of your light.

And so, in your presence are countless hosts of Angels,
who serve you day and night

and, gazing upon the glory of your face,
glorify you without ceasing.

With them we, too, confess your name in exultation,
giving voice to every creature under heaven,
as we acclaim:

**Holy, Holy, Holy Lord God of hosts.**
**Heaven and earth are full of your glory.**
**Hosanna in the highest.**
**Blessed is he who comes in the name of the Lord.**
**Hosanna in the highest.**

Priest:

We give you praise, Father most holy,
for you are great
and you have fashioned all your works
in wisdom and in love.
You formed man in your own image
and entrusted the whole world to his care,
so that in serving you alone, the Creator,
he might have dominion over all creatures.
And when through disobedience he had lost your friendship,
you did not abandon him to the domain of death.
For you came in mercy to the aid of all,
so that those who seek might find you.
Time and again you offered them covenants
and through the prophets
taught them to look forward to salvation.

And you so loved the world, Father most holy,
that in the fullness of time
you sent your Only Begotten Son to be our Savior.
Made incarnate by the Holy Spirit
and born of the Virgin Mary,
he shared our human nature
in all things but sin.
To the poor he proclaimed the good news of salvation,
to prisoners, freedom,
and to the sorrowful of heart, joy.
To accomplish your plan,
he gave himself up to death,
and, rising from the dead,
he destroyed death and restored life.

And that we might live no longer for ourselves
but for him who died and rose again for us,
he sent the Holy Spirit from you, Father,

as the first fruits for those who believe,
so that, bringing to perfection his work in the world,
he might sanctify creation to the full.

Therefore, O Lord, we pray:
may this same Holy Spirit
graciously sanctify these offerings,
that they may become
the Body and ✠ Blood of our Lord Jesus Christ
for the celebration of this great mystery,
which he himself left us
as an eternal covenant.

For when the hour had come
for him to be glorified by you, Father most holy,
having loved his own who were in the world,
he loved them to the end:
and while they were at supper,
he took bread, blessed and broke it,
and gave it to his disciples, saying:

Take this, all of you, and eat of it,
for this is my Body,
which will be given up for you.

In a similar way,
taking the chalice filled with the fruit of the vine,
he gave thanks,
and gave the chalice to his disciples, saying:

Take this, all of you, and drink from it,
for this is the chalice of my Blood,
the Blood of the new and eternal covenant,
which will be poured out for you and for many
for the forgiveness of sins.

Do this in memory of me.

The mystery of faith.

People:

**A** We proclaim your Death, O Lord,
and profess your Resurrection
until you come again.

**B** When we eat this Bread and drink this Cup,
we proclaim your Death, O Lord,
until you come again.

EUCH IV

**C**   **Save us, Savior of the world,**
      **for by your Cross and Resurrection**
      **you have set us free.**

Priest:

Therefore, O Lord,
as we now celebrate the memorial of our redemption,
we remember Christ's Death
and his descent to the realm of the dead,
we proclaim his Resurrection
and his Ascension to your right hand,
and, as we await his coming in glory,
we offer you his Body and Blood,
the sacrifice acceptable to you
which brings salvation to the whole world.

Look, O Lord, upon the Sacrifice
which you yourself have provided for your Church,
and grant in your loving kindness
to all who partake of this one Bread and one Chalice
that, gathered into one body by the Holy Spirit,
they may truly become a living sacrifice in Christ
to the praise of your glory.

Therefore, Lord, remember now
all for whom we offer this sacrifice:
especially your servant N. our Pope,
N. our Bishop,* and the whole Order of Bishops,
all the clergy,
those who take part in this offering,
those gathered here before you,
your entire people,
and all who seek you with a sincere heart.

Remember also
those who have died in the peace of your Christ
and all the dead,
whose faith you alone have known.

To all of us, your children,
grant, O merciful Father,
that we may enter into a heavenly inheritance
with the Blessed Virgin Mary, Mother of God,
with blessed Joseph, her Spouse,
and with your Apostles and Saints in your kingdom.

---

* Mention may be made here of the Coadjutor Bishop, or Auxiliary Bishops,
  as noted in the *General Instruction of the Roman Missal*, no. 149.

There, with the whole of creation,
freed from the corruption of sin and death,
may we glorify you through Christ our Lord,
through whom you bestow on the world all that is good.

Through him, and with him, and in him,
O God, almighty Father,
in the unity of the Holy Spirit,
all glory and honor is yours,
for ever and ever.

People: **Amen.**

# THE COMMUNION RITE

STAND

## THE LORD'S PRAYER

Priest: At the Savior's command
and formed by divine teaching,
we dare to say:

All: **Our Father, who art in heaven,
hallowed be thy name;
thy kingdom come,
thy will be done
on earth as it is in heaven.
Give us this day our daily bread,
and forgive us our trespasses,
as we forgive those who trespass against us;
and lead us not into temptation,
but deliver us from evil.**

Priest: Deliver us, Lord, we pray, from every evil,
graciously grant peace in our days,
that, by the help of your mercy,
we may be always free from sin
and safe from all distress,
as we await the blessed hope
and the coming of our Savior, Jesus Christ.

All: **For the kingdom,
the power and the glory are yours
now and for ever.**

## SIGN OF PEACE

Priest: Lord Jesus Christ,
who said to your Apostles:
Peace I leave you, my peace I give you,
look not on our sins,
but on the faith of your Church,
and graciously grant her peace and unity
in accordance with your will.
Who live and reign for ever and ever.

People: **Amen.**

Priest: The peace of the Lord be with you always.

People: **And with your spirit.**

Then, if appropriate, the Deacon, or the Priest, adds:
Let us offer each other the sign of peace.

## FRACTION OF THE BREAD

The Priest says quietly:

Priest: May this mingling of the Body and Blood
of our Lord Jesus Christ
bring eternal life to us who receive it.

All: **Lamb of God, you take away the sins of the world,
have mercy on us.**

**Lamb of God, you take away the sins of the world,
have mercy on us.**

**Lamb of God, you take away the sins of the world,
grant us peace.**

The Priest says quietly: **KNEEL**

Lord Jesus Christ, Son of the living God,
who, by the will of the Father
and the work of the Holy Spirit,
through your Death gave life to the world,
free me by this, your most holy Body and Blood,
from all my sins and from every evil;
keep me always faithful to your commandments,
and never let me be parted from you.

Or:

May the receiving of your Body and Blood,
Lord Jesus Christ,
not bring me to judgment and condemnation,
but through your loving mercy
be for me protection in mind and body
and a healing remedy.

## INVITATION TO COMMUNION

Priest:    Behold the Lamb of God,
           behold him who takes away the sins of the world.
           Blessed are those called to the supper of the Lamb.

All:    **Lord, I am not worthy**
        **that you should enter under my roof,**
        **but only say the word**
        **and my soul shall be healed.**

## COMMUNION

The Priest says quietly:    May the Body of Christ
                            keep me safe for eternal life.

The Priest says quietly:    May the Blood of Christ
                            keep me safe for eternal life.    **STAND**

The Priest says to each of the communicants:    **The Body of Christ.**
The communicant replies:    **Amen.**

Priest says quietly:    What has passed our lips as food, O Lord,
                        may we possess in purity of heart,
                        that what has been given to us in time
                        may be our healing for eternity.

## PRAYER AFTER COMMUNION                                        **STAND**

The Priest says:    Let us pray.
At the end the people acclaim:    **Amen.**

# THE CONCLUDING RITES

## FINAL BLESSING

Priest:    The Lord be with you.
People:    **And with your spirit.**

Priest:   May almighty God bless you,
          the Father, and the Son, ✝ and the Holy Spirit.

People:   **Amen.**

DISMISSAL

The Deacon, or the Priest himself:

> Go forth, the Mass is ended.

> Or:

> Go and announce the Gospel of the Lord.

> Or:

> Go in peace, glorifying the Lord by your life.

> Or:

> Go in peace.

People:   **Thanks be to God.**

---

### A PRAYER FOR VOCATIONS

"O Lord, send us chosen messengers and teachers,
lovers of worship and of art
who will restore with chaste and noble works
the beauty of your house!
May they teach us to see with pure heart
the splendor of your Son Jesus Christ
and to express what we have seen
in images worthy of so great a vision."

*Thomas Merton, OCSO*

# Celebration of the Liturgy of the Word
## [With Holy Communion]

## INTRODUCTORY RITES

### INTRODUCTION
Deacon or lay leader:

We gather here to celebrate the Lord's Day.
Sunday has been called the Lord's Day because
    it was on this day
that Jesus conquered sin and death and rose to new life.
Unfortunately, we are not able to celebrate the Mass today
because we do not have a Priest.
Let us be united in the spirit of Christ with
    the Church around the world
and celebrate our redemption in Christ's suffering,
    Death and Resurrection.

### SIGN OF THE CROSS                                    **STAND**
Deacon or lay leader:

In the name of the Father, and of the Son, and of the
Holy Spirit.

All respond:  **Amen.**

### GREETING
Deacon or lay leader:

Grace to you and peace from God our Father
and the Lord Jesus Christ.
Blessed be God for ever.

All:  **Blessed be God for ever.**

### COLLECT

## LITURGY OF THE WORD                                   **SIT**

### FIRST READING

### RESPONSORIAL PSALM

SECOND READING

GOSPEL ACCLAMATION                                    **STAND**

GOSPEL

HOMILY OR REFLECTION ON THE READINGS                 **SIT**

PERIOD OF SILENCE

PROFESSION OF FAITH                                  **STAND**
[The Nicene Creed can be found on page 5]

Apostles' Creed

**I believe in God,
the Father almighty,
Creator of heaven and earth,
and in Jesus Christ, his only Son, our Lord,**

> At the words that follow, up to and including the Virgin Mary,
> all bow.

**who was conceived by the Holy Spirit,
born of the Virgin Mary,
suffered under Pontius Pilate,
was crucified, died and was buried;
he descended into hell;
on the third day he rose again from the dead;
he ascended into heaven,
and is seated at the right hand of God the Father
      almighty;
from there he will come to judge the living and the
      dead.**

**I believe in the Holy Spirit,
the holy catholic Church,
the communion of saints,
the forgiveness of sins,
the resurrection of the body,
and life everlasting. Amen.**

PRAYER OF THE FAITHFUL

# COMMUNION RITE

## LORD'S PRAYER

Deacon or lay leader:

The Father provides us with food
for eternal life.
Let us pray for nourishment
and strength.

All say:

**Our Father, who art in heaven,**
**hallowed be thy name;**
**thy kingdom come,**
**thy will be done**
**on earth as it is in heaven.**
**Give us this day our daily bread,**
**and forgive us our trespasses,**
**as we forgive those who trespass against us;**
**and lead us not into temptation,**
**but deliver us from evil.**
**Amen.**

## INVITATION TO COMMUNION                           **KNEEL**

Deacon or lay leader:

Behold the Lamb of God,
behold him who takes away the sins of the world.
Blessed are those called to the supper of the Lamb.

All say:

**Lord, I am not worthy**
**that you should enter under my roof,**
**but only say the word**
**and my soul shall be healed.**

## COMMUNION

## ACT OF THANKSGIVING                                **STAND**

# CONCLUDING RITES

## INVITATION TO PRAY FOR VOCATIONS TO THE PRIESTHOOD
Deacon or lay leader:

Mindful of the Lord's word, "Ask the Master of the harvest to send out laborers for the harvest," let us pray for an increase of vocations to the Priesthood. May our prayer hasten the day when we will be able to take part in the celebration of the Holy Eucharist every Sunday.

## BLESSING

## SIGN OF PEACE

---

### A PRAYER FOR GENEROSITY

Dear Lord, teach me to be generous,
teach me to serve you as you deserve,
to give and not to count the cost,
to fight and not to heed the wound,
to toil and not to seek for rest,
to labor and not to seek reward,
save that of knowing that I do your will.

*St. Ignatius Loyola*

# First Sunday of Advent

*November 27, 2016*

## Reflection on the Gospel

*Daily living is filled with planned events at set hours: eating, drinking, marrying, working. In this way, we human beings measure time. There is, however, another time that cannot be measured: God's time, the fullness of time in which is the fullness of Life. How we live in our time is a doorway into God's time. Advent calls us to immerse ourselves in God's time and to stay awake for the Life that is yet to come—and is already now.*

- *Our time is a doorway into God's time, when I . . .*

—Living Liturgy™, *First Sunday of Advent 2016*

## ENTRANCE ANTIPHON (Cf. Psalm 25[24]:1-3)

To you, I lift up my soul, O my God.
In you, I have trusted; let me not be put to shame.
Nor let my enemies exult over me;
and let none who hope in you be put to shame.

## COLLECT

Grant your faithful, we pray, almighty God,
the resolve to run forth to meet your Christ
with righteous deeds at his coming,
so that, gathered at his right hand,
they may be worthy to possess the heavenly Kingdom.
Through our Lord Jesus Christ, your Son,
who lives and reigns with you in the unity of the Holy Spirit,
one God, for ever and ever. All: **Amen.**

## READING I (L 1) (Isaiah 2:1-5)

### A reading from the Book of the Prophet Isaiah

*The Lord will gather all nations into the eternal peace of the kingdom of God.*

This is what Isaiah, son of Amoz,
  saw concerning Judah and Jerusalem.
    In days to come,
  the mountain of the L<small>ORD</small>'s house
    shall be established as the highest mountain
    and raised above the hills.
All nations shall stream toward it;
  many peoples shall come and say:
"Come, let us climb the L<small>ORD</small>'s mountain,
  to the house of the God of Jacob,
that he may instruct us in his ways,
  and we may walk in his paths."
For from Zion shall go forth instruction,
  and the word of the L<small>ORD</small> from Jerusalem.
He shall judge between the nations,
  and impose terms on many peoples.
They shall beat their swords into plowshares
  and their spears into pruning hooks;
one nation shall not raise the sword against another,
  nor shall they train for war again.
O house of Jacob, come,
  let us walk in the light of the L<small>ORD</small>!

The word of the Lord. All: Thanks be to God.

R<small>ESPONSORIAL</small> P<small>SALM</small> 122

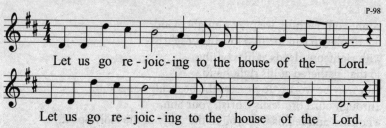

P-98

Let us go re-joic-ing to the house of the___ Lord.

Let us go re-joic-ing to the house of the Lord.

Psalm 122:1-2, 3-4, 4-5, 6-7, 8-9

R̶7̶. **Let us go rejoicing to the house of the Lord.**

  I rejoiced because they said to me,
    "We will go up to the house of the L<small>ORD</small>."

And now we have set foot
within your gates, O Jerusalem. ℟.

Jerusalem, built as a city
with compact unity.
To it the tribes go up,
the tribes of the LORD. ℟.

According to the decree for Israel,
to give thanks to the name of the LORD.
In it are set up judgment seats,
seats for the house of David. ℟.

Pray for the peace of Jerusalem!
May those who love you prosper!
May peace be within your walls,
prosperity in your buildings. ℟.

Because of my brothers and friends
I will say, "Peace be within you!"
Because of the house of the LORD, our God,
I will pray for your good. ℟.

READING II (Romans 13:11-14)

**A reading from the Letter of Saint Paul to the Romans**

*Our salvation is nearer.*

**Brothers and sisters:**
**You know the time;**
**it is the hour now for you to awake from sleep.**
**For our salvation is nearer now than when we first**
**believed;**
**the night is advanced, the day is at hand.**
**Let us then throw off the works of darkness**
**and put on the armor of light;**
**let us conduct ourselves properly as in the day,**
**not in orgies and drunkenness,**
**not in promiscuity and lust,**
**not in rivalry and jealousy.**
**But put on the Lord Jesus Christ,**
**and make no provision for the desires of the flesh.**

**The word of the Lord.** All: **Thanks be to God.**

GOSPEL (Matthew 24:37-44)

ALLELUIA (*See* Psalm 85:8)

℣. Alleluia, alleluia.  ℟. **Alleluia, alleluia.**

℣. Show us Lord, your love;
and grant us your salvation. ℟.

✠ **A reading from the holy Gospel according to Matthew**

All: **Glory to you, O Lord.**

*Stay awake, that you may be prepared!*

**Jesus said to his disciples:**
**"As it was in the days of Noah,**
**so it will be at the coming of the Son of Man.**
**In those days before the flood,**
**they were eating and drinking,**
**marrying and giving in marriage,**
**up to the day that Noah entered the ark.**
**They did not know until the flood came and carried**
**them all away.**
**So will it be also at the coming of the Son of Man.**
**Two men will be out in the field;**
**one will be taken, and one will be left.**
**Two women will be grinding at the mill;**
**one will be taken, and one will be left.**
**Therefore, stay awake!**
**For you do not know on which day your Lord will come.**
**Be sure of this: if the master of the house**
**had known the hour of night when the thief was**
**coming,**
**he would have stayed awake**
**and not let his house be broken into.**
**So too, you also must be prepared,**
**for at an hour you do not expect, the Son of Man will**
**come."**

**The Gospel of the Lord.** All: **Praise to you, Lord Jesus Christ.**

Prayer over the Offerings
Accept, we pray, O Lord, these offerings we make,
gathered from among your gifts to us,
and may what you grant us to celebrate devoutly here below
gain for us the prize of eternal redemption.
Through Christ our Lord. All: **Amen.**

Communion Antiphon (Psalm 85[84]:13)
The Lord will bestow his bounty, and our earth shall yield
     its increase.

Prayer after Communion
May these mysteries, O Lord,
in which we have participated,
profit us, we pray,
for even now, as we walk amid passing things,
you teach us by them to love the things of heaven
and hold fast to what endures.
Through Christ our Lord. All: **Amen.**

# Second Sunday
# of Advent

*December 4, 2016*

*Reflection on the Gospel*

*Repentance always changes one's life. Our attitudes and behaviors noticeably change for the better when we choose to repent. Some in John the Baptist's time repented by acknowledging their sins, expressing a desire to live "in the kingdom of heaven," and submitting to his baptism with water. Others resisted repentance. John's challenge to repent elicits two responses. Which response do we choose? Whether Jesus will gather us as wheat or burn us as chaff depends upon our choice.*

• *My response to the preaching of John the Baptist is . . .*

—Living Liturgy™, *Second Sunday of Advent 2016*

Entrance Antiphon (Cf. Isaiah 30:19, 30)
O people of Sion, behold,
the Lord will come to save the nations,
and the Lord will make the glory of his voice heard
in the joy of your heart.

Collect
Almighty and merciful God,
may no earthly undertaking hinder those
who set out in haste to meet your Son,
but may our learning of heavenly wisdom
gain us admittance to his company.
Who lives and reigns with you in the unity of the Holy Spirit,
one God, for ever and ever. All: **Amen.**

Reading I (L 4) (Isaiah 11:1-10)

## A reading from the Book of the Prophet Isaiah

*He shall judge the poor with justice.*

On that day, a shoot shall sprout from the stump
of Jesse,
and from his roots a bud shall blossom.
The spirit of the LORD shall rest upon him:
a spirit of wisdom and of understanding,
a spirit of counsel and of strength,
a spirit of knowledge and of fear of the LORD,
and his delight shall be the fear of the LORD.
Not by appearance shall he judge,
nor by hearsay shall he decide,
but he shall judge the poor with justice,
and decide aright for the land's afflicted.
He shall strike the ruthless with the rod of his mouth,
and with the breath of his lips he shall slay the wicked.
Justice shall be the band around his waist,
and faithfulness a belt upon his hips.
Then the wolf shall be a guest of the lamb,
and the leopard shall lie down with the kid;
the calf and the young lion shall browse together,
with a little child to guide them.

The cow and the bear shall be neighbors,
   together their young shall rest;
   the lion shall eat hay like the ox.
The baby shall play by the cobra's den,
   and the child lay his hand on the adder's lair.
There shall be no harm or ruin on all my holy
      mountain;
   for the earth shall be filled with knowledge of
      the LORD,
   as water covers the sea.
On that day, the root of Jesse,
   set up as a signal for the nations,
the Gentiles shall seek out,
   for his dwelling shall be glorious.

**The word of the Lord.** All: **Thanks be to God.**

RESPONSORIAL PSALM 72

P-99

Jus - tice shall flou-rish in his time,
and full - ness of peace for - ev - er.

Music: Jay F. Hunstiger, © 1990, administered by Liturgical Press. All rights reserved.

Psalm 72:1-2, 7-8, 12-13, 17

R̤. (*See* 7) **Justice shall flourish in his time, and fullness
   of peace forever.**

O God, with your judgment endow the king,
   and with your justice, the king's son;
he shall govern your people with justice
   and your afflicted ones with judgment. R̤.

Justice shall flower in his days,
   and profound peace, till the moon be no more.
May he rule from sea to sea,
   and from the River to the ends of the earth. R̤.

*(continued)*

For he shall rescue the poor when he cries out,
  and the afflicted when he has no one to help him.
He shall have pity for the lowly and the poor;
  the lives of the poor he shall save. R̶⁊.

May his name be blessed forever;
  as long as the sun his name shall remain.
In him shall all the tribes of the earth be blessed;
  all the nations shall proclaim his happiness. R̶⁊.

## READING II (Romans 15:4-9)

**A reading from the Letter of Saint Paul to the Romans**

*Christ saves everyone.*

**Brothers and sisters:**
**Whatever was written previously was written for our**
**    instruction,**
**    that by endurance and by the encouragement of the**
**        Scriptures**
**    we might have hope.**
**May the God of endurance and encouragement**
**    grant you to think in harmony with one another,**
**    in keeping with Christ Jesus,**
**    that with one accord you may with one voice**
**    glorify the God and Father of our Lord Jesus Christ.**

**Welcome one another, then, as Christ welcomed you,**
**    for the glory of God.**

**For I say that Christ became a minister of the circumcised**
**    to show God's truthfulness,**
**    to confirm the promises to the patriarchs,**
**    but so that the Gentiles might glorify God for his**
**        mercy.**
**As it is written:**
*Therefore, I will praise you among the Gentiles*
*and sing praises to your name.*

**The word of the Lord.** All: **Thanks be to God.**

GOSPEL (Matthew 3:1-12)
ALLELUIA (Luke 3:4, 6)

℣. Alleluia, alleluia.  ℟. **Alleluia, alleluia.**

℣. Prepare the way of the Lord, make straight his paths:
all flesh shall see the salvation of God. ℟.

✝ **A reading from the holy Gospel according to Matthew**

All: **Glory to you, O Lord.**

*Repent, for the kingdom of heaven is at hand!*

**John the Baptist appeared, preaching in the desert of
Judea
and saying, "Repent, for the kingdom of heaven is at
hand!"**

**It was of him that the prophet Isaiah had spoken when
he said:**

*A voice of one crying out in the desert,*
*Prepare the way of the Lord,*
*make straight his paths.*

**John wore clothing made of camel's hair
and had a leather belt around his waist.**

**His food was locusts and wild honey.**

**At that time Jerusalem, all Judea,
and the whole region around the Jordan
were going out to him
and were being baptized by him in the Jordan River
as they acknowledged their sins.**

**When he saw many of the Pharisees and Sadducees
coming to his baptism, he said to them, "You brood
of vipers!**

**Who warned you to flee from the coming wrath?**

**Produce good fruit as evidence of your repentance.**

**And do not presume to say to yourselves,
'We have Abraham as our father.'**

**For I tell you,
God can raise up children to Abraham from these
stones.**

**Even now the ax lies at the root of the trees.**
**Therefore every tree that does not bear good fruit**
   **will be cut down and thrown into the fire.**
**I am baptizing you with water, for repentance,**
   **but the one who is coming after me is mightier than I.**
**I am not worthy to carry his sandals.**
**He will baptize you with the Holy Spirit and fire.**
**His winnowing fan is in his hand.**
**He will clear his threshing floor**
   **and gather his wheat into his barn,**
   **but the chaff he will burn with unquenchable fire."**

**The Gospel of the Lord.** All: **Praise to you, Lord Jesus Christ.**

PRAYER OVER THE OFFERINGS
Be pleased, O Lord, with our humble prayers and offerings,
and, since we have no merits to plead our cause,
come, we pray, to our rescue
with the protection of your mercy.
Through Christ our Lord. All: **Amen.**

COMMUNION ANTIPHON (Baruch 5:5; 4:36)
Jerusalem, arise and stand upon the heights,
and behold the joy which comes to you from God.

PRAYER AFTER COMMUNION
Replenished by the food of spiritual nourishment,
we humbly beseech you, O Lord,
that, through our partaking in this mystery,
you may teach us to judge wisely the things of earth
and hold firm to the things of heaven.
Through Christ our Lord. All: **Amen.**

# The Immaculate Conception of the Blessed Virgin Mary

*December 8, 2016*

## Reflection on the Gospel

*Mary, sinless and "full of grace" from the moment of her conception, responded to Gabriel's words "Do not be afraid" and embraced what God would accomplish in her. Mary said yes and bore "the Son of God" for the world. Despite our own sinfulness, when we say yes, we too have nothing to fear. If we open ourselves to God's Presence, we can also hear said to us, "Do not be afraid." We too can say yes to God. We too can bear God for the world.*

- *I respond to the Lord's "Do not be afraid" when I . . .*

—*Living Liturgy*™, *Immaculate Conception 2016*

## ENTRANCE ANTIPHON (Isaiah 61:10)

I rejoice heartily in the Lord,
in my God is the joy of my soul;
for he has clothed me with a robe of salvation,
and wrapped me in a mantle of justice,
like a bride adorned with her jewels.

## COLLECT

O God, who by the Immaculate Conception of the Blessed Virgin
prepared a worthy dwelling for your Son,
grant, we pray,
that, as you preserved her from every stain
by virtue of the Death of your Son, which you foresaw,
so, through her intercession,
we, too, may be cleansed and admitted to your presence.
Through our Lord Jesus Christ, your Son,
who lives and reigns with you in the unity of the Holy Spirit,
one God, for ever and ever. All: **Amen.**

READING I (L 689) (Genesis 3:9-15, 20)

## A reading from the Book of Genesis

*I will put enmity between your offspring and hers.*

After the man, Adam, had eaten of the tree,
  the LORD God called to the man and asked him,
    "Where are you?"
He answered, "I heard you in the garden;
  but I was afraid, because I was naked,
  so I hid myself."
Then he asked, "Who told you that you were naked?
You have eaten, then,
  from the tree of which I had forbidden you to eat!"
The man replied, "The woman whom you put here
    with me—
  she gave me fruit from the tree, and so I ate it."
The LORD God then asked the woman,
  "Why did you do such a thing?"
The woman answered, "The serpent tricked me into it,
    so I ate it."

Then the LORD God said to the serpent:
  "Because you have done this, you shall be banned
    from all the animals
    and from all the wild creatures;
  on your belly shall you crawl,
    and dirt shall you eat
    all the days of your life.
  I will put enmity between you and the woman,
    and between your offspring and hers;
  he will strike at your head,
    while you strike at his heel."

The man called his wife Eve,
  because she became the mother of all the living.

The word of the Lord. All: Thanks be to God.

RESPONSORIAL PSALM 98

P-189

Sing to the Lord a new song, for he has done marv-'lous deeds.

Psalm 98:1, 2-3ab, 3cd-4

R̰. (1a) **Sing to the Lord a new song, for he has done marvelous deeds.**

Sing to the LORD a new song,
    for he has done wondrous deeds;
His right hand has won victory for him,
    his holy arm. R̰.

The LORD has made his salvation known:
    in the sight of the nations he has revealed his justice.
He has remembered his kindness and his faithfulness
    toward the house of Israel. R̰.

All the ends of the earth have seen
    the salvation by our God.
Sing joyfully to the LORD, all you lands;
    break into song; sing praise. R̰.

READING II (Ephesians 1:3-6, 11-12)

**A reading from the Letter of Saint Paul to the Ephesians**

*He chose us in Christ before the foundation of the world.*

**Brothers and sisters:**
**Blessed be the God and Father of our Lord Jesus Christ,**
    **who has blessed us in Christ**
    **with every spiritual blessing in the heavens,**
    **as he chose us in him, before the foundation of the**
        **world,**
    **to be holy and without blemish before him.**

In love he destined us for adoption to himself through
    Jesus Christ,
  in accord with the favor of his will,
  for the praise of the glory of his grace
  that he granted us in the beloved.

In him we were also chosen,
  destined in accord with the purpose of the One
  who accomplishes all things according to the intention
    of his will,
  so that we might exist for the praise of his glory,
  we who first hoped in Christ.

The word of the Lord. All: **Thanks be to God.**

GOSPEL (Luke 1:26-38)
ALLELUIA (*See* Luke 1:28)

℣. Alleluia, alleluia.  ℟. **Alleluia, alleluia.**
℣. Hail, Mary, full of grace, the Lord is with you;
  blessed are you among women. ℟.

✠ **A reading from the holy Gospel according to Luke**

All: **Glory to you, O Lord.**

*Hail, full of grace! The Lord is with you.*

The angel Gabriel was sent from God
  to a town of Galilee called Nazareth,
  to a virgin betrothed to a man named Joseph,
  of the house of David,
  and the virgin's name was Mary.
And coming to her, he said,
  "Hail, full of grace! The Lord is with you."
But she was greatly troubled at what was said
  and pondered what sort of greeting this might be.
Then the angel said to her,
  "Do not be afraid, Mary,
  for you have found favor with God.
Behold, you will conceive in your womb and bear a son,
  and you shall name him Jesus.

He will be great and will be called Son of the Most High,
>and the Lord God will give him the throne of David
>>his father,
>and he will rule over the house of Jacob forever,
>and of his Kingdom there will be no end."

But Mary said to the angel,
>"How can this be,
>since I have no relations with a man?"

And the angel said to her in reply,
>"The Holy Spirit will come upon you,
>and the power of the Most High will overshadow you.

Therefore the child to be born
>will be called holy, the Son of God.

And behold, Elizabeth, your relative,
>has also conceived a son in her old age,
>and this is the sixth month for her who was called
>>barren;
>for nothing will be impossible for God."

Mary said, "Behold, I am the handmaid of the Lord.
May it be done to me according to your word."
Then the angel departed from her.

The Gospel of the Lord. All: **Praise to you, Lord Jesus Christ.**

PRAYER OVER THE OFFERINGS
Graciously accept the saving sacrifice
which we offer you, O Lord,
on the Solemnity of the Immaculate Conception
of the Blessed Virgin Mary,
and grant that, as we profess her,
on account of your prevenient grace,
to be untouched by any stain of sin,
so, through her intercession,
we may be delivered from all our faults.
Through Christ our Lord. All: **Amen.**

COMMUNION ANTIPHON
Glorious things are spoken of you, O Mary,
for from you arose the sun of justice,
Christ our God.

Prayer after Communion

May the Sacrament we have received,
O Lord our God,
heal in us the wounds of that fault
from which in a singular way
you preserved Blessed Mary in her Immaculate Conception.
Through Christ our Lord. All: **Amen.**

# Third Sunday of Advent

## December 11, 2016

*Reflection on the Gospel*

*Three identities are revealed in this gospel. John seeks to know if Jesus is "the one who is to come." Jesus does not respond with a simple yes, but invites John and his disciples to discover his identity by hearing and seeing his good works. Then Jesus reveals who John is. Even "more than a prophet," he is the messenger of the Messiah. Finally Jesus reveals who we are. We, "the least in the kingdom of heaven," are greater than John. How can this be?*

• *I follow Jesus, when I . . .*

—Living Liturgy™, *Third Sunday of Advent 2016*

Entrance Antiphon (Philippians 4:4-5)

Rejoice in the Lord always; again I say, rejoice.
Indeed, the Lord is near.

Collect

O God, who see how your people
faithfully await the feast of the Lord's Nativity,
enable us, we pray,
to attain the joys of so great a salvation
and to celebrate them always
with solemn worship and glad rejoicing.
Through our Lord Jesus Christ, your Son,
who lives and reigns with you in the unity of the Holy Spirit,
one God, for ever and ever. All: **Amen.**

READING I (L 7) (Isaiah 35:1-6a, 10)

## A reading from the Book of the Prophet Isaiah

*God himself will come to save us.*

The desert and the parched land will exult;
    the steppe will rejoice and bloom.
They will bloom with abundant flowers,
    and rejoice with joyful song.
The glory of Lebanon will be given to them,
    the splendor of Carmel and Sharon;
they will see the glory of the LORD,
    the splendor of our God.
Strengthen the hands that are feeble,
    make firm the knees that are weak,
say to those whose hearts are frightened:
    Be strong, fear not!
Here is your God,
    he comes with vindication;
with divine recompense
    he comes to save you.
Then will the eyes of the blind be opened,
    the ears of the deaf be cleared;
then will the lame leap like a stag,
    then the tongue of the mute will sing.

Those whom the LORD has ransomed will return
    and enter Zion singing,
    crowned with everlasting joy;
they will meet with joy and gladness,
    sorrow and mourning will flee.

The word of the Lord. All: Thanks be to God.

RESPONSORIAL PSALM 146

P-100

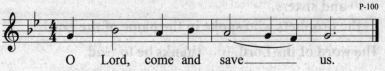

O Lord, come and save us.

Psalm 146:6-7, 8-9, 9-10

℟. (*See* Isaiah 35:4) **Lord, come and save us.** *or:* ℟. **Alleluia.**

The LORD God keeps faith forever,
　　secures justice for the oppressed,
　　gives food to the hungry.
The LORD sets captives free. ℟.

The LORD gives sight to the blind;
　　the LORD raises up those who were bowed down.
The LORD loves the just;
　　the LORD protects strangers. ℟.

The fatherless and the widow he sustains,
　　but the way of the wicked he thwarts.
The LORD shall reign forever;
　　your God, O Zion, through all generations. ℟.

## READING II (James 5:7-10)

**A reading from the Letter of Saint James**

*Make your hearts firm, because the coming of the Lord is at hand.*

**Be patient, brothers and sisters,**
　　**until the coming of the Lord.**
**See how the farmer waits for the precious fruit of the**
　　　　**earth,**
　　**being patient with it**
　　**until it receives the early and the late rains.**
**You too must be patient.**
**Make your hearts firm,**
　　**because the coming of the Lord is at hand.**
**Do not complain, brothers and sisters, about one another,**
　　**that you may not be judged.**
**Behold, the Judge is standing before the gates.**
**Take as an example of hardship and patience, brothers**
　　　　**and sisters,**
　　**the prophets who spoke in the name of the Lord.**

**The word of the Lord.** All: **Thanks be to God.**

GOSPEL (Matthew 11:2-11)

ALLELUIA (Isaiah 61:1 cited in Luke 4:18)

℣. Alleluia, alleluia.   ℟. **Alleluia, alleluia.**

℣. The Spirit of the LORD is upon me,
    because he has anointed me
    to bring glad tidings to the poor. ℟.

✛ **A reading from the holy Gospel according to Matthew**

All: **Glory to you, O Lord.**

*Are you the one who is to come or should we look for another?*

**When John the Baptist heard in prison of the works of
    the Christ,
    he sent his disciples to Jesus with this question,
    "Are you the one who is to come,
    or should we look for another?"
Jesus said to them in reply,
    "Go and tell John what you hear and see:
    the blind regain their sight,
    the lame walk,
    lepers are cleansed,
    the deaf hear,
    the dead are raised,
    and the poor have the good news proclaimed to them.
And blessed is the one who takes no offense at me."**

**As they were going off,
    Jesus began to speak to the crowds about John,
    "What did you go out to the desert to see?
A reed swayed by the wind?
Then what did you go out to see?
Someone dressed in fine clothing?
Those who wear fine clothing are in royal palaces.
Then why did you go out? To see a prophet?
Yes, I tell you, and more than a prophet.
This is the one about whom it is written:**
    *Behold, I am sending my messenger ahead of you;
        he will prepare your way before you.*

**Amen, I say to you,**
    **among those born of women**
        **there has been none greater than John the Baptist;**
    **yet the least in the kingdom of heaven is greater**
            **than he."**

**The Gospel of the Lord.** All: **Praise to you, Lord Jesus Christ.**

PRAYER OVER THE OFFERINGS
May the sacrifice of our worship, Lord, we pray,
be offered to you unceasingly,
to complete what was begun in sacred mystery
and powerfully accomplish for us your saving work.
Through Christ our Lord. All: **Amen.**

COMMUNION ANTIPHON (Cf. Isaiah 35:4)
Say to the faint of heart: Be strong and do not fear.
Behold, our God will come, and he will save us.

PRAYER AFTER COMMUNION
We implore your mercy, Lord,
that this divine sustenance may cleanse us of our faults
and prepare us for the coming feasts.
Through Christ our Lord. All: **Amen.**

# Fourth Sunday of Advent

*December 18, 2016*

*Reflection on the Gospel*

*This gospel describes events that led to a whole new in-breaking of God into human history. The Virgin Mary conceived by "the Holy Spirit" and the reassured Joseph "took his wife into his home." Mary and Joseph typify how we ourselves give "birth" to Jesus in our own time. By opening* ourselves to the Holy Spirit and cooperating with God's plan for our life, we, like Mary and Joseph, usher in a whole new in-breaking of God into human history. Truly, Emmanuel, "God is with us."

• *I open myself to the Holy Spirit by . . .*

—*Living Liturgy*™, *Fourth Sunday of Advent 2016*

## Entrance Antiphon (Cf. Isaiah 45:8)

Drop down dew from above, you heavens,
and let the clouds rain down the Just One;
let the earth be opened and bring forth a Savior.

## Collect

Pour forth, we beseech you, O Lord,
your grace into our hearts,
that we, to whom the Incarnation of Christ your Son
was made known by the message of an Angel,
may by his Passion and Cross
be brought to the glory of his Resurrection.
Who lives and reigns with you in the unity of the Holy Spirit,
one God, for ever and ever. All: **Amen.**

## Reading I (L 10) (Isaiah 7:10-14)

## A reading from the Book of the Prophet Isaiah

*Behold, the virgin shall conceive.*

The Lord spoke to Ahaz, saying:
Ask for a sign from the Lord, your God;
let it be deep as the netherworld, or high as the sky!
But Ahaz answered,
"I will not ask! I will not tempt the Lord!"
Then Isaiah said:
Listen, O house of David!
Is it not enough for you to weary people,
must you also weary my God?
Therefore the Lord himself will give you this sign:
the virgin shall conceive, and bear a son,
and shall name him Emmanuel.

The word of the Lord. All: **Thanks be to God.**

RESPONSIVE PSALM 24

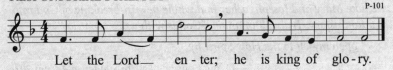

Let the Lord— en-ter; he is king of glo-ry.

Psalm 24:1-2, 3-4, 5-6

℟. (7c and 10b) **Let the Lord enter; he is king of glory.**

The LORD's are the earth and its fullness;
    the world and those who dwell in it.
For he founded it upon the seas
    and established it upon the rivers. ℟.

Who can ascend the mountain of the LORD?
    or who may stand in his holy place?
One whose hands are sinless, whose heart is clean,
    who desires not what is vain. ℟.

He shall receive a blessing from the LORD,
    a reward from God his savior.
Such is the race that seeks for him,
    that seeks the face of the God of Jacob. ℟.

READING II (Romans 1:1-7)

**A reading from the beginning of the Letter of Saint Paul to the Romans**

*Jesus Christ, descended from David, is the Son of God.*

**Paul, a slave of Christ Jesus,**
    **called to be an apostle and set apart for the gospel of**
        **God,**
    **which he promised previously through his prophets**
        **in the holy Scriptures,**
**the gospel about his Son, descended from David**
    **according to the flesh,**
    **but established as Son of God in power**
    **according to the Spirit of holiness**
    **through resurrection from the dead, Jesus Christ our**
        **Lord.**

Through him we have received the grace of apostleship,
> to bring about the obedience of faith,
>> for the sake of his name, among all the Gentiles,
>> among whom are you also, who are called to belong
>>> to Jesus Christ;
>> to all the beloved of God in Rome, called to be holy.

Grace to you and peace from God our Father
> and the Lord Jesus Christ.

The word of the Lord. All: Thanks be to God.

GOSPEL (Matthew 1:18-24)
ALLELUIA (Matthew 1:23)
℣. Alleluia, alleluia.  ℟. **Alleluia, alleluia.**
℣. The virgin shall conceive, and bear a son,
> and they shall name him Emmanuel. ℟.

☩ **A reading from the holy Gospel according to Matthew**

All: **Glory to you, O Lord.**

*Jesus will be born of Mary, the betrothed of Joseph, a son of David.*

This is how the birth of Jesus Christ came about.
When his mother Mary was betrothed to Joseph,
> but before they lived together,
>> she was found with child through the Holy Spirit.

Joseph her husband, since he was a righteous man,
> yet unwilling to expose her to shame,
>> decided to divorce her quietly.

Such was his intention when, behold,
> the angel of the Lord appeared to him in a dream and
>> said,
> "Joseph, son of David,
> do not be afraid to take Mary your wife into your
>> home.

For it is through the Holy Spirit
> that this child has been conceived in her.

She will bear a son and you are to name him Jesus,
> because he will save his people from their sins."

**All this took place to fulfill what the Lord had said
 through the prophet:**
 *Behold, the virgin shall conceive and bear a son,*
 *and they shall name him Emmanuel,*
 **which means "God is with us."**
**When Joseph awoke,**
 **he did as the angel of the Lord had commanded him**
 **and took his wife into his home.**

**The Gospel of the Lord.** All: **Praise to you, Lord Jesus Christ.**

PRAYER OVER THE OFFERINGS
May the Holy Spirit, O Lord,
sanctify these gifts laid upon your altar,
just as he filled with his power the womb of the Blessed Virgin Mary.
Through Christ our Lord. All: **Amen.**

COMMUNION ANTIPHON (Isaiah 7:14)
Behold, a Virgin shall conceive and bear a son;
and his name will be called Emmanuel.

PRAYER AFTER COMMUNION
Having received this pledge of eternal redemption,
we pray, almighty God,
that, as the feast day of our salvation draws ever nearer,
so we may press forward all the more eagerly
to the worthy celebration of the mystery of your Son's Nativity.
Who lives and reigns for ever and ever. All: **Amen.**

# The Nativity of the Lord (Christmas)

## AT THE VIGIL MASS

*December 24, 2016*

The Mass of the Vigil of Christmas is to be used on Saturday evening in those places where the Sunday (holy day of) obligation may be fulfilled on Saturday evening.

*Reflection on the Gospel*

*From the exalted heavenly host of angels to the lowly shepherds "living in the fields," a newness of God's Presence and glory are announced. This Good News cannot be contained in highest heavens, but must be made known to all creatures on earth. Although it is Mystery ever so rich that God should be clothed in human likeness, it is nonetheless a Mystery that touches all people of all times. Angels and shepherds: they trusted the Mystery we celebrate. So must all of God's creatures.*

* *Christ is born for us, "God with us" . . .*

—*Living Liturgy*™, *Vigil of Christmas 2016*

## ENTRANCE ANTIPHON (Cf. Exodus 16:6-7)

Today you will know that the Lord will come, and he will save us,
and in the morning you will see his glory.

## COLLECT

O God, who gladden us year by year
as we wait in hope for our redemption,
grant that, just as we joyfully welcome
your Only Begotten Son as our Redeemer,
we may also merit to face him confidently
when he comes again as our Judge.
Who lives and reigns with you in the unity of the Holy Spirit,
one God, for ever and ever. All: **Amen.**

## READING I (L 13) (Isaiah 62:1-5)

## A reading from the Book of the Prophet Isaiah

*The Lord delights in you.*

For Zion's sake I will not be silent,
   for Jerusalem's sake I will not be quiet,
until her vindication shines forth like the dawn
   and her victory like a burning torch.

Nations shall behold your vindication,
   and all the kings your glory;
you shall be called by a new name
   pronounced by the mouth of the LORD.
You shall be a glorious crown in the hand of the LORD,
   a royal diadem held by your God.
No more shall people call you "Forsaken,"
   or your land "Desolate,"
but you shall be called "My Delight,"
   and your land "Espoused."
For the LORD delights in you
   and makes your land his spouse.
As a young man marries a virgin,
   your Builder shall marry you;
and as a bridegroom rejoices in his bride
   so shall your God rejoice in you.

The word of the Lord. All: Thanks be to God.

RESPONSORIAL PSALM 89

P-102

For ev - er I will sing the good - ness of the Lord.

Psalm 89:4-5, 16-17, 27, 29

R̸. (2a) **For ever I will sing the goodness of the Lord.**

I have made a covenant with my chosen one,
   I have sworn to David my servant:

forever will I confirm your posterity
  and establish your throne for all generations. R̸.

Blessed the people who know the joyful shout;
  in the light of your countenance, O LORD, they walk.
At your name they rejoice all the day,
  and through your justice they are exalted. R̸.

He shall say of me, "You are my father,
  my God, the Rock, my savior."
Forever I will maintain my kindness toward him,
  and my covenant with him stands firm. R̸.

READING II (Acts of the Apostles 13:16-17, 22-25)

**A reading from the Acts of the Apostles**

*Paul bears witness to Christ, the Son of David.*

**When Paul reached Antioch in Pisidia and entered the
      synagogue,**
  **he stood up, motioned with his hand, and said,**
  **"Fellow Israelites and you others who are God-fearing,
      listen.**
**The God of this people Israel chose our ancestors**
  **and exalted the people during their sojourn in the
      land of Egypt.**
**With uplifted arm he led them out of it.**
**Then he removed Saul and raised up David as king;**
  **of him he testified,**
  **'I have found David, son of Jesse, a man after my own
      heart;**
  **he will carry out my every wish.'**
**From this man's descendants God, according to his
      promise,**
  **has brought to Israel a savior, Jesus.**
**John heralded his coming by proclaiming a baptism of
      repentance**
  **to all the people of Israel;**
  **and as John was completing his course, he would say,**
  **'What do you suppose that I am? I am not he.**

**Behold, one is coming after me;**
   **I am not worthy to unfasten the sandals of his feet.'"**

**The word of the Lord.** All: **Thanks be to God.**

GOSPEL (Matthew 1:1-25) *or* Shorter Form [ ] (Matthew 1:18-25)
ALLELUIA

℣. Alleluia, alleluia.  ℟. **Alleluia, alleluia.**
℣. Tomorrow the wickedness of the earth will be destroyed:
   the Savior of the world will reign over us. ℟.

✠ **A reading from the beginning of the holy Gospel**
**according to Matthew**

All: **Glory to you, O Lord.**

*The genealogy of Jesus Christ, the Son of David.*

**The book of the genealogy of Jesus Christ,**
   **the son of David, the son of Abraham.**

**Abraham became the father of Isaac,**
   **Isaac the father of Jacob,**
   **Jacob the father of Judah and his brothers.**
**Judah became the father of Perez and Zerah,**
   **whose mother was Tamar.**
**Perez became the father of Hezron,**
   **Hezron the father of Ram,**
   **Ram the father of Amminadab.**
**Amminadab became the father of Nahshon,**
   **Nahshon the father of Salmon,**
   **Salmon the father of Boaz,**
   **whose mother was Rahab.**
**Boaz became the father of Obed,**
   **whose mother was Ruth.**
**Obed became the father of Jesse,**
   **Jesse the father of David the king.**

**David became the father of Solomon,**
   **whose mother had been the wife of Uriah.**
**Solomon became the father of Rehoboam,**
   **Rehoboam the father of Abijah,**

Abijah the father of Asaph.
Asaph became the father of Jehoshaphat,
  Jehoshaphat the father of Joram,
  Joram the father of Uzziah.
Uzziah became the father of Jotham,
  Jotham the father of Ahaz,
  Ahaz the father of Hezekiah.
Hezekiah became the father of Manasseh,
  Manasseh the father of Amos,
  Amos the father of Josiah.
Josiah became the father of Jechoniah and his brothers
  at the time of the Babylonian exile.

After the Babylonian exile,
  Jechoniah became the father of Shealtiel,
  Shealtiel the father of Zerubbabel,
  Zerubbabel the father of Abiud.
Abiud became the father of Eliakim,
  Eliakim the father of Azor,
  Azor the father of Zadok.
Zadok became the father of Achim,
  Achim the father of Eliud,
  Eliud the father of Eleazar.
Eleazar became the father of Matthan,
  Matthan the father of Jacob,
  Jacob the father of Joseph, the husband of Mary.
Of her was born Jesus who is called the Christ.

Thus the total number of generations
  from Abraham to David
  is fourteen generations;
  from David to the Babylonian exile,
  fourteen generations;
  from the Babylonian exile to the Christ,
  fourteen generations.

[Now this is how the birth of Jesus Christ came about.
When his mother Mary was betrothed to Joseph,

but before they lived together,
she was found with child through the Holy Spirit.
Joseph her husband, since he was a righteous man,
yet unwilling to expose her to shame,
decided to divorce her quietly.
Such was his intention when, behold,
the angel of the Lord appeared to him in a dream
and said,
"Joseph, son of David,
do not be afraid to take Mary your wife into your home.
For it is through the Holy Spirit
that this child has been conceived in her.
She will bear a son and you are to name him Jesus,
because he will save his people from their sins."
All this took place to fulfill
what the Lord had said through the prophet:
*Behold, the virgin shall conceive and bear a son,*
*and they shall name him Emmanuel,*
which means "God is with us."
When Joseph awoke,
he did as the angel of the Lord had commanded him
and took his wife into his home.
He had no relations with her until she bore a son,
and he named him Jesus.]

**The Gospel of the Lord.** All: **Praise to you, Lord Jesus Christ.**

PRAYER OVER THE OFFERINGS
As we look forward, O Lord,
to the coming festivities,
may we serve you all the more eagerly
for knowing that in them
you make manifest the beginnings of our redemption.
Through Christ our Lord. All: **Amen.**

COMMUNION ANTIPHON (Cf. Isaiah 40:5)
The glory of the Lord will be revealed,
and all flesh will see the salvation of our God.

PRAYER AFTER COMMUNION

Grant, O Lord, we pray,
that we may draw new vigor
from celebrating the Nativity of your Only Begotten Son,
by whose heavenly mystery we receive both food and drink.
Who lives and reigns for ever and ever. All: **Amen.**

# The Nativity
# of the Lord
## AT THE MASS
## DURING THE NIGHT

*December 25, 2016*

ENTRANCE ANTIPHON (Psalm 2:7)

The Lord said to me: You are my Son.
It is I who have begotten you this day.

Or:

Let us all rejoice in the Lord, for our Savior has been born
   in the world.
Today true peace has come down to us from heaven.

COLLECT

O God, who have made this most sacred night
radiant with the splendor of the true light,
grant, we pray, that we, who have known the mysteries of his light on
   earth,
may also delight in his gladness in heaven.
Who lives and reigns with you in the unity of the Holy Spirit,
one God, for ever and ever. All: **Amen.**

## Reading I (L 14) (Isaiah 9:1-6)

**A reading from the Book of the Prophet Isaiah**

*A son is given us.*

The people who walked in darkness
  have seen a great light;
upon those who dwelt in the land of gloom
  a light has shone.
You have brought them abundant joy
  and great rejoicing,
as they rejoice before you as at the harvest,
  as people make merry when dividing spoils.
For the yoke that burdened them,
  the pole on their shoulder,
and the rod of their taskmaster
  you have smashed, as on the day of Midian.
For every boot that tramped in battle,
  every cloak rolled in blood,
  will be burned as fuel for flames.
For a child is born to us, a son is given us;
  upon his shoulder dominion rests.
They name him Wonder-Counselor, God-Hero,
  Father-Forever, Prince of Peace.
His dominion is vast
  and forever peaceful,
from David's throne, and over his kingdom,
  which he confirms and sustains
by judgment and justice,
  both now and forever.
The zeal of the Lord of hosts will do this!

**The word of the Lord.** All: **Thanks be to God.**

## Responsorial Psalm 96

P-103

To - day is born our Sav - ior, Christ the Lord.

Psalm 96:1-2, 2-3, 11-12, 13

R℣. (Luke 2:11) **Today is born our Savior, Christ the Lord.**

Sing to the LORD a new song;
   sing to the LORD, all you lands.
Sing to the LORD; bless his name. R℣.

Announce his salvation, day after day.
   Tell his glory among the nations;
   among all peoples, his wondrous deeds. R℣.

Let the heavens be glad and the earth rejoice;
   let the sea and what fills it resound;
   let the plains be joyful and all that is in them!
Then shall all the trees of the forest exult. R℣.

They shall exult before the LORD, for he comes;
   for he comes to rule the earth.
He shall rule the world with justice
   and the peoples with his constancy. R℣.

READING II (Titus 2:11-14)

**A reading from the Letter of Saint Paul to Titus**

*The grace of God has appeared to all.*

**Beloved:**
   **The grace of God has appeared, saving all**
**and training us to reject godless ways and worldly**
     **desires**
**and to live temperately, justly, and devoutly in this age,**
**as we await the blessed hope,**
   **the appearance of the glory of our great God**
**and savior Jesus Christ,**
   **who gave himself for us to deliver us from all lawlessness**
**and to cleanse for himself a people as his own,**
   **eager to do what is good.**

The word of the Lord. All: **Thanks be to God.**

GOSPEL (Luke 2:1-14)

ALLELUIA (Luke 2:10-11)

℣. Alleluia, alleluia.  ℟. **Alleluia, alleluia.**

℣. I proclaim to you good news of great joy:
today a Savior is born for us,
Christ the Lord. ℟.

✢ **A reading from the holy Gospel according to Luke**

All: **Glory to you, O Lord.**

*Today a Savior has been born for you.*

**In those days a decree went out from Caesar Augustus
that the whole world should be enrolled.
This was the first enrollment,
when Quirinius was governor of Syria.
So all went to be enrolled, each to his own town.
And Joseph too went up from Galilee from the town of
Nazareth
to Judea, to the city of David that is called Bethlehem,
because he was of the house and family of David,
to be enrolled with Mary, his betrothed, who was with
child.
While they were there,
the time came for her to have her child,
and she gave birth to her firstborn son.
She wrapped him in swaddling clothes and laid him in a
manger,
because there was no room for them in the inn.
Now there were shepherds in that region living in the fields
and keeping the night watch over their flock.
The angel of the Lord appeared to them
and the glory of the Lord shone around them,
and they were struck with great fear.
The angel said to them,
"Do not be afraid;
for behold, I proclaim to you good news of great joy
that will be for all the people.**

For today in the city of David
    a savior has been born for you who is Christ and Lord.
And this will be a sign for you:
    you will find an infant wrapped in swaddling clothes
    and lying in a manger."
And suddenly there was a multitude of the heavenly host
      with the angel,
    praising God and saying:
      "Glory to God in the highest
        and on earth peace to those on whom his favor
          rests."

**The Gospel of the Lord.** All: **Praise to you, Lord Jesus Christ.**

PRAYER OVER THE OFFERINGS
May the oblation of this day's feast
be pleasing to you, O Lord, we pray,
that through this most holy exchange
we may be found in the likeness of Christ,
in whom our nature is united to you.
Who lives and reigns for ever and ever. All: **Amen.**

COMMUNION ANTIPHON (John 1:14)
The Word became flesh, and we have seen his glory.

PRAYER AFTER COMMUNION
Grant us, we pray, O Lord our God,
that we, who are gladdened by participation
in the feast of our Redeemer's Nativity,
may through an honorable way of life become worthy of union with
   him.
Who lives and reigns for ever and ever. All: **Amen.**

## AT THE MASS AT DAWN

<small>ENTRANCE ANTIPHON</small> (Cf. Isaiah 9:1, 5; Luke 1:33)
Today a light will shine upon us, for the Lord is born for us;
and he will be called Wondrous God,
Prince of peace, Father of future ages:
and his reign will be without end.

<small>COLLECT</small>
Grant, we pray, almighty God,
that, as we are bathed in the new radiance of your incarnate Word,
the light of faith, which illumines our minds,
may also shine through in our deeds.
Through our Lord Jesus Christ, your Son,
who lives and reigns with you in the unity of the Holy Spirit,
one God, for ever and ever. All: **Amen.**

<small>READING I</small> (L 15) (Isaiah 62:11-12)
### A reading from the Book of the Prophet Isaiah

*Behold, your Savior comes!*

> See, the LORD proclaims
>     to the ends of the earth:
> say to daughter Zion,
>     your savior comes!
> Here is his reward with him,
>     his recompense before him.
> They shall be called the holy people,
>     the redeemed of the LORD,
> and you shall be called "Frequented,"
>     a city that is not forsaken.

The word of the Lord. All: **Thanks be to God.**

RESPONSORIAL PSALM 97

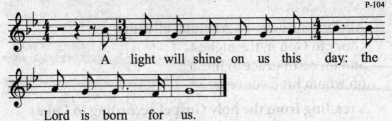

A light will shine on us this day: the Lord is born for us.

Psalm 97:1, 6, 11-12

℟. **A light will shine on us this day: the Lord is born for us.**

The LORD is king; let the earth rejoice;
　　let the many isles be glad.
The heavens proclaim his justice,
　　and all peoples see his glory. ℟.

Light dawns for the just;
　　and gladness, for the upright of heart.
Be glad in the LORD, you just,
　　and give thanks to his holy name. ℟.

READING II (Titus 3:4-7)

**A reading from the Letter of Saint Paul to Titus**

*Because of his mercy, he saved us.*

**Beloved:**
**When the kindness and generous love**
　　**of God our savior appeared,**
**not because of any righteous deeds we had done**
　　**but because of his mercy,**
**he saved us through the bath of rebirth**
　　**and renewal by the Holy Spirit,**
**whom he richly poured out on us**
　　**through Jesus Christ our savior,**
**so that we might be justified by his grace**
　　**and become heirs in hope of eternal life.**

The word of the Lord. All: Thanks be to God.

GOSPEL (Luke 2:15-20)
ALLELUIA (Luke 2:14)

℣. Alleluia, alleluia.  ℟. **Alleluia, alleluia.**
℣. Glory to God in the highest,
    and on earth peace to those
    on whom his favor rests. ℟.

✠ **A reading from the holy Gospel according to Luke**

All: **Glory to you, O Lord.**

*The shepherds found Mary and Joseph and the infant.*

**When the angels went away from them to heaven,**
    **the shepherds said to one another,**
    **"Let us go, then, to Bethlehem**
    **to see this thing that has taken place,**
    **which the Lord has made known to us."**
**So they went in haste and found Mary and Joseph,**
    **and the infant lying in the manger.**
**When they saw this,**
    **they made known the message**
    **that had been told them about this child.**
**All who heard it were amazed**
    **by what had been told them by the shepherds.**
**And Mary kept all these things,**
    **reflecting on them in her heart.**
**Then the shepherds returned,**
    **glorifying and praising God**
    **for all they had heard and seen,**
    **just as it had been told to them.**

**The Gospel of the Lord.** All: **Praise to you, Lord Jesus Christ.**

PRAYER OVER THE OFFERINGS
May our offerings be worthy, we pray, O Lord,
of the mysteries of the Nativity this day,
that, just as Christ was born a man and also shone forth as God,
so these earthly gifts may confer on us what is divine.
Through Christ our Lord. All: **Amen.**

## Communion Antiphon (Cf. Zechariah 9:9)

Rejoice, O Daughter Sion; lift up praise, Daughter Jerusalem:
Behold, your King will come, the Holy One and Savior of
the world.

## Prayer after Communion

Grant us, Lord, as we honor with joyful devotion
the Nativity of your Son,
that we may come to know with fullness of faith
the hidden depths of this mystery
and to love them ever more and more.
Through Christ our Lord. All: **Amen.**

# AT THE MASS
# DURING THE DAY

## Entrance Antiphon (Cf. Isaiah 9:5)

A child is born for us, and a son is given to us;
his scepter of power rests upon his shoulder,
and his name will be called Messenger of great counsel.

## Collect

O God, who wonderfully created the dignity of human nature
and still more wonderfully restored it,
grant, we pray,
that we may share in the divinity of Christ,
who humbled himself to share in our humanity.
Who lives and reigns with you in the unity of the Holy Spirit,
one God, for ever and ever. All: **Amen.**

## READING I (L 16) (Isaiah 52:7-10)

**A reading from the Book of the Prophet Isaiah**

*All the ends of the earth will behold the salvation of our God.*

> How beautiful upon the mountains
> > are the feet of him who brings glad tidings,
> announcing peace, bearing good news,
> > announcing salvation, and saying to Zion,
> > "Your God is King!"
>
> Hark! Your sentinels raise a cry,
> > together they shout for joy,
> for they see directly, before their eyes,
> > the LORD restoring Zion.
> Break out together in song,
> > O ruins of Jerusalem!
> For the LORD comforts his people,
> > he redeems Jerusalem.
> The LORD has bared his holy arm
> > in the sight of all the nations;
> all the ends of the earth will behold
> > the salvation of our God.

**The word of the Lord.** All: **Thanks be to God.**

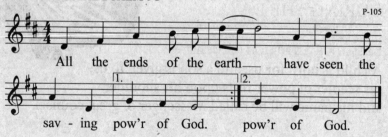

P-105

All the ends of the earth have seen the sav-ing pow'r of God. pow'r of God.

Music: Jay F. Hunstiger, © 1990, administered by Liturgical Press. All rights reserved.

Psalm 98:1, 2-3, 3-4, 5-6

℟. (3c) **All the ends of the earth have seen the saving power of God.**

> Sing to the LORD a new song,
> > for he has done wondrous deeds;

his right hand has won victory for him,
    his holy arm. ℟.

The LORD has made his salvation known:
    in the sight of the nations he has revealed his justice.
He has remembered his kindness and his faithfulness
    toward the house of Israel. ℟.

All the ends of the earth have seen
    the salvation by our God.
Sing joyfully to the LORD, all you lands;
    break into song; sing praise. ℟.

Sing praise to the LORD with the harp,
    with the harp and melodious song.
With trumpets and the sound of the horn
    sing joyfully before the King, the LORD. ℟.

## READING II (Hebrews 1:1-6)

**A reading from the beginning of the Letter to the Hebrews**

*God has spoken to us through the Son.*

**Brothers and sisters:**
**In times past, God spoke in partial and various ways**
    **to our ancestors through the prophets;**
    **in these last days, he has spoken to us through the Son,**
    **whom he made heir of all things**
    **and through whom he created the universe,**
        **who is the refulgence of his glory,**
            **the very imprint of his being,**
        **and who sustains all things by his mighty word.**
        **When he had accomplished purification from sins,**
        **he took his seat at the right hand of the Majesty**
            **on high,**
        **as far superior to the angels**
        **as the name he has inherited is more excellent than**
            **theirs.**

**For to which of the angels did God ever say:**
    *You are my son; this day I have begotten you?*

**Or again:**

> *I will be a father to him, and he shall be a son to me?*

**And again, when he leads the firstborn into the world,**
**he says:**

> *Let all the angels of God worship him.*

**The word of the Lord.** All: **Thanks be to God.**

GOSPEL (John 1:1-18) *or* Shorter Form [ ] (John 1:1-5, 9-14)
ALLELUIA

℣. Alleluia, alleluia.  ℟. **Alleluia, alleluia.**
℣. A holy day has dawned upon us.
    Come, you nations, and adore the Lord.
    For today a great light has come upon the earth. ℟.

✣ **A reading from the holy Gospel according to John**

All: **Glory to you, O Lord.**

*The Word became flesh and made his dwelling among us.*

**[In the beginning was the Word,**
    **and the Word was with God,**
    **and the Word was God.**
**He was in the beginning with God.**
**All things came to be through him,**
    **and without him nothing came to be.**
**What came to be through him was life,**
    **and this life was the light of the human race;**
    **the light shines in the darkness,**
    **and the darkness has not overcome it.]**
**A man named John was sent from God.**
**He came for testimony, to testify to the light,**
    **so that all might believe through him.**
**He was not the light,**
    **but came to testify to the light.**
**[The true light, which enlightens everyone,**
    **was coming into the world.**
    **He was in the world,**
        **and the world came to be through him,**
        **but the world did not know him.**

He came to what was his own,
　　but his own people did not accept him.

But to those who did accept him
　　he gave power to become children of God,
　　to those who believe in his name,
　　who were born not by natural generation
　　nor by human choice nor by a man's decision
　　but of God.
　　　And the Word became flesh
　　　　and made his dwelling among us,
　　　　and we saw his glory,
　　　　the glory as of the Father's only Son,
　　　　full of grace and truth.]

John testified to him and cried out, saying,
　　"This was he of whom I said,
　　'The one who is coming after me ranks ahead of me
　　because he existed before me.'"

From his fullness we have all received,
　　grace in place of grace,
　　because while the law was given through Moses,
　　grace and truth came through Jesus Christ.

No one has ever seen God.

The only Son, God, who is at the Father's side,
　　has revealed him.

The Gospel of the Lord. All: **Praise to you, Lord Jesus Christ.**

**PRAYER OVER THE OFFERINGS**

Make acceptable, O Lord, our oblation on this solemn day,
when you manifested the reconciliation
that makes us wholly pleasing in your sight
and inaugurated for us the fullness of divine worship.
Through Christ our Lord. All: **Amen.**

**COMMUNION ANTIPHON** (Cf. Psalm 98[97]:3)

All the ends of the earth have seen the salvation of our God.

**PRAYER AFTER COMMUNION**

Grant, O merciful God,
that, just as the Savior of the world, born this day,

is the author of divine generation for us,
so he may be the giver even of immortality.
Who lives and reigns for ever and ever. All: **Amen.**

# The Holy Family of Jesus, Mary and Joseph

## FRIDAY WITHIN THE OCTAVE OF THE NATIVITY OF THE LORD (Christmas)

## December 30, 2016

---

*Reflection on the Gospel*

*All the wonderful gifts of grace bestowed upon the Holy Family—Jesus' miraculous conception by the Holy Spirit, the virgin birth—did not preserve this family from hardship. They faced challenges and pressures. Yet they responded faithfully and obediently to God's messages and will for them. The Holy Family was not exempt from life-threatening difficulties. Rather, it was in the midst of difficulty that their holiness was tested, deepened, and revealed as a faithful and obedient response to God. This feast calls us to be this same kind of holy family.*

• *Daily life and our response calls us to holiness . . .*

—*Living Liturgy™, Holy Family 2016*

ENTRANCE ANTIPHON (Luke 2:16)
The shepherds went in haste,
and found Mary and Joseph and the Infant lying in a
    manger.

COLLECT

O God, who were pleased to give us
the shining example of the Holy Family,
graciously grant that we may imitate them
in practicing the virtues of family life and in the bonds of charity,
and so, in the joy of your house,
delight one day in eternal rewards.
Through our Lord Jesus Christ, your Son,
who lives and reigns with you in the unity of the Holy Spirit,
one God, for ever and ever. All: **Amen.**

READING I

A  (L 17) (Sirach 3:2-6, 12-14) *for this year additional options
can be found in the Lectionary*

**A reading from the Book of Sirach**

*Those who fear the Lord honor their parents.*

> **God sets a father in honor over his children;**
> **a mother's authority he confirms over her sons.**
> **Whoever honors his father atones for sins,**
> **and preserves himself from them.**
> **When he prays, he is heard;**
> **he stores up riches who reveres his mother.**
> **Whoever honors his father is gladdened by children,**
> **and, when he prays, is heard.**
> **Whoever reveres his father will live a long life;**
> **he who obeys his father brings comfort to his mother.**
>
> **My son, take care of your father when he is old;**
> **grieve him not as long as he lives.**
> **Even if his mind fail, be considerate of him;**
> **revile him not all the days of his life;**
> **kindness to a father will not be forgotten,**
> **firmly planted against the debt of your sins**
> **—a house raised in justice to you.**

The word of the Lord. All: **Thanks be to God.**

Or:

B (Colossians 3:12-21) *or* Shorter Form [ ] (Colossians 3:12-17)
*for this year additional options can be found in the Lectionary*

# A reading from the Letter of Saint Paul to the Colossians

*Family life in the Lord.*

[Brothers and sisters:
Put on, as God's chosen ones, holy and beloved,
   heartfelt compassion, kindness, humility, gentleness,
      and patience,
   bearing with one another and forgiving one another,
   if one has a grievance against another;
   as the Lord has forgiven you, so must you also do.
And over all these put on love,
   that is, the bond of perfection.
And let the peace of Christ control your hearts,
   the peace into which you were also called in one body.
And be thankful.
Let the word of Christ dwell in you richly,
   as in all wisdom you teach and admonish one another,
   singing psalms, hymns, and spiritual songs
   with gratitude in your hearts to God.
And whatever you do, in word or in deed,
   do everything in the name of the Lord Jesus,
   giving thanks to God the Father through him.]

Wives, be subordinate to your husbands,
   as is proper in the Lord.
Husbands, love your wives,
   and avoid any bitterness toward them.
Children, obey your parents in everything,
   for this is pleasing to the Lord.
Fathers, do not provoke your children,
   so they may not become discouraged.

The word of the Lord. All: **Thanks be to God.**

RESPONSORIAL PSALM 128

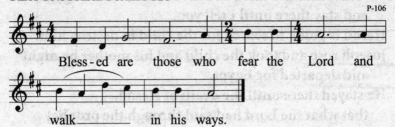

P-106

Bless - ed are those who fear the Lord and walk _____ in his ways.

Psalm 128:1-2, 3, 4-5

℟. (*See* 1) **Blessed are those who fear the Lord and walk in his ways.**

Blessed is everyone who fears the LORD,
    who walks in his ways!
For you shall eat the fruit of your handiwork;
    blessed shall you be, and favored. ℟.

Your wife shall be like a fruitful vine
    in the recesses of your home;
your children like olive plants
    around your table. ℟.

Behold, thus is the man blessed
    who fears the LORD.
The LORD bless you from Zion:
    may you see the prosperity of Jerusalem
    all the days of your life. ℟.

GOSPEL (Matthew 2:13-15, 19-23)
ALLELUIA (Colossians 3:15a, 16a)

℣. Alleluia, alleluia.  ℟. **Alleluia, alleluia.**
℣. Let the peace of Christ control your hearts;
    let the word of Christ dwell in you richly. ℟.

☩ **A reading from the holy Gospel according to Matthew**

All: **Glory to you, O Lord.**

*Take the child and his mother, and flee into Egypt.*

**When the magi had departed, behold,**
    **the angel of the Lord appeared to Joseph in a dream**
        **and said,**

"Rise, take the child and his mother, flee to Egypt,
and stay there until I tell you."
Herod is going to search for the child to destroy him."
Joseph rose and took the child and his mother by night
and departed for Egypt.
He stayed there until the death of Herod,
that what the Lord had said through the prophet
might be fulfilled,
*Out of Egypt I called my son.*

When Herod had died, behold,
the angel of the Lord appeared in a dream
to Joseph in Egypt and said,
"Rise, take the child and his mother and go to the
land of Israel,
for those who sought the child's life are dead."
He rose, took the child and his mother,
and went to the land of Israel.
But when he heard that Archelaus was ruling over Judea
in place of his father Herod,
he was afraid to go back there.
And because he had been warned in a dream,
he departed for the region of Galilee.
He went and dwelt in a town called Nazareth,
so that what had been spoken through the prophets
might be fulfilled,
*He shall be called a Nazorean.*

The Gospel of the Lord. All: **Praise to you, Lord Jesus Christ.**

PRAYER OVER THE OFFERINGS
We offer you, Lord, the sacrifice of conciliation,
humbly asking that,
through the intercession of the Virgin Mother of God and Saint Joseph,
you may establish our families firmly in your grace and your peace.
Through Christ our Lord. All: **Amen.**

COMMUNION ANTIPHON (Baruch 3:38)
Our God has appeared on the earth, and lived among us.

PRAYER AFTER COMMUNION

Bring those you refresh with this heavenly Sacrament,
most merciful Father,
to imitate constantly the example of the Holy Family,
so that, after the trials of this world,
we may share their company for ever.
Through Christ our Lord. All: **Amen.**

# Solemnity of Mary, the Holy Mother of God

## OCTAVE DAY OF THE NATIVITY OF THE LORD (Christmas)

*January 1, 2017*

World Day of Peace

*Reflection on the Gospel*

*Mary was present when the shepherds encountered her Son, received the
Good News into their hearts, and then "made known the message" to all
"who heard it." Likewise, Mary is present when we encounter her Son,
reflect on the Good News in our hearts, and make known the message of
Life to all we meet. Mary is not only the Mother of God. She also is our
mother who mothers us into her kind of contemplative love.*

• *Like Mary I can respond to God's Presence by . . .*

—Living Liturgy™, *Mary, Mother of God 2017*

ENTRANCE ANTIPHON

Hail, Holy Mother, who gave birth to the King
who rules heaven and earth for ever.

Or:

(Cf. Isaiah 9:1, 5; Luke 1:33)

Today a light will shine upon us, for the Lord is born for us;
and he will be called Wondrous God,
Prince of peace, Father of future ages:
and his reign will be without end.

## COLLECT

O God, who through the fruitful virginity of Blessed Mary
bestowed on the human race
the grace of eternal salvation,
grant, we pray,
that we may experience the intercession of her,
through whom we were found worthy
to receive the author of life,
our Lord Jesus Christ, your Son.
Who lives and reigns with you in the unity of the Holy Spirit,
one God, for ever and ever. All: **Amen.**

## READING I (L 18) (Numbers 6:22-27)

**A reading from the Book of Numbers**

*They shall invoke my name upon the Israelites, and I will bless them.*

**The LORD said to Moses:**
 "**Speak to Aaron and his sons and tell them:**
 **This is how you shall bless the Israelites.**
**Say to them:**
 **The LORD bless you and keep you!**
 **The LORD let his face shine upon**
 **you, and be gracious to you!**
 **The LORD look upon you kindly and**
 **give you peace!**
**So shall they invoke my name upon the Israelites,**
 **and I will bless them."**

**The word of the Lord. All: Thanks be to God.**

## RESPONSORIAL PSALM 67

P-107

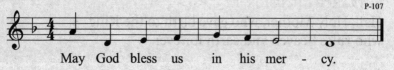

May God bless us in his mer - cy.

Music: Jay F. Hunstiger, © 1990, administered by Liturgical Press. All rights reserved.

Psalm 67:2-3, 5, 6, 8

R℣. (2a) **May God bless us in his mercy.**

May God have pity on us and bless us;
    may he let his face shine upon us.
So may your way be known upon earth;
    among all nations, your salvation. R℣.

May the nations be glad and exult
    because you rule the peoples in equity;
    the nations on the earth you guide. R℣.

May the peoples praise you, O God;
    may all the peoples praise you!
May God bless us,
    and may all the ends of the earth fear him! R℣.

READING II (Galatians 4:4-7)

**A reading from the Letter of Saint Paul to the Galatians**

*God sent his Son, born of a woman.*

**Brothers and sisters:**
**When the fullness of time had come, God sent his Son,**
    **born of a woman, born under the law,**
    **to ransom those under the law,**
    **so that we might receive adoption as sons.**
**As proof that you are sons,**
    **God sent the Spirit of his Son into our hearts,**
    **crying out, "Abba, Father!"**
**So you are no longer a slave but a son,**
    **and if a son then also an heir, through God.**

**The word of the Lord. All: Thanks be to God.**

GOSPEL (Luke 2:16-21)

ALLELUIA (Hebrews 1:1-2)

℣. Alleluia, alleluia. R℣. **Alleluia, alleluia.**
℣. In the past God spoke to our ancestors through the
        prophets;
    in these last days, he has spoken to us through the Son. R℣.

✢ **A reading from the holy Gospel according to Luke**

All: **Glory to you, O Lord.**

*They found Mary and Joseph and the infant. When the eight days were completed, he was named Jesus.*

**The shepherds went in haste to Bethlehem and found**
    **Mary and Joseph,**
  **and the infant lying in the manger.**
**When they saw this,**
  **they made known the message**
  **that had been told them about this child.**
**All who heard it were amazed**
  **by what had been told them by the shepherds.**
**And Mary kept all these things,**
  **reflecting on them in her heart.**
**Then the shepherds returned,**
  **glorifying and praising God**
  **for all they had heard and seen,**
  **just as it had been told to them.**

**When eight days were completed for his circumcision,**
    **he was named Jesus, the name given him by the angel**
    **before he was conceived in the womb.**

**The Gospel of the Lord.** All: **Praise to you, Lord Jesus Christ.**

PRAYER OVER THE OFFERINGS

O God, who in your kindness begin all good things
and bring them to fulfillment,
grant to us, who find joy in the Solemnity of the holy Mother of God,
that, just as we glory in the beginnings of your grace,
so one day we may rejoice in its completion.
Through Christ our Lord. All: **Amen.**

COMMUNION ANTIPHON (Hebrews 13:8)

Jesus Christ is the same yesterday, today, and for ever.

PRAYER AFTER COMMUNION

We have received this heavenly Sacrament with joy, O Lord:
grant, we pray,
that it may lead us to eternal life,
for we rejoice to proclaim the blessed ever-Virgin Mary
Mother of your Son and Mother of the Church.
Through Christ our Lord. All: **Amen.**

# The Epiphany of the Lord

## AT THE VIGIL MASS

*January 7, 2017*

This Mass is used on the evening of the day before the Solemnity,
either before or after First Vespers (Evening Prayer I) of the Epiphany.

*Reflection on the Gospel*

*Who is this newborn Child for whom the magi are searching, being led
by a star? He is "the newborn king of the Jews." But in reality the One
they seek is more: he is ruler, shepherd—the Christ. Do we ever ask, as
did the magi, "Where is the newborn king of the Jews?" How diligently
do we search? What star leads us? Whom do we find? How do we fit
into this astounding story? How do we encounter the Light of the world?*

• *"Where is the newborn king of the Jews?"* . . .

—*Living Liturgy*™, *Epiphany 2017*

ENTRANCE ANTIPHON (Cf. Baruch 5:5)

Arise, Jerusalem, and look to the East
and see your children gathered from the rising to the
    setting of the sun.

COLLECT

May the splendor of your majesty, O Lord, we pray,
shed its light upon our hearts,
that we may pass through the shadows of this world
and reach the brightness of our eternal home.
Through our Lord Jesus Christ, your Son,
who lives and reigns with you in the unity of the Holy Spirit,
one God, for ever and ever. All: **Amen.**

(Note readings are those of the day.)

PRAYER OVER THE OFFERINGS

Accept we pray, O Lord, our offerings,
in honor of the appearing of your Only Begotten Son
and the first fruits of the nations,
that to you praise may be rendered
and eternal salvation be ours.
Through Christ our Lord. All: **Amen.**

COMMUNION ANTIPHON (Cf. Revelation 21:23)

The brightness of God illumined the holy city Jerusalem,
and the nations will walk by its light.

PRAYER AFTER COMMUNION

Renewed by sacred nourishment,
we implore your mercy, O Lord,
that the star of your justice
may shine always bright in our minds
and that our true treasure may ever consist in our confession of you.
Through Christ our Lord. All: **Amen.**

*January 8*

# AT THE MASS DURING THE DAY

ENTRANCE ANTIPHON (Cf. Malachi 3:1; 1 Chronicles 29:12)

Behold, the Lord, the Mighty One, has come;
and kingship is in his grasp, and power and dominion.

COLLECT

O God, who on this day
revealed your Only Begotten Son to the nations
by the guidance of a star,
grant in your mercy
that we, who know you already by faith,

may be brought to behold the beauty of your sublime glory.
Through our Lord Jesus Christ, your Son,
who lives and reigns with you in the unity of the Holy Spirit,
one God, for ever and ever. All: **Amen.**

READING I (L 20) (Isaiah 60:1-6)

## A reading from the Book of the Prophet Isaiah

*The glory of the Lord shines upon you.*

> Rise up in splendor, Jerusalem! Your light has come,
> the glory of the Lord shines upon you.
> See, darkness covers the earth,
> and thick clouds cover the peoples;
> but upon you the LORD shines,
> and over you appears his glory.
> Nations shall walk by your light,
> and kings by your shining radiance.
> Raise your eyes and look about;
> they all gather and come to you:
> your sons come from afar,
> and your daughters in the arms of their nurses.
>
> Then you shall be radiant at what you see,
> your heart shall throb and overflow,
> for the riches of the sea shall be emptied out before you,
> the wealth of nations shall be brought to you.
> Caravans of camels shall fill you,
> dromedaries from Midian and Ephah;
> all from Sheba shall come
> bearing gold and frankincense,
> and proclaiming the praises of the LORD.

The word of the Lord. All: **Thanks be to God.**

RESPONSORIAL PSALM 72

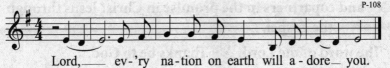

P-108

Lord,— ev-'ry na-tion on earth will a-dore— you.

Psalm 72:1-2, 7-8, 10-11, 12-13

R℣. (*See* 11) **Lord, every nation on earth will adore you.**

O God, with your judgment endow the king,
    and with your justice, the king's son;
he shall govern your people with justice
    and your afflicted ones with judgment. R℣.

Justice shall flower in his days,
    and profound peace, till the moon be no more.
May he rule from sea to sea,
    and from the River to the ends of the earth. R℣.

The kings of Tarshish and the Isles shall offer gifts;
    the kings of Arabia and Seba shall bring tribute.
All kings shall pay him homage,
    all nations shall serve him. R℣.

For he shall rescue the poor when he cries out,
    and the afflicted when he has no one to help him.
He shall have pity for the lowly and the poor;
    the lives of the poor he shall save. R℣.

READING II (Ephesians 3:2-3a, 5-6)

**A reading from the Letter of Saint Paul to the Ephesians**

*Now it has been revealed that the Gentiles are coheirs of the promise.*

**Brothers and sisters:**
**You have heard of the stewardship of God's grace**
    **that was given to me for your benefit,**
        **namely, that the mystery was made known to me by**
            **revelation.**
**It was not made known to people in other generations**
    **as it has now been revealed**
    **to his holy apostles and prophets by the Spirit:**
    **that the Gentiles are coheirs, members of the same body,**
    **and copartners in the promise in Christ Jesus through**
        **the gospel.**

The word of the Lord. All: **Thanks be to God.**

GOSPEL (Matthew 2:1-12)
ALLELUIA (Matthew 2:2)

℣. Alleluia, alleluia. ℟. **Alleluia, alleluia.**
℣. We saw his star at its rising
    and have come to do him homage. ℟.

✛ **A reading from the holy Gospel according to Matthew**

All: **Glory to you, O Lord.**

*We saw his star at its rising and have come to do him homage.*

**When Jesus was born in Bethlehem of Judea,**
    **in the days of King Herod,**
      **behold, magi from the east arrived in Jerusalem, saying,**
      **"Where is the newborn king of the Jews?**
**We saw his star at its rising**
    **and have come to do him homage."**
**When King Herod heard this,**
    **he was greatly troubled,**
    **and all Jerusalem with him.**
**Assembling all the chief priests and the scribes of the**
      **people,**
    **he inquired of them where the Christ was to be born.**
**They said to him, "In Bethlehem of Judea,**
    **for thus it has been written through the prophet:**
      ***And you, Bethlehem, land of Judah,***
        ***are by no means least among the rulers of Judah;***
      ***since from you shall come a ruler,***
        ***who is to shepherd my people Israel."***
**Then Herod called the magi secretly**
    **and ascertained from them the time of the star's**
      **appearance.**
**He sent them to Bethlehem and said,**
    **"Go and search diligently for the child.**
**When you have found him, bring me word,**
    **that I too may go and do him homage."**
**After their audience with the king they set out.**

And behold, the star that they had seen at its rising
   preceded them,
   until it came and stopped over the place where the
      child was.
They were overjoyed at seeing the star,
   and on entering the house
   they saw the child with Mary his mother.
They prostrated themselves and did him homage.
Then they opened their treasures
   and offered him gifts of gold, frankincense, and myrrh.
And having been warned in a dream not to return to
   Herod,
   they departed for their country by another way.

The Gospel of the Lord. All: **Praise to you, Lord Jesus Christ.**

PRAYER OVER THE OFFERINGS
Look with favor, Lord, we pray,
on these gifts of your Church,
in which are offered now not gold or frankincense or myrrh,
but he who by them is proclaimed,
sacrificed and received, Jesus Christ.
Who lives and reigns for ever and ever. All: **Amen.**

COMMUNION ANTIPHON (Cf. Matthew 2:2)
We have seen his star in the East,
and have come with gifts to adore the Lord.

PRAYER AFTER COMMUNION
Go before us with heavenly light, O Lord,
always and everywhere,
that we may perceive with clear sight
and revere with true affection
the mystery in which you have willed us to participate.
Through Christ our Lord. All: **Amen.**

# The Baptism of the Lord

*January 9, 2017*

*Reflection on the Gospel*

*Jesus comes to John who is baptizing in the River Jordan. John is pointing to a baptism greater than his and to a person greater than he. Jesus asks John to baptize him in order to "fulfill all righteousness" and thus show forth his continuity with the tradition in which John stands. But more happens. When the heavens open, the Spirit descends, and Jesus is announced as the "beloved Son," a new tradition is born and humanity's relationship with God is changed forever. Through baptism we are invited into this new tradition.*

- *Like Jesus, Baptism has invited me to . . . .*

—Living Liturgy™, *Baptism of the Lord 2017*

## Entrance Antiphon (Cf. Matthew 3:16-17)

After the Lord was baptized, the heavens were opened,
and the Spirit descended upon him like a dove,
and the voice of the Father thundered:
This is my beloved Son, with whom I am well pleased.

## Collect

Almighty ever-living God,
who, when Christ had been baptized in the River Jordan
and as the Holy Spirit descended upon him,
solemnly declared him your beloved Son,
grant that your children by adoption,
reborn of water and the Holy Spirit,
may always be well pleasing to you.
Through our Lord Jesus Christ, your Son,

who lives and reigns with you in the unity of the Holy Spirit,
one God, for ever and ever. All: **Amen.**

Or:

O God, whose Only Begotten Son
has appeared in our very flesh,
grant, we pray, that we may be inwardly transformed
through him whom we recognize as outwardly like ourselves.
Who lives and reigns with you in the unity of the Holy Spirit,
one God, for ever and ever. All: **Amen.**

## READING I

*A* (L 21) (Isaiah 42:1-4, 6-7) *for this year additional options can be found in the Lectionary*

## A reading from the Book of the Prophet Isaiah

*Behold my servant with whom I am well pleased.*

> Thus says the LORD:
> Here is my servant whom I uphold,
>> my chosen one with whom I am pleased,
> upon whom I have put my spirit;
>> he shall bring forth justice to the nations,
> not crying out, not shouting,
>> not making his voice heard in the street.
> A bruised reed he shall not break,
>> and a smoldering wick he shall not quench,
> until he establishes justice on the earth;
>> the coastlands will wait for his teaching.
>
> I, the LORD, have called you for the victory of justice,
>> I have grasped you by the hand;
> I formed you, and set you
>> as a covenant of the people,
>> a light for the nations,
> to open the eyes of the blind,
>> to bring out prisoners from confinement,
>> and from the dungeon, those who live in darkness.

The word of the Lord. All: **Thanks be to God.**

Or:

*B* (Acts of the Apostles 10:34-38) *for this year additional options can be found in the Lectionary*

## A reading from the Acts of the Apostles

*God anointed him with the Holy Spirit.*

**Peter proceeded to speak to those gathered**
    **in the house of Cornelius, saying:**
    **"In truth, I see that God shows no partiality.**
**Rather, in every nation whoever fears him and acts**
        **uprightly**
    **is acceptable to him.**
**You know the word that he sent to the Israelites**
    **as he proclaimed peace through Jesus Christ, who is**
            **Lord of all,**
    **what has happened all over Judea,**
    **beginning in Galilee after the baptism**
    **that John preached,**
    **how God anointed Jesus of Nazareth**
    **with the Holy Spirit and power.**
**He went about doing good**
    **and healing all those oppressed by the devil,**
    **for God was with him."**

**The word of the Lord.** All: **Thanks be to God.**

RESPONSORIAL PSALM 29

P-109

The Lord will bless his peo-ple with peace.

peace, ___ his peo - ple with peace. ___

Music: Jay F. Hunstiger, © 1990, administered by Liturgical Press. All rights reserved.

Psalm 29:1-2, 3-4, 3, 9-10

R̸. (11b) **The Lord will bless his people with peace.**

    Give to the LORD, you sons of God,
        give to the LORD glory and praise,        *(continued)*

give to the LORD the glory due his name;
   adore the LORD in holy attire. R7.

The voice of the LORD is over the waters,
   the LORD, over vast waters.
The voice of the LORD is mighty;
   the voice of the LORD is majestic. R7.

The God of glory thunders,
   and in his temple all say, "Glory!"
The LORD is enthroned above the flood;
   the LORD is enthroned as king forever. R7.

GOSPEL (Matthew 3:13-17)
ALLELUIA (*See* Mark 9:7)
V̷. Alleluia, alleluia.   R7. **Alleluia, alleluia.**
V̷. The heavens were opened and the voice of the Father
         thundered:
   This is my beloved Son, listen to him. R7.

✠ **A reading from the holy Gospel according to Matthew**

All: **Glory to you, O Lord.**

*After Jesus was baptized, he saw the Spirit of God coming upon him.*

**Jesus came from Galilee to John at the Jordan**
   **to be baptized by him.**
**John tried to prevent him, saying,**
   **"I need to be baptized by you,**
   **and yet you are coming to me?"**
**Jesus said to him in reply,**
   **"Allow it now, for thus it is fitting for us**
   **to fulfill all righteousness."**
**Then he allowed him.**
**After Jesus was baptized,**
   **he came up from the water and behold,**
   **the heavens were opened for him,**
   **and he saw the Spirit of God descending like a dove**
   **and coming upon him.**

**And a voice came from the heavens, saying,**
**"This is my beloved Son, with whom I am well pleased."**

**The Gospel of the Lord.** All: **Praise to you, Lord Jesus Christ.**

PRAYER OVER THE OFFERINGS
Accept, O Lord, the offerings
we have brought to honor the revealing of your beloved Son,
so that the oblation of your faithful
may be transformed into the sacrifice of him
who willed in his compassion
to wash away the sins of the world.
Who lives and reigns for ever and ever. All: **Amen.**

COMMUNION ANTIPHON (John 1:32, 34)
Behold the One of whom John said:
I have seen and testified that this is the Son of God.

PRAYER AFTER COMMUNION
Nourished with these sacred gifts,
we humbly entreat your mercy, O Lord,
that, faithfully listening to your Only Begotten Son,
we may be your children in name and in truth.
Through Christ our Lord. All: **Amen.**

# Second Sunday in Ordinary Time

## January 15, 2017

*Reflection on the Gospel*

*John's prophetic announcement, "Behold, the Lamb of God," reveals two things about Jesus. He is "the Lamb" who will be sacrificed for the remission of sins. He is "of God" who will "baptize with the Holy Spirit." Further, the gospel reveals two things about baptism. Baptism with water washes away our sin. Baptism with the Holy Spirit empowers us to come to know who Jesus is. Like John, we do not know Jesus—until our baptism initiates us into a lifelong encounter with him.*

*• As I learn more about Jesus, I have discovered . . .*

—Living Liturgy™, *Second Sunday in Ordinary Time 2017*

ENTRANCE ANTIPHON (Psalm 66[65]:4)

All the earth shall bow down before you, O God,
and shall sing to you,
shall sing to your name, O Most High!

COLLECT

Almighty ever-living God,
who govern all things,
both in heaven and on earth,
mercifully hear the pleading of your people
and bestow your peace on our times.
Through our Lord Jesus Christ, your Son,
who lives and reigns with you in the unity of the Holy Spirit,
one God, for ever and ever. All: **Amen.**

READING I (L 64-A) (Isaiah 49:3, 5-6)

## A reading from the Book of the Prophet Isaiah

*I will make you a light to the nations, that my salvation may reach to the ends of the earth.*

**The LORD said to me: You are my servant,
Israel, through whom I show my glory.**

Now the Lord has spoken
    who formed me as his servant from the womb,
that Jacob may be brought back to him
    and Israel gathered to him;
and I am made glorious in the sight of the Lord,
    and my God is now my strength!
It is too little, the Lord says, for you to be my servant,
    to raise up the tribes of Jacob,
    and restore the survivors of Israel;
I will make you a light to the nations,
    that my salvation may reach to the ends of the earth.

The word of the Lord. All: **Thanks be to God.**

Responsorial Psalm 40

P-139

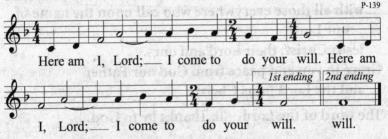

Here am I, Lord; — I come to do your will. Here am I, Lord; — I come to do your will. will.

1st ending  2nd ending

Music: Jay F. Hunstiger, © 1992, administered by Liturgical Press. All rights reserved.

Psalm 40:2, 4, 7-8, 8-9, 10

R̸. (8a and 9a) **Here am I, Lord; I come to do your will.**

I have waited, waited for the Lord,
    and he stooped toward me and heard my cry.
And he put a new song into my mouth,
    a hymn to our God. R̸.

Sacrifice or offering you wished not,
    but ears open to obedience you gave me.
Holocausts or sin-offerings you sought not;
    then said I, "Behold I come." R̸.

"In the written scroll it is prescribed for me,
    to do your will, O my God, is my delight,
    and your law is within my heart!" R̸.

*(continued)*

I announced your justice in the vast assembly;
    I did not restrain my lips, as you, O LORD, know. R℣.

## READING II (1 Corinthians 1:1-3)

**A reading from the beginning of the first Letter of Saint Paul to the Corinthians**

*Grace to you and peace from God our Father and the Lord Jesus Christ.*

**Paul, called to be an apostle of Christ Jesus by the will of God,**
    **and Sosthenes our brother,**
    **to the church of God that is in Corinth,**
    **to you who have been sanctified in Christ Jesus, called to be holy,**
    **with all those everywhere who call upon the name of our Lord**
    **Jesus Christ, their Lord and ours.**
**Grace to you and peace from God our Father**
    **and the Lord Jesus Christ.**

**The word of the Lord.** All: **Thanks be to God.**

## GOSPEL (John 1:29-34)
### ALLELUIA (John 1:14a, 12a)

℣. Alleluia, alleluia. R℣. **Alleluia, alleluia.**
℣. The Word of God became flesh and dwelt among us.
    To those who accepted him,
    he gave power to become children of God. R℣.

✠ **A reading from the holy Gospel according to John**

All: **Glory to you, O Lord.**

*Behold, the Lamb of God, who takes away the sin of the world.*

**John the Baptist saw Jesus coming toward him and said,**
    **"Behold, the Lamb of God, who takes away the sin of the world.**
**He is the one of whom I said,**
    **'A man is coming after me who ranks ahead of me because he existed before me.'**

I did not know him,

but the reason why I came baptizing with water
was that he might be made known to Israel."

John testified further, saying,

"I saw the Spirit come down like a dove from heaven
and remain upon him.

I did not know him,

but the one who sent me to baptize with water told me,
'On whomever you see the Spirit come down and
remain,

he is the one who will baptize with the Holy Spirit.'

Now I have seen and testified that he is the Son of God."

**The Gospel of the Lord.** All: **Praise to you, Lord Jesus Christ.**

PRAYER OVER THE OFFERINGS

Grant us, O Lord, we pray,
that we may participate worthily in these mysteries,
for whenever the memorial of this sacrifice is celebrated
the work of our redemption is accomplished.
Through Christ our Lord. All: **Amen.**

COMMUNION ANTIPHON (Cf. Psalm 23[22]:5)

You have prepared a table before me,
and how precious is the chalice that quenches my thirst.

Or:

(1 John 4:16)

We have come to know and to believe
in the love that God has for us.

PRAYER AFTER COMMUNION

Pour on us, O Lord, the Spirit of your love,
and in your kindness
make those you have nourished
by this one heavenly Bread
one in mind and heart.
Through Christ our Lord. All: **Amen.**

# Third Sunday in Ordinary Time

*January 22, 2017*

*Reflection on the Gospel*

*This gospel passage tells of a turning point in Jesus' life. "From that time on . . . the kingdom of heaven is at hand." "From that time on" the ful-fillment of Isaiah's prophecy that "light has arisen" to dispel darkness is coming to completion. "From that time on" Jesus' public ministry is set in motion. "From that time on" disciples are called. "From that time on" encounters with Jesus lead to changed lives. Then and now. From this time on . . .*

- *I hear and follow Jesus by . . .*

—*Living Liturgy™, Third Sunday in Ordinary Time 2017*

## Entrance Antiphon (Cf. Psalm 96[95]:1, 6)

O sing a new song to the Lord;
sing to the Lord, all the earth.
In his presence are majesty and splendor,
strength and honor in his holy place.

## Collect

Almighty ever-living God,
direct our actions according to your good pleasure,
that in the name of your beloved Son
we may abound in good works.
Through our Lord Jesus Christ, your Son,
who lives and reigns with you in the unity of the Holy Spirit,
one God, for ever and ever. All: **Amen.**

## Reading I (L 67-A) (Isaiah 8:23—9:3)

### A reading from the Book of the Prophet Isaiah

*In Galilee of the Gentiles, the people have seen a great light.*

**First the LORD degraded the land of Zebulun**
**and the land of Naphtali;**
**but in the end he has glorified the seaward road,**
**the land west of the Jordan,**
**the District of the Gentiles.**

**Anguish has taken wing, dispelled is darkness:**
**for there is no gloom where but now there was distress.**
**The people who walked in darkness**
**have seen a great light;**
**upon those who dwelt in the land of gloom**
**a light has shone.**
**You have brought them abundant joy**
**and great rejoicing,**
**as they rejoice before you as at the harvest,**
**as people make merry when dividing spoils.**
**For the yoke that burdened them,**
**the pole on their shoulder,**
**and the rod of their taskmaster**
**you have smashed, as on the day of Midian.**

**The word of the Lord.** All: **Thanks be to God.**

RESPONSORIAL PSALM 27

P-140

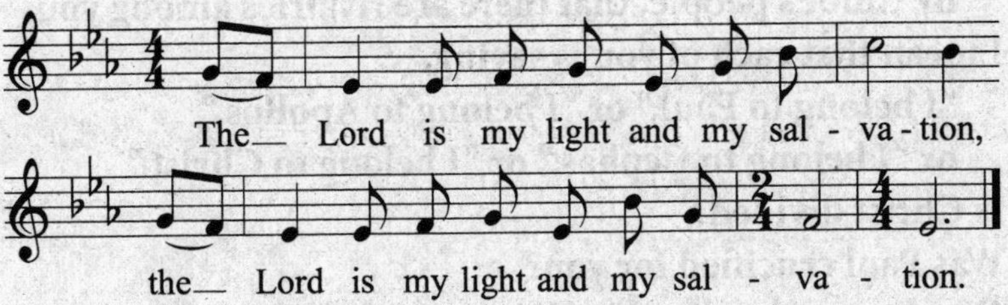




Psalm 27:1, 4, 13-14

℟. (1a) **The Lord is my light and my salvation.**

The LORD is my light and my salvation;
whom should I fear?
The LORD is my life's refuge;
of whom should I be afraid? ℟.

*(continued)*

One thing I ask of the LORD;
  this I seek:
to dwell in the house of the LORD
  all the days of my life,
that I may gaze on the loveliness of the LORD
  and contemplate his temple. R̷.

I believe that I shall see the bounty of the LORD
  in the land of the living.
Wait for the LORD with courage;
  be stouthearted, and wait for the LORD. R̷.

## READING II (1 Corinthians 1:10-13, 17)

**A reading from the first Letter of Saint Paul to the Corinthians**

*That all of you may agree in what you say, and that there be no divisions among you.*

**I urge you, brothers and sisters, in the name of our Lord Jesus Christ,**
  **that all of you agree in what you say,**
  **and that there be no divisions among you,**
  **but that you be united in the same mind and in the same purpose.**
**For it has been reported to me about you, my brothers and sisters,**
  **by Chloe's people, that there are rivalries among you.**
**I mean that each of you is saying,**
  **"I belong to Paul," or "I belong to Apollos,"**
  **or "I belong to Cephas," or "I belong to Christ."**
**Is Christ divided?**
**Was Paul crucified for you?**
**Or were you baptized in the name of Paul?**
**For Christ did not send me to baptize but to preach the gospel,**
  **and not with the wisdom of human eloquence,**
  **so that the cross of Christ might not be emptied of its meaning.**

**The word of the Lord.** All: **Thanks be to God.**

GOSPEL (Matthew 4:12-23) *or* Shorter Form [ ]
(Matthew 4:12-17)

ALLELUIA (*See* Matthew 4:23)

℣. Alleluia, alleluia.  ℟. **Alleluia, alleluia.**

℣. Jesus proclaimed the Gospel of the kingdom
  and cured every disease among the people. ℟.

✠ **A reading from the holy Gospel according to Matthew**

All: **Glory to you, O Lord.**

*Jesus went to Capernaum, so that what had been said through*
*Isaiah might be fulfilled.*

[**When Jesus heard that John had been arrested,**
  **he withdrew to Galilee.**
**He left Nazareth and went to live in Capernaum by the**
    **sea,**
  **in the region of Zebulun and Naphtali,**
  **that what had been said through Isaiah the prophet**
  **might be fulfilled:**
    *Land of Zebulun and land of Naphtali,*
      *the way to the sea, beyond the Jordan,*
      *Galilee of the Gentiles,*
    *the people who sit in darkness have seen a great light,*
    *on those dwelling in a land overshadowed by death*
      *light has arisen.*
**From that time on, Jesus began to preach and say,**
  **"Repent, for the kingdom of heaven is at hand."**]

**As he was walking by the Sea of Galilee, he saw two**
    **brothers,**
  **Simon who is called Peter, and his brother Andrew,**
  **casting a net into the sea; they were fishermen.**
**He said to them,**
  **"Come after me, and I will make you fishers of men."**
**At once they left their nets and followed him.**
**He walked along from there and saw two other brothers,**
  **James, the son of Zebedee, and his brother John.**

They were in a boat, with their father Zebedee, mending
their nets.
He called them, and immediately they left their boat and
their father
and followed him.
He went around all of Galilee,
teaching in their synagogues, proclaiming the gospel
of the kingdom,
and curing every disease and illness among the people.

**The Gospel of the Lord.** All: **Praise to you, Lord Jesus Christ.**

PRAYER OVER THE OFFERINGS
Accept our offerings, O Lord, we pray,
and in sanctifying them
grant that they may profit us for salvation.
Through Christ our Lord. All: **Amen.**

COMMUNION ANTIPHON (Cf. Psalm 34[33]:6)
Look toward the Lord and be radiant;
let your faces not be abashed.

Or:

(John 8:12)
I am the light of the world, says the Lord;
whoever follows me will not walk in darkness,
but will have the light of life.

PRAYER AFTER COMMUNION
Grant, we pray, almighty God,
that, receiving the grace
by which you bring us to new life,
we may always glory in your gift.
Through Christ our Lord. All: **Amen.**

# Fourth Sunday in Ordinary Time

*January 29, 2017*

*Reflection on the Gospel*

In the Beatitudes Jesus describes the qualities that mark true disciple-ship: poor in spirit, mourning loss, meek, seekers of justice, merciful, clean of heart, peacemakers, bearers of insults and persecution. To be so blessed, so happy, so fortunate requires letting go of self. All these qualities exhibit the self-emptying of Jesus himself. Blessedness is of, in, and with Jesus—and his followers. Our blessedness is both a quality of who we are and a blueprint for how we are to be and live as followers of Jesus.

- *Blessedness is both a quality of who we are and a blueprint for how we are to live . . .*

—Living Liturgy™, *Fourth Sunday in Ordinary Time 2017*

## ENTRANCE ANTIPHON (Psalm 106[105]:47)

Save us, O Lord our God!
And gather us from the nations,
to give thanks to your holy name,
and make it our glory to praise you.

## COLLECT

Grant us, Lord our God,
that we may honor you with all our mind,
and love everyone in truth of heart.
Through our Lord Jesus Christ, your Son,
who lives and reigns with you in the unity of the Holy Spirit,
one God, for ever and ever. All: **Amen.**

## READING I (L 70) (Zephaniah 2:3; 3:12-13)

### A reading from the Book of the Prophet Zephaniah

*I will leave in your midst a people humble and lowly.*

**Seek the LORD, all you humble of the earth,**
    **who have observed his law;**
**seek justice, seek humility;**
    **perhaps you may be sheltered**
    **on the day of the LORD's anger.**

**But I will leave as a remnant in your midst**
    **a people humble and lowly,**
**who shall take refuge in the name of the LORD:**
    **the remnant of Israel.**
**They shall do no wrong**
    **and speak no lies;**
**nor shall there be found in their mouths**
    **a deceitful tongue;**
**they shall pasture and couch their flocks**
    **with none to disturb them.**

**The word of the Lord.** All: **Thanks be to God.**

RESPONSORIAL PSALM 146

P-141

Bless - ed are the poor in spir - it; the king - dom of heav'n is theirs, the king - dom of heav'n is theirs!

Music: Jay F. Hunstiger, © 1990, administered by Liturgical Press. All rights reserved.

Psalm 146:6-7, 8-9, 9-10

R̶/. (Matthew 5:3) **Blessed are the poor in spirit; the**
    **kingdom of heaven is theirs!** *or:* R̶/. **Alleluia.**

The LORD keeps faith forever,
    secures justice for the oppressed,
        gives food to the hungry.
The LORD sets captives free. R̶/.

The LORD gives sight to the blind;
    the LORD raises up those who were bowed down.
The LORD loves the just;
    the LORD protects strangers. R̶/.

The fatherless and the widow the LORD sustains,
> but the way of the wicked he thwarts.

The LORD shall reign forever;
> your God, O Zion, through all generations.
>> Alleluia. R̸.

## READING II (1 Corinthians 1:26-31)

### A reading from the first Letter of Saint Paul to the Corinthians

*God chose the weak of the world.*

Consider your own calling, brothers and sisters.
Not many of you were wise by human standards,
> not many were powerful,
> not many were of noble birth.
Rather, God chose the foolish of the world to shame the
>> wise,
> and God chose the weak of the world to shame the
>> strong,
> and God chose the lowly and despised of the world,
> those who count for nothing,
> to reduce to nothing those who are something,
> so that no human being might boast before God.
It is due to him that you are in Christ Jesus,
> who became for us wisdom from God,
> as well as righteousness, sanctification, and
>> redemption,
> so that, as it is written,
> "Whoever boasts, should boast in the Lord."

The word of the Lord. All: Thanks be to God.

## GOSPEL (Matthew 5:1-12a)
### ALLELUIA (Matthew 5:12a)

℣. Alleluia, alleluia.  R̸. **Alleluia, alleluia.**
℣. Rejoice and be glad;
> your reward will be great in heaven. R̸.

✠ **A reading from the holy Gospel according to Matthew**

All: **Glory to you, O Lord.**

*Blessed are the poor in spirit.*

When Jesus saw the crowds, he went up the mountain,
  and after he had sat down, his disciples came to him.
He began to teach them, saying:
  "Blessed are the poor in spirit,
    for theirs is the kingdom of heaven.
  Blessed are they who mourn,
    for they will be comforted.
  Blessed are the meek,
    for they will inherit the land.
  Blessed are they who hunger and thirst for
    righteousness,
    for they will be satisfied.
  Blessed are the merciful,
    for they will be shown mercy.
  Blessed are the clean of heart,
    for they will see God.
  Blessed are the peacemakers,
    for they will be called children of God.
  Blessed are they who are persecuted for the sake of
    righteousness,
    for theirs is the kingdom of heaven.
  Blessed are you when they insult you and persecute
    you
    and utter every kind of evil against you falsely
      because of me.
  Rejoice and be glad,
    for your reward will be great in heaven."

**The Gospel of the Lord.** All: **Praise to you, Lord Jesus Christ.**

PRAYER OVER THE OFFERINGS
O Lord, we bring to your altar
these offerings of our service:
be pleased to receive them, we pray,

and transform them
into the Sacrament of our redemption.
Through Christ our Lord. All: **Amen.**

COMMUNION ANTIPHON (Cf. Psalm 31[30]:17-18)
Let your face shine on your servant.
Save me in your merciful love.
O Lord, let me never be put to shame, for I call on you.

Or:

(Matthew 5:3-4)
Blessed are the poor in spirit,
for theirs is the Kingdom of Heaven.
Blessed are the meek, for they shall possess the land.

PRAYER AFTER COMMUNION
Nourished by these redeeming gifts,
we pray, O Lord,
that through this help to eternal salvation
true faith may ever increase.
Through Christ our Lord. All: **Amen.**

# Fifth Sunday
# in Ordinary Time

*February 5, 2017*

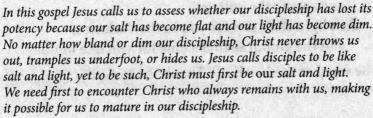

*Reflection on the Gospel*

*In this gospel Jesus calls us to assess whether our discipleship has lost its
potency because our salt has become flat and our light has become dim.
No matter how bland or dim our discipleship, Christ never throws us
out, tramples us underfoot, or hides us. Jesus calls disciples to be like
salt and light, yet to be such, Christ must first be our salt and light.
We need first to encounter Christ who always remains with us, making
it possible for us to mature in our discipleship.*

• *In truly following Jesus I must . . .*

—Living Liturgy™, *Fifth Sunday in Ordinary Time 2017*

O come, let us worship God
and bow low before the God who made us,
for he is the Lord our God.

COLLECT

Keep your family safe, O Lord, with unfailing care,
that, relying solely on the hope of heavenly grace,
they may be defended always by your protection.
Through our Lord Jesus Christ, your Son,
who lives and reigns with you in the unity of the Holy Spirit,
one God, for ever and ever. All: **Amen.**

READING I (L 73) (Isaiah 58:7-10)

**A reading from the Book of the Prophet Isaiah**

*Your light shall break forth like the dawn.*

Thus says the LORD:
  Share your bread with the hungry,
      shelter the oppressed and the homeless;
  clothe the naked when you see them,
      and do not turn your back on your own.
  Then your light shall break forth like the dawn,
      and your wound shall quickly be healed;
  your vindication shall go before you,
      and the glory of the LORD shall be your rear guard.
  Then you shall call, and the LORD will answer,
      you shall cry for help, and he will say: Here I am!
  If you remove from your midst
      oppression, false accusation and malicious speech;
  if you bestow your bread on the hungry
      and satisfy the afflicted;
  then light shall rise for you in the darkness,
      and the gloom shall become for you like midday.
The word of the Lord. All: **Thanks be to God.**

## RESPONSORIAL PSALM 112

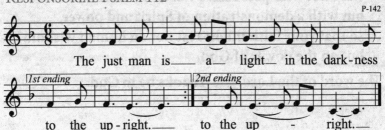

The just man is___ a___ light___ in the dark-ness

**1st ending** to the up-right.___ **2nd ending** to the up - right.___

Psalm 112:4-5, 6-7, 8-9

℟. (4a) **The just man is a light in darkness to the upright.**
   *or:* ℟. **Alleluia.**

Light shines through the darkness for the upright;
   he is gracious and merciful and just.
Well for the man who is gracious and lends,
   who conducts his affairs with justice. ℟.

He shall never be moved;
   the just one shall be in everlasting remembrance.
An evil report he shall not fear;
   his heart is firm, trusting in the LORD. ℟.

His heart is steadfast; he shall not fear.
   Lavishly he gives to the poor;
his justice shall endure forever;
   his horn shall be exalted in glory. ℟.

## READING II (1 Corinthians 2:1-5)

**A reading from the first Letter of Saint Paul to the Corinthians**

*I have announced to you the mystery of Christ crucified.*

**When I came to you, brothers and sisters,**
   **proclaiming the mystery of God,**
   **I did not come with sublimity of words or of wisdom.**
**For I resolved to know nothing while I was with you**
   **except Jesus Christ, and him crucified.**
**I came to you in weakness and fear and much trembling,**
   **and my message and my proclamation**

were not with persuasive words of wisdom,
but with a demonstration of Spirit and power,
so that your faith might rest not on human wisdom
but on the power of God.

**The word of the Lord.** All: **Thanks be to God.**

GOSPEL (Matthew 5:13-16)
ALLELUIA (John 8:12)

℣. Alleluia, alleluia.  ℟. **Alleluia, alleluia.**
℣. I am the light of the world, says the Lord;
whoever follows me will have the light of life. ℟.

✝ **A reading from the holy Gospel according to Matthew**

All: **Glory to you, O Lord.**

*You are the light of the world.*

**Jesus said to his disciples:**
**"You are the salt of the earth.**
**But if salt loses its taste, with what can it be seasoned?**
**It is no longer good for anything**
**but to be thrown out and trampled underfoot.**
**You are the light of the world.**
**A city set on a mountain cannot be hidden.**
**Nor do they light a lamp and then put it under a bushel**
**basket;**
**it is set on a lampstand,**
**where it gives light to all in the house.**
**Just so, your light must shine before others,**
**that they may see your good deeds**
**and glorify your heavenly Father."**

**The Gospel of the Lord.** All: **Praise to you, Lord Jesus Christ.**

PRAYER OVER THE OFFERINGS
O Lord our God,
who once established these created things
to sustain us in our frailty,
grant, we pray,
that they may become for us now
the Sacrament of eternal life.
Through Christ our Lord. All: **Amen.**

COMMUNION ANTIPHON (Cf. Psalm 107[106]:8-9)
Let them thank the Lord for his mercy,
his wonders for the children of men,
for he satisfies the thirsty soul,
and the hungry he fills with good things.

Or:

(Matthew 5:5-6)
Blessed are those who mourn, for they shall be consoled.
Blessed are those who hunger and thirst for righteousness,
for they shall have their fill.

PRAYER AFTER COMMUNION
O God, who have willed that we be partakers
in the one Bread and the one Chalice,
grant us, we pray, so to live
that, made one in Christ,
we may joyfully bear fruit
for the salvation of the world.
Through Christ our Lord. All: **Amen.**

# Sixth Sunday
# in Ordinary Time

*February 12, 2017*

*Reflection on the Gospel*

*Jesus urges his hearers to live the law to God's intended fulfillment of it. The fulfillment of the law is the "righteousness" (right relationship with God and others) that identifies those who are the "greatest in the kingdom of heaven." The "greatest in the kingdom of heaven" is Jesus himself, who is the fulfillment of the law in his very Person. If we are to be "greatest in the kingdom of heaven," we must encounter Jesus himself, the righteous One, the fulfillment of the law.*

• *Right relationship in the kingdom of heaven means . . .*

—*Living Liturgy*™, *Sixth Sunday in Ordinary Time 2017*

ENTRANCE ANTIPHON (Cf. Psalm 31[30]:3-4)

Be my protector, O God,
a mighty stronghold to save me.
For you are my rock, my stronghold!
Lead me, guide me, for the sake of your name.

## COLLECT

O God, who teach us that you abide
in hearts that are just and true,
grant that we may be so fashioned by your grace
as to become a dwelling pleasing to you.
Through our Lord Jesus Christ, your Son,
who lives and reigns with you in the unity of the Holy Spirit,
one God, for ever and ever. All: **Amen.**

## READING I (L 76-A) (Sirach 15:15-20)

**A reading from the Book of Sirach**

*No one does he command to act unjustly.*

**If you choose you can keep the commandments, they
　　will save you;
　if you trust in God, you too shall live;
he has set before you fire and water;
　to whichever you choose, stretch forth your hand.
Before man are life and death, good and evil,
　whichever he chooses shall be given him.
Immense is the wisdom of the Lord;
　he is mighty in power, and all-seeing.
The eyes of God are on those who fear him;
　he understands man's every deed.
No one does he command to act unjustly,
　to none does he give license to sin.**

**The word of the Lord. All: Thanks be to God.**

## RESPONSORIAL PSALM 119

P-143

Bless-ed are they who fol-low the law____ of the Lord.

Psalm 119:1-2, 4-5, 17-18, 33-34

℟. (1b) **Blessed are they who follow the law of the Lord!**

Blessed are they whose way is blameless,
    who walk in the law of the LORD.
Blessed are they who observe his decrees,
    who seek him with all their heart. ℟.

You have commanded that your precepts
    be diligently kept.
Oh, that I might be firm in the ways
    of keeping your statutes! ℟.

Be good to your servant, that I may live
    and keep your words.
Open my eyes, that I may consider
    the wonders of your law. ℟.

Instruct me, O LORD, in the way of your statutes,
    that I may exactly observe them.
Give me discernment, that I may observe your law
    and keep it with all my heart. ℟.

READING II (1 Corinthians 2:6-10)

**A reading from the first Letter of Saint Paul to the Corinthians**

*God predestined wisdom before the ages for our glory.*

**Brothers and sisters:**
**We speak a wisdom to those who are mature,**
    **not a wisdom of this age,**
    **nor of the rulers of this age who are passing away.**
**Rather, we speak God's wisdom, mysterious, hidden,**
    **which God predetermined before the ages for our glory,**
    **and which none of the rulers of this age knew;**
    **for, if they had known it,**
    **they would not have crucified the Lord of glory.**
**But as it is written:**
    *What eye has not seen, and ear has not heard,*
      *and what has not entered the human heart,*
      *what God has prepared for those who love him,*
      *this God has revealed to us through the Spirit.*

For the Spirit scrutinizes everything, even the depths
of God.

**The word of the Lord.** All: **Thanks be to God.**

GOSPEL (Matthew 5:17-37) *or* Shorter Form [ ] (Matthew 5:20-
22a, 27-28, 33-34a, 37)
ALLELUIA (*See* Matthew 11:25)
℣. Alleluia, alleluia. ℟. **Alleluia, alleluia.**
℣. Blessed are you, Father, Lord of heaven and earth;
you have revealed to little ones the mysteries of the
kingdom. ℟.

✠ **A reading from the holy Gospel according to Matthew**

All: **Glory to you, O Lord.**

*So it was said to your ancestors; but I say this to you.*

[Jesus said to his disciples:]
"Do not think that I have come to abolish the law or
the prophets.
I have come not to abolish but to fulfill.
Amen, I say to you, until heaven and earth pass away,
not the smallest letter or the smallest part of a letter
will pass from the law,
until all things have taken place.
Therefore, whoever breaks one of the least of these
commandments
and teaches others to do so
will be called least in the kingdom of heaven.
But whoever obeys and teaches these commandments
will be called greatest in the kingdom of heaven.
[I tell you, unless your righteousness surpasses
that of the scribes and Pharisees,
you will not enter the kingdom of heaven.

"You have heard that it was said to your ancestors,
*You shall not kill; and whoever kills will be liable to
judgment.*

But I say to you,
> whoever is angry with brother
> will be liable to judgment;]
> and whoever says to his brother, 'Raqa,'
> will be answerable to the Sanhedrin;
> and whoever says, 'You fool,'
> will be liable to fiery Gehenna.

Therefore, if you bring your gift to the altar,
> and there recall that your brother
> has anything against you,
> leave your gift there at the altar,
> go first and be reconciled with your brother,
> and then come and offer your gift.

Settle with your opponent quickly while on the way to
> court.

Otherwise your opponent will hand you over to the judge,
> and the judge will hand you over to the guard,
> and you will be thrown into prison.

Amen, I say to you,
> you will not be released until you have paid the last
> penny.

["You have heard that it was said,
> *You shall not commit adultery.*

But I say to you,
> everyone who looks at a woman with lust
> has already committed adultery with her in his heart.]

If your right eye causes you to sin,
> tear it out and throw it away.

It is better for you to lose one of your members
> than to have your whole body thrown into Gehenna.

And if your right hand causes you to sin,
> cut it off and throw it away.

It is better for you to lose one of your members
> than to have your whole body go into Gehenna.

"It was also said,
*Whoever divorces his wife must give her a bill of divorce.*
But I say to you,
whoever divorces his wife—unless the marriage is
unlawful—
causes her to commit adultery,
and whoever marries a divorced woman commits
adultery.

["Again you have heard that it was said to your ancestors,
*Do not take a false oath,*
*but make good to the Lord all that you vow.*
But I say to you, do not swear at all;]
not by heaven, for it is God's throne;
nor by the earth, for it is his footstool;
nor by Jerusalem, for it is the city of the great King.
Do not swear by your head,
for you cannot make a single hair white or black.
[Let your 'Yes' mean 'Yes,' and your 'No' mean 'No.'
Anything more is from the evil one."]

**The Gospel of the Lord.** All: **Praise to you, Lord Jesus Christ.**

PRAYER OVER THE OFFERINGS
May this oblation, O Lord, we pray,
cleanse and renew us
and may it become for those who do your will
the source of eternal reward.
Through Christ our Lord. All: **Amen.**

COMMUNION ANTIPHON (Cf. Psalm 78[77]:29-30)
They ate and had their fill,
and what they craved the Lord gave them;
they were not disappointed in what they craved.

Or:

(John 3:16)
God so loved the world
that he gave his Only Begotten Son,
so that all who believe in him may not perish,
but may have eternal life.

PRAYER AFTER COMMUNION

Having fed upon these heavenly delights,
we pray, O Lord,
that we may always long
for that food by which we truly live.
Through Christ our Lord. All: **Amen.**

# Seventh Sunday in Ordinary Time

## February 19, 2017

---

*Reflection on the Gospel*

*Jesus commands us to keep the law in a radically different way. We are duty-bound as "children of [the] heavenly Father" to do more than simply what is mandated. We are to go beyond our natural expectation about keeping laws to embrace the divine excess with which God treats us. Acting toward others as God acts toward us transforms us to "be perfect" as God. This radical living of the law makes divine blessings, grace, and holiness to be real, visible, and at hand for us.*

• *I do more than what is expected when I . . .*

—*Living Liturgy*™, *Seventh Sunday in Ordinary Time 2017*

ENTRANCE ANTIPHON (Psalm 13[12]:6)

O Lord, I trust in your merciful love.
My heart will rejoice in your salvation.
I will sing to the Lord who has been bountiful with me.

COLLECT

Grant, we pray, almighty God,
that, always pondering spiritual things,
we may carry out in both word and deed
that which is pleasing to you.
Through our Lord Jesus Christ, your Son,
who lives and reigns with you in the unity of the Holy Spirit,
one God, for ever and ever. All: **Amen.**

## Reading I (L 79-A) (Leviticus 19:1-2, 17-18)

**A reading from the Book of Leviticus**

*You shall love your neighbor as yourself.*

**The Lord said to Moses,
"Speak to the whole Israelite community and tell them:
Be holy, for I, the Lord, your God, am holy.**

**"You shall not bear hatred for your brother or sister in
your heart.
Though you may have to reprove your fellow citizen,
do not incur sin because of him.
Take no revenge and cherish no grudge against any of
your people.
You shall love your neighbor as yourself.
I am the Lord."**

**The word of the Lord.** All: **Thanks be to God.**

## Responsorial Psalm 103

P-144

The Lord is kind and mer-ci-ful, is kind and mer-ci-ful.

Psalm 103:1-2, 3-4, 8, 10, 12-13

℟. (8a) **The Lord is kind and merciful.**

Bless the Lord, O my soul;
    and all my being, bless his holy name.
Bless the Lord, O my soul,
    and forget not all his benefits. ℟.

He pardons all your iniquities,
    heals all your ills.
He redeems your life from destruction,
    crowns you with kindness and compassion. ℟.

Merciful and gracious is the Lord,
    slow to anger and abounding in kindness.
Not according to our sins does he deal with us,
    nor does he requite us according to our crimes. ℟.

As far as the east is from the west,
>    so far has he put our transgressions from us.
As a father has compassion on his children,
>    so the LORD has compassion on those who fear him. ℟.

## READING II (1 Corinthians 3:16-23)

**A reading from the first Letter of Saint Paul to the Corinthians**

*All things belong to you, and you to Christ, and Christ to God.*

**Brothers and sisters:**

**Do you not know that you are the temple of God,**
>    **and that the Spirit of God dwells in you?**

**If anyone destroys God's temple, God will destroy that person;**
>    **for the temple of God, which you are, is holy.**

**Let no one deceive himself.**

**If any one among you considers himself wise in this age,**
>    **let him become a fool, so as to become wise.**

**For the wisdom of this world is foolishness in the eyes of God,**
>    **for it is written:**
>    ***God catches the wise in their own ruses,***
>    **and again:**
>    ***The Lord knows the thoughts of the wise,***
>    ***that they are vain.***

**So let no one boast about human beings, for everything belongs to you,**
>    **Paul or Apollos or Cephas,**
>    **or the world or life or death,**
>    **or the present or the future:**
>    **all belong to you, and you to Christ, and Christ to God.**

The word of the Lord. All: **Thanks be to God.**

Gospel (Matthew 5:38-48)

Alleluia (1 John 2:5)

℣. Alleluia, alleluia.　℟. **Alleluia, alleluia.**

℣. Whoever keeps the word of Christ,
　the love of God is truly perfected in him. ℟.

✠ **A reading from the holy Gospel according to Matthew**

All: **Glory to you, O Lord.**

*Love your enemies.*

Jesus said to his disciples:
　"You have heard that it was said,
　*An eye for an eye and a tooth for a tooth.*
But I say to you, offer no resistance to one who is evil.
When someone strikes you on your right cheek,
　turn the other one as well.
If anyone wants to go to law with you over your tunic,
　hand over your cloak as well.
Should anyone press you into service for one mile,
　go for two miles.
Give to the one who asks of you,
　and do not turn your back on one who wants to borrow.

"You have heard that it was said,
　*You shall love your neighbor and hate your enemy.*
But I say to you, love your enemies
　and pray for those who persecute you,
　that you may be children of your heavenly Father,
　for he makes his sun rise on the bad and the good,
　and causes rain to fall on the just and the unjust.
For if you love those who love you, what recompense
　will you have?
Do not the tax collectors do the same?
And if you greet your brothers only,
　what is unusual about that?
Do not the pagans do the same?
So be perfect, just as your heavenly Father is perfect."

The Gospel of the Lord. All: **Praise to you, Lord Jesus Christ.**

PRAYER OVER THE OFFERINGS

As we celebrate your mysteries, O Lord,
with the observance that is your due,
we humbly ask you,
that what we offer to the honor of your majesty
may profit us for salvation.
Through Christ our Lord. All: **Amen.**

COMMUNION ANTIPHON (Psalm 9:2-3)

I will recount all your wonders,
I will rejoice in you and be glad,
and sing psalms to your name, O Most High.

Or:

(John 11:27)

Lord, I have come to believe that you are the Christ,
the Son of the living God, who is coming into this world.

PRAYER AFTER COMMUNION

Grant, we pray, almighty God,
that we may experience the effects of the salvation
which is pledged to us by these mysteries.
Through Christ our Lord. All: **Amen.**

# Eighth Sunday in Ordinary Time

*February 26, 2017*

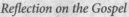

*Reflection on the Gospel*

*Jesus tells us that we cannot serve "two masters." Clearly, he is pitting exclusive concern ("worry") with ourselves, our wants, our needs against single-mindedly seeking "the kingdom of God and his righteousness." We are not to neglect our legitimate needs, but to keep them in proper perspective. We must "not worry" but look beyond today and even tomorrow. In everything we do, we must serve only one Master, the God who lavishly provides and cares for us—today, tomorrow, and even unto fullness of Life forever.*

- *Choose life, choose between God and mammon, means . . .*

—*Living Liturgy*™, *Eighth Sunday in Ordinary Time 2017*

## ENTRANCE ANTIPHON (Cf. Psalm 18[17]:19-20)

The Lord became my protector.
He brought me out to a place of freedom;
he saved me because he delighted in me.

## COLLECT

Grant us, O Lord, we pray,
that the course of our world
may be directed by your peaceful rule
and that your Church may rejoice,
untroubled in her devotion.
Through our Lord Jesus Christ, your Son,
who lives and reigns with you in the unity of the Holy Spirit,
one God, for ever and ever. All: **Amen.**

## READING I (L 82-A) (Isaiah 49:14-15)

**A reading from the Book of the Prophet Isaiah**

*I will never forget you.*

Zion said, "The LORD has forsaken me;
  my LORD has forgotten me."
Can a mother forget her infant,
  be without tenderness for the child of her womb?
Even should she forget,
  I will never forget you.

**The word of the Lord.** All: **Thanks be to God.**

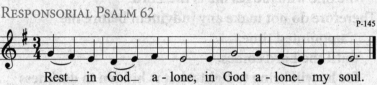

Rest in God alone, in God alone my soul.

Psalm 62:2-3, 6-7, 8-9

R̥. (6a) **Rest in God alone, my soul.**

Only in God is my soul at rest;
  from him comes my salvation.
He only is my rock and my salvation,
  my stronghold; I shall not be disturbed at all. R̥.

Only in God be at rest, my soul,
  for from him comes my hope.
He only is my rock and my salvation,
  my stronghold; I shall not be disturbed. R̥.

With God is my safety and my glory,
  he is the rock of my strength; my refuge is in God.
Trust in him at all times, O my people!
  Pour out your hearts before him. R̥.

READING II (1 Corinthians 4:1-5)

**A reading from the first Letter of Saint Paul to the Corinthians**

*The Lord will manifest the motives of our hearts.*

**Brothers and sisters:**
**Thus should one regard us: as servants of Christ**
  **and stewards of the mysteries of God.**

Now it is of course required of stewards
    that they be found trustworthy.
It does not concern me in the least
    that I be judged by you or any human tribunal;
    I do not even pass judgment on myself;
    I am not conscious of anything against me,
    but I do not thereby stand acquitted;
    the one who judges me is the Lord.
Therefore do not make any judgment before the
      appointed time,
    until the Lord comes,
    for he will bring to light what is hidden in darkness
    and will manifest the motives of our hearts,
    and then everyone will receive praise from God.

The word of the Lord. All: Thanks be to God.

GOSPEL (Matthew 6:24-34)
ALLELUIA (Hebrews 4:12)
℣. Alleluia, alleluia. ℟. **Alleluia, alleluia.**
℣. The word of God is living and effective;
    discerning reflections and thoughts of the heart. ℟.

✢ **A reading from the holy Gospel according to Matthew**

All: **Glory to you, O Lord.**

*Do not worry about tomorrow.*

Jesus said to his disciples:
    "No one can serve two masters.
He will either hate one and love the other,
    or be devoted to one and despise the other.
You cannot serve God and mammon.

"Therefore I tell you, do not worry about your life,
    what you will eat or drink,
    or about your body, what you will wear.
Is not life more than food and the body more than
      clothing?
Look at the birds in the sky;
    they do not sow or reap, they gather nothing into barns,

yet your heavenly Father feeds them.
Are not you more important than they?
Can any of you by worrying add a single moment to
your life-span?
Why are you anxious about clothes?
Learn from the way the wild flowers grow.
They do not work or spin.
But I tell you that not even Solomon in all his splendor
was clothed like one of them.
If God so clothes the grass of the field,
which grows today and is thrown into the oven
tomorrow,
will he not much more provide for you, O you of little
faith?
So do not worry and say, 'What are we to eat?'
or 'What are we to drink?' or 'What are we to wear?'
All these things the pagans seek.
Your heavenly Father knows that you need them all.
But seek first the kingdom of God and his righteousness,
and all these things will be given you besides.
Do not worry about tomorrow; tomorrow will take care
of itself.
Sufficient for a day is its own evil."

**The Gospel of the Lord.** All: **Praise to you, Lord Jesus Christ.**

PRAYER OVER THE OFFERINGS
O God, who provide gifts to be offered to your name
and count our oblations as signs
of our desire to serve you with devotion,
we ask of your mercy
that what you grant as the source of merit
may also help us to attain merit's reward.
Through Christ our Lord. All: **Amen.**

COMMUNION ANTIPHON (Cf. Psalm 13[12]:6)
I will sing to the Lord who has been bountiful with me,
sing psalms to the name of the Lord Most High.

Or:

(Matthew 28:20)

Behold, I am with you always,
even to the end of the age, says the Lord.

PRAYER AFTER COMMUNION

Nourished by your saving gifts,
we beseech your mercy, Lord,
that by this same Sacrament
with which you feed us in the present age,
you may make us partakers of life eternal.
Through Christ our Lord. All: **Amen.**

# Ash Wednesday

*March 1, 2017*

*Reflection on the Gospel*

*In this gospel Jesus tells us what others ought not to see in us: penitential acts aimed at gaining adulation from others. Instead, what ought others to see in us through our Lenten penance? They should see unwavering care for others through our "secret" almsgiving, prevailing love for God through our "secret" prayer, persistent self-emptying through our "secret" fasting. Lent is about developing these habits of a heart seeking conversion, these habits of a life turned toward God and others.*

 • *I am transformed by . . .*

—Living Liturgy™, *Ash Wednesday 2017*

ENTRANCE ANTIPHON (Wisdom 11:24, 25, 27)

You are merciful to all, O Lord,
and despise nothing that you have made.
You overlook people's sins, to bring them to repentance,
and you spare them, for you are the Lord our God.

## Collect

Grant, O Lord, that we may begin with holy fasting
this campaign of Christian service,
so that, as we take up battle against spiritual evils,
we may be armed with weapons of self-restraint.
Through our Lord Jesus Christ, your Son,
who lives and reigns with you in the unity of the Holy Spirit,
one God, for ever and ever. All: **Amen.**

## Reading I (L 219) (Joel 2:12-18)

### A reading from the Book of the Prophet Joel

*Rend your hearts, not your garments.*

**Even now, says the Lord,**
    **return to me with your whole heart,**
    **with fasting, and weeping, and mourning;**
**Rend your hearts, not your garments,**
    **and return to the Lord, your God.**
**For gracious and merciful is he,**
    **slow to anger, rich in kindness,**
    **and relenting in punishment.**
**Perhaps he will again relent**
    **and leave behind him a blessing,**
**Offerings and libations**
    **for the Lord, your God.**

**Blow the trumpet in Zion!**
    **proclaim a fast,**
    **call an assembly;**
**Gather the people,**
    **notify the congregation;**
**Assemble the elders,**
    **gather the children**
    **and the infants at the breast;**
**Let the bridegroom quit his room**
    **and the bride her chamber.**
**Between the porch and the altar**
    **let the priests, the ministers of the Lord, weep,**

And say, "Spare, O LORD, your people,
   and make not your heritage a reproach,
   with the nations ruling over them!
Why should they say among the peoples,
   'Where is their God?'"

Then the LORD was stirred to concern for his land
   and took pity on his people.

**The word of the Lord.** All: **Thanks be to God.**

RESPONSORIAL PSALM 51

P-174

Be mer-ci-ful, O Lord, for__ we have sinned.__

Psalm 51:3-4, 5-6ab, 12-13, 14 and 17

R̸. (*See* 3a) **Be merciful, O Lord, for we have sinned.**

Have mercy on me, O God, in your goodness;
   in the greatness of your compassion wipe out my
      offense.
Thoroughly wash me from my guilt
   and of my sin cleanse me. R̸.

For I acknowledge my offense,
   and my sin is before me always:
"Against you only have I sinned,
   and done what is evil in your sight." R̸.

A clean heart create for me, O God,
   and a steadfast spirit renew within me.
Cast me not out from your presence,
   and your Holy Spirit take not from me. R̸.

Give me back the joy of your salvation,
   and a willing spirit sustain in me.
O Lord, open my lips,
   and my mouth shall proclaim your praise. R̸.

Reading II (2 Corinthians 5:20—6:2)

## A reading from the second Letter of Saint Paul to the Corinthians

*Be reconciled to God. Behold, now is the acceptable time.*

Brothers and sisters:
We are ambassadors for Christ,
    as if God were appealing through us.
We implore you on behalf of Christ,
    be reconciled to God.
For our sake he made him to be sin who did not know sin,
    so that we might become the righteousness of God
        in him.

Working together, then,
    we appeal to you not to receive the grace of God in vain.
For he says:

    *In an acceptable time I heard you,*
        *and on the day of salvation I helped you.*

Behold, now is a very acceptable time;
    behold, now is the day of salvation.

The word of the Lord. All: Thanks be to God.

Gospel (Matthew 6:1-6, 16-18)
Verse before the Gospel (*See* Psalm 95:8)
℣. Praise to you, Lord Jesus Christ, King of endless glory!
℟. **Praise to you, Lord Jesus Christ, King of endless glory!**
℣. If today you hear his voice,
    harden not your hearts. ℟.

✠ A reading from the holy Gospel according to Matthew

All: **Glory to you, O Lord.**

*Your Father who sees in secret will repay you.*

Jesus said to his disciples:
    "Take care not to perform righteous deeds
    in order that people may see them;
    otherwise, you will have no recompense from your
        heavenly Father.

When you give alms,
do not blow a trumpet before you,
as the hypocrites do in the synagogues and in the streets
to win the praise of others.
Amen, I say to you,
they have received their reward.
But when you give alms,
do not let your left hand know what your right is doing,
so that your almsgiving may be secret.
And your Father who sees in secret will repay you.

"When you pray,
do not be like the hypocrites,
who love to stand and pray in the synagogues and on
street corners
so that others may see them.
Amen, I say to you,
they have received their reward.
But when you pray, go to your inner room,
close the door, and pray to your Father in secret.
And your Father who sees in secret will repay you.

"When you fast,
do not look gloomy like the hypocrites.
They neglect their appearance,
so that they may appear to others to be fasting.
Amen, I say to you, they have received their reward.
But when you fast,
anoint your head and wash your face,
so that you may not appear to be fasting,
except to your Father who is hidden.
And your Father who sees what is hidden will repay you."

The Gospel of the Lord. All: **Praise to you, Lord Jesus Christ.**

BLESSING AND DISTRIBUTION OF ASHES
Dear brethren (brothers and sisters), let us humbly ask God our Father
that he be pleased to bless with the abundance of his grace
these ashes, which we will put on our heads in penitence.

O God, who are moved by acts of humility
and respond with forgiveness to works of penance,
lend your merciful ear to our prayers
and in your kindness pour out the grace of your ☩ blessing
on your servants who are marked with these ashes,
that, as they follow the Lenten observances,
they may be worthy to come with minds made pure
to celebrate the Paschal Mystery of your Son.
Through Christ our Lord. All: **Amen.**

Or:

O God, who desire not the death of sinners,
but their conversion,
mercifully hear our prayers
and in your kindness be pleased to bless ☩ these ashes,
which we intend to receive upon our heads,
that we, who acknowledge we are but ashes
and shall return to dust,
may, through a steadfast observance of Lent,
gain pardon for sins and newness of life
after the likeness of your Risen Son.
Who lives and reigns for ever and ever. All: **Amen.**

To each who receives the ashes:
Repent, and believe in the Gospel.

or:

Remember that you are dust, and to dust you shall return.

The rite concludes with the Prayer of the Faithful.

PRAYER OVER THE OFFERINGS
As we solemnly offer
the annual sacrifice for the beginning of Lent,
we entreat you, O Lord,
that, through works of penance and charity,
we may turn away from harmful pleasures
and, cleansed from our sins, may become worthy
to celebrate devoutly the Passion of your Son.
Who lives and reigns for ever and ever. All: **Amen.**

COMMUNION ANTIPHON (Cf. Psalm 1:2-3)
He who ponders the law of the Lord day and night
will yield fruit in due season.

PRAYER AFTER COMMUNION

May the Sacrament we have received sustain us, O Lord,
that our Lenten fast may be pleasing to you
and be for us a healing remedy.
Through Christ our Lord. All: **Amen.**

# First Sunday of Lent

### *March 5, 2017*

*Reflection on the Gospel*

*That same Spirit that led Jesus into the desert leads us into the desert of
ourselves to encounter the demons within us, to encounter the Father's
mercy and forgiveness, to encounter Jesus calling us to align our lives
more closely with his. We are first grafted onto Christ at our baptism.
We are plunged into the cleansing waters to be raised up to new Life.
The strength of our baptismal commitment to God must be honed in the
desert of ourselves where, stripped of all that distracts us, we stand
naked and hungry before God.*

- *God comes to my aid when I . . .*

—Living Liturgy™, *First Sunday of Lent 2017*

ENTRANCE ANTIPHON (Cf. Psalm 91[90]:15-16)

When he calls on me, I will answer him;
I will deliver him and give him glory,
I will grant him length of days.

COLLECT

Grant, almighty God,
through the yearly observances of holy Lent,
that we may grow in understanding
of the riches hidden in Christ
and by worthy conduct pursue their effects.
Through our Lord Jesus Christ, your Son,

who lives and reigns with you in the unity of the Holy Spirit,
one God, for ever and ever. All: **Amen.**

READING I (L 22-A) (Genesis 2:7-9; 3:1-7)

### A reading from the Book of Genesis

*The creation of our first parents, and sin.*

The LORD God formed man out of the clay of the ground
and blew into his nostrils the breath of life,
and so man became a living being.

Then the LORD God planted a garden in Eden, in the east,
and placed there the man whom he had formed.
Out of the ground the LORD God made various trees grow
that were delightful to look at and good for food,
with the tree of life in the middle of the garden
and the tree of the knowledge of good and evil.

Now the serpent was the most cunning of all the animals
that the LORD God had made.
The serpent asked the woman,
"Did God really tell you not to eat
from any of the trees in the garden?"
The woman answered the serpent:
"We may eat of the fruit of the trees in the garden;
it is only about the fruit of the tree
in the middle of the garden that God said,
'You shall not eat it or even touch it, lest you die.'"
But the serpent said to the woman:
"You certainly will not die!
No, God knows well that the moment you eat of it
your eyes will be opened and you will be like gods
who know what is good and what is evil."
The woman saw that the tree was good for food,
pleasing to the eyes, and desirable for gaining wisdom.
So she took some of its fruit and ate it;
and she also gave some to her husband, who was with
her,
and he ate it.

**Then the eyes of both of them were opened,**
> **and they realized that they were naked;**
> **so they sewed fig leaves together**
> **and made loincloths for themselves.**

**The word of the Lord.** All: **Thanks be to God.**

RESPONSORIAL PSALM 51

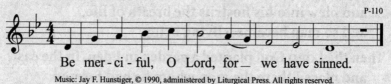

P-110

Be mer - ci - ful, O Lord, for — we have sinned.

Psalm 51:3-4, 5-6, 12-13, 17

℟. (*See* 3a) **Be merciful, O Lord, for we have sinned.**

Have mercy on me, O God, in your goodness;
> in the greatness of your compassion wipe out my
> offense.
Thoroughly wash me from my guilt
> and of my sin cleanse me. ℟.

For I acknowledge my offense,
> and my sin is before me always:
"Against you only have I sinned,
> and done what is evil in your sight." ℟.

A clean heart create for me, O God,
> and a steadfast spirit renew within me.
Cast me not out from your presence,
> and your Holy Spirit take not from me. ℟.

Give me back the joy of your salvation,
> and a willing spirit sustain in me.
O Lord, open my lips,
> and my mouth shall proclaim your praise. ℟.

READING II (Romans 5:12-19) *or* Shorter Form [ ] (Romans 5:12, 17-19)

**A reading from the Letter of Saint Paul to the Romans**

*Where sin increased, there grace increased all the more.*

[Brothers and sisters:
Through one man sin entered the world,
    and through sin, death,
    and thus death came to all men, inasmuch as all
        sinned—]
    for up to the time of the law, sin was in the world,
    though sin is not accounted when there is no law.
But death reigned from Adam to Moses,
    even over those who did not sin
    after the pattern of the trespass of Adam,
    who is the type of the one who was to come.

But the gift is not like the transgression.
For if by the transgression of the one, the many died,
    how much more did the grace of God
    and the gracious gift of the one man Jesus Christ
    overflow for the many.
And the gift is not like the result of the one who sinned.
For after one sin there was the judgment that brought
        condemnation;
    but the gift, after many transgressions, brought
        acquittal.
[For if, by the transgression of the one,
    death came to reign through that one,
    how much more will those who receive the abundance
        of grace
    and of the gift of justification
    come to reign in life through the one Jesus Christ.
In conclusion, just as through one transgression
    condemnation came upon all,
    so, through one righteous act,
    acquittal and life came to all.
For just as through the disobedience of the one man
    the many were made sinners,
    so, through the obedience of the one,
    the many will be made righteous.]

The word of the Lord. All: Thanks be to God.

GOSPEL (Matthew 4:1-11)

VERSE BEFORE THE GOSPEL (Matthew 4:4b)

℣. Praise to you, Lord Jesus Christ, king of endless glory!

℟. **Praise to you, Lord Jesus Christ, king of endless glory!**

℣. One does not live on bread alone,
but on every word that comes forth from the mouth of
God. ℟.

✠ **A reading from the holy Gospel according to Matthew**

All: **Glory to you, O Lord.**

*Jesus fasted for forty days and forty nights and was tempted.*

**At that time Jesus was led by the Spirit into the desert
to be tempted by the devil.**

**He fasted for forty days and forty nights,
and afterwards he was hungry.**

**The tempter approached and said to him,
"If you are the Son of God,
command that these stones become loaves of bread."**

**He said in reply,
"It is written:**
***One does not live on bread alone,
but on every word that comes forth
from the mouth of God."***

**Then the devil took him to the holy city,
and made him stand on the parapet of the temple,
and said to him, "If you are the Son of God, throw
yourself down.**

**For it is written:**
***He will command his angels concerning you
and with their hands they will support you,
lest you dash your foot against a stone."***

**Jesus answered him,
"Again it is written,**
***You shall not put the Lord, your God, to the test."***

Then the devil took him up to a very high mountain,
and showed him all the kingdoms of the world in
their magnificence,
and he said to him, "All these I shall give to you,
if you will prostrate yourself and worship me."
At this, Jesus said to him,
"Get away, Satan!
It is written:
*The Lord, your God, shall you worship*
*and him alone shall you serve."*

Then the devil left him and, behold,
angels came and ministered to him.

**The Gospel of the Lord.** All: **Praise to you, Lord Jesus Christ.**

PRAYER OVER THE OFFERINGS
Give us the right dispositions, O Lord, we pray,
to make these offerings,
for with them we celebrate the beginning
of this venerable and sacred time.
Through Christ our Lord. All: **Amen.**

COMMUNION ANTIPHON (Matthew 4:4)
One does not live by bread alone,
but by every word that comes forth from the mouth of God.

Or:

(Cf. Psalm 91[90]:4)
The Lord will conceal you with his pinions,
and under his wings you will trust.

PRAYER AFTER COMMUNION
Renewed now with heavenly bread,
by which faith is nourished, hope increased,
and charity strengthened,
we pray, O Lord,
that we may learn to hunger for Christ,
the true and living Bread,
and strive to live by every word
which proceeds from your mouth.
Through Christ our Lord. All: **Amen.**

# Second Sunday of Lent

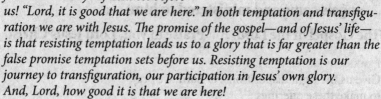

## March 12, 2017

*Reflection on the Gospel*

*Last week, temptation; this week, transfiguration. Such contrasts these first two Sundays of Lent set before us! "Lord, it is good that we are here." In both temptation and transfiguration we are with Jesus. The promise of the gospel—and of Jesus' life— is that resisting temptation leads us to a glory that is far greater than the false promise temptation sets before us. Resisting temptation is our journey to transfiguration, our participation in Jesus' own glory. And, Lord, how good it is that we are here!*

• *I am transformed when I . . .*

—Living Liturgy™, *Second Sunday of Lent 2017*

ENTRANCE ANTIPHON (Cf. Psalm 27[26]:8-9)
Of you my heart has spoken: Seek his face.
It is your face, O Lord, that I seek;
hide not your face from me.

Or:

(Cf. Psalm 25[24]:6, 2, 22)
Remember your compassion, O Lord,
and your merciful love, for they are from of old.
Let not our enemies exult over us.
Redeem us, O God of Israel, from all our distress.

COLLECT
O God, who have commanded us
to listen to your beloved Son,
be pleased, we pray,
to nourish us inwardly by your word,
that, with spiritual sight made pure,
we may rejoice to behold your glory.
Through our Lord Jesus Christ, your Son,

who lives and reigns with you in the unity of the Holy Spirit,
one God, for ever and ever. All: **Amen.**

<small>READING I (L 25-A)</small> (Genesis 12:1-4a)

**A reading from the Book of Genesis**

*The call of Abraham, the father of God's people.*

**The L**ORD** said to Abram:**

  **"Go forth from the land of your kinsfolk**

    **and from your father's house to a land that I will**

      **show you.**

    **"I will make of you a great nation,**

      **and I will bless you;**

  **I will make your name great,**

    **so that you will be a blessing.**

  **I will bless those who bless you**

    **and curse those who curse you.**

  **All the communities of the earth**

    **shall find blessing in you."**

**Abram went as the L**ORD** directed him.**

**The word of the Lord.** All: **Thanks be to God.**

<small>RESPONSORIAL PSALM 33</small>

P-111

Lord, let your mer-cy be on us, as we place our trust in you.

<small>Music: Jay F. Hunstiger, © 1991, administered by Liturgical Press. All rights reserved.</small>

Psalm 33:4-5, 18-19, 20, 22

℟. (22) **Lord, let your mercy be on us, as we place our**
    **trust in you.**

  Upright is the word of the L**ORD**,

    and all his works are trustworthy.

  He loves justice and right;

    of the kindness of the L**ORD** the earth is full. ℟.

*(continued)*

See, the eyes of the L<small>ORD</small> are upon those who fear him,
   upon those who hope for his kindness,
to deliver them from death
   and preserve them in spite of famine. ℟.

Our soul waits for the L<small>ORD</small>,
   who is our help and our shield.
May your kindness, O L<small>ORD</small>, be upon us
   who have put our hope in you. ℟.

R<small>EADING</small> II (2 Timothy 1:8b-10)

## A reading from the second Letter of Saint Paul to Timothy

*God has saved us and called us to be holy.*

**Beloved:**
**Bear your share of hardship for the gospel**
   **with the strength that comes from God.**

**He saved us and called us to a holy life,**
   **not according to our works**
   **but according to his own design**
   **and the grace bestowed on us in Christ Jesus before**
      **time began,**
   **but now made manifest**
   **through the appearance of our savior Christ Jesus,**
   **who destroyed death and brought life and immortality**
   **to light through the gospel.**

**The word of the Lord.** All: **Thanks be to God.**

G<small>OSPEL</small> (Matthew 17:1-9)
V<small>ERSE BEFORE THE</small> G<small>OSPEL</small> (See Matthew 17:5)
℣. Praise and honor to you, Lord Jesus Christ!
℟. **Praise and honor to you, Lord Jesus Christ!**
℣. From the shining cloud the Father's voice is heard:
   This is my beloved Son, hear him. ℟.

✢ **A reading from the holy Gospel according to Matthew**

All: **Glory to you, O Lord.**

*Jesus' face shone like the sun.*

Jesus took Peter, James, and John his brother,
  and led them up a high mountain by themselves.
And he was transfigured before them;
  his face shone like the sun
  and his clothes became white as light.
And behold, Moses and Elijah appeared to them,
  conversing with him.
Then Peter said to Jesus in reply,
  "Lord, it is good that we are here.
If you wish, I will make three tents here,
  one for you, one for Moses, and one for Elijah."
While he was still speaking, behold,
  a bright cloud cast a shadow over them,
  then from the cloud came a voice that said,
  "This is my beloved Son, with whom I am well pleased;
  listen to him."
When the disciples heard this, they fell prostrate
  and were very much afraid.
But Jesus came and touched them, saying,
  "Rise, and do not be afraid."
And when the disciples raised their eyes,
  they saw no one else but Jesus alone.

As they were coming down from the mountain,
  Jesus charged them,
  "Do not tell the vision to anyone
    until the Son of Man has been raised from the dead."

The Gospel of the Lord. All: **Praise to you, Lord Jesus Christ.**

PRAYER OVER THE OFFERINGS
May this sacrifice, O Lord, we pray,
cleanse us of our faults
and sanctify your faithful in body and mind
for the celebration of the paschal festivities.
Through Christ our Lord. All: **Amen.**

COMMUNION ANTIPHON (Matthew 17:5)
This is my beloved Son, with whom I am well pleased;
listen to him.

PRAYER AFTER COMMUNION

As we receive these glorious mysteries,
we make thanksgiving to you, O Lord,
for allowing us while still on earth
to be partakers even now of the things of heaven.
Through Christ our Lord. All: **Amen.**

# Third Sunday of Lent

*March 19, 2017*

*Reflection on the Gospel*

*Jesus himself is the well of "living water" who draws the Samaritan woman into deeper "worship in Spirit and truth." He draws the disciples into the deeper mission of reaping the harvest that is already sown and ripe. He draws the townspeople into deeper belief in him as "the Christ" who "is truly the savior of the world." Worship, mission, and believing are the way to "eternal life." We need only to drink of Jesus, the "living water."*

• *Jesus transforms me, when I . . .*

—*Living Liturgy*™, *Third Sunday of Lent 2017*

ENTRANCE ANTIPHON (Cf. Psalm 25[24]:15-16)

My eyes are always on the Lord,
for he rescues my feet from the snare.
Turn to me and have mercy on me,
for I am alone and poor.

Or:

(Cf. Ezekiel 36:23-26)

When I prove my holiness among you,
I will gather you from all the foreign lands;
and I will pour clean water upon you
and cleanse you from all your impurities,
and I will give you a new spirit, says the Lord.

COLLECT

O God, author of every mercy and of all goodness,
who in fasting, prayer and almsgiving
have shown us a remedy for sin,
look graciously on this confession of our lowliness,
that we, who are bowed down by our conscience,
may always be lifted up by your mercy.
Through our Lord Jesus Christ, your Son,
who lives and reigns with you in the unity of the Holy Spirit,
one God, for ever and ever. All: **Amen.**

READING I (L 28-A) (Exodus 17:3-7)

**A reading from the Book of Exodus**

*Give us water, so that we may drink.*

**In those days, in their thirst for water,
the people grumbled against Moses,
saying, "Why did you ever make us leave Egypt?
Was it just to have us die here of thirst
with our children and our livestock?"
So Moses cried out to the LORD,
"What shall I do with this people?
A little more and they will stone me!"
The LORD answered Moses,
"Go over there in front of the people,
along with some of the elders of Israel,
holding in your hand, as you go,
the staff with which you struck the river.
I will be standing there in front of you on the rock in
Horeb.
Strike the rock, and the water will flow from it
for the people to drink."
This Moses did, in the presence of the elders of Israel.**

The place was called Massah and Meribah,
   because the Israelites quarreled there
   and tested the LORD, saying,
"Is the LORD in our midst or not?"

**The word of the Lord.** All: **Thanks be to God.**

RESPONSORIAL PSALM 95

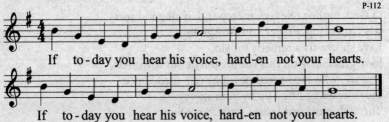

If to-day you hear his voice, hard-en not your hearts.

If to-day you hear his voice, hard-en not your hearts.

Psalm 95:1-2, 6-7, 8-9

℟. (8) **If today you hear his voice, harden not your hearts.**

Come, let us sing joyfully to the LORD;
   let us acclaim the Rock of our salvation.
Let us come into his presence with thanksgiving;
   let us joyfully sing psalms to him. ℟.

Come, let us bow down in worship;
   let us kneel before the LORD who made us.
For he is our God,
   and we are the people he shepherds, the flock he
      guides. ℟.

Oh, that today you would hear his voice:
   "Harden not your hearts as at Meribah,
   as in the day of Massah in the desert.
Where your fathers tempted me;
   they tested me though they had seen my works." ℟.

READING II (Romans 5:1-2, 5-8)

**A reading from the Letter of Saint Paul to the Romans**

*The love of God has been poured into our hearts through the Holy Spirit that has been given to us.*

Brothers and sisters:
Since we have been justified by faith,
> we have peace with God through our Lord Jesus Christ,
> through whom we have gained access by faith
> to this grace in which we stand,
> and we boast in hope of the glory of God.

And hope does not disappoint,
> because the love of God has been poured out into our
> > hearts
> through the Holy Spirit who has been given to us.

For Christ, while we were still helpless,
> died at the appointed time for the ungodly.

Indeed, only with difficulty does one die for a just person,
> though perhaps for a good person one might even
> > find courage to die.

But God proves his love for us
> in that while we were still sinners Christ died for us.

The word of the Lord. All: Thanks be to God.

GOSPEL (John 4:5-42) *or* Shorter Form [ ] (John 4:5-15, 19b-26, 39a, 40-42)

VERSE BEFORE THE GOSPEL (*See* John 4:42, 15)

℣. Praise to you, Lord Jesus Christ, King of endless glory!
℟. **Praise to you, Lord Jesus Christ, King of endless glory!**
℣. Lord, you are truly the Savior of the world;
> give me living water, that I may never thirst again. ℟.

✠ **A reading from the holy Gospel according to John**

All: **Glory to you, O Lord.**

*The water that I shall give will become a spring of eternal life.*

[Jesus came to a town of Samaria called Sychar,
> near the plot of land that Jacob had given to his son
> > Joseph.

Jacob's well was there.
Jesus, tired from his journey, sat down there at the well.
It was about noon.

A woman of Samaria came to draw water.
Jesus said to her,
  "Give me a drink."
His disciples had gone into the town to buy food.
The Samaritan woman said to him,
  "How can you, a Jew, ask me, a Samaritan woman, for
    a drink?"
—For Jews use nothing in common with Samaritans.—
Jesus answered and said to her,
  "If you knew the gift of God
  and who is saying to you, 'Give me a drink,'
  you would have asked him
  and he would have given you living water."
The woman said to him,
  "Sir, you do not even have a bucket and the cistern is
    deep;
  where then can you get this living water?
Are you greater than our father Jacob,
  who gave us this cistern and drank from it himself
  with his children and his flocks?"
Jesus answered and said to her,
  "Everyone who drinks this water will be thirsty again;
  but whoever drinks the water I shall give will never
    thirst;
  the water I shall give will become in him
  a spring of water welling up to eternal life."
The woman said to him,
  "Sir, give me this water, so that I may not be thirsty
  or have to keep coming here to draw water."]

Jesus said to her,
  "Go call your husband and come back."
The woman answered and said to him,
  "I do not have a husband."
Jesus answered her,
  "You are right in saying, 'I do not have a husband.'

For you have had five husbands,
>and the one you have now is not your husband.
What you have said is true."
The woman said to him,
>["Sir, I can see that you are a prophet.
Our ancestors worshiped on this mountain;
>but you people say that the place to worship is in
>>Jerusalem."
Jesus said to her,
>"Believe me, woman, the hour is coming
>when you will worship the Father
>neither on this mountain nor in Jerusalem.
You people worship what you do not understand;
>we worship what we understand,
>because salvation is from the Jews.
But the hour is coming, and is now here,
>when true worshipers will worship the Father in
>>Spirit and truth;
>and indeed the Father seeks such people to worship
>>him.
God is Spirit, and those who worship him
>must worship in Spirit and truth."
The woman said to him,
>"I know that the Messiah is coming, the one called the
>>Christ;
>when he comes, he will tell us everything."
Jesus said to her,
>"I am he, the one speaking with you."]

At that moment his disciples returned,
>and were amazed that he was talking with a woman,
>but still no one said, "What are you looking for?"
>or "Why are you talking with her?"
The woman left her water jar
>and went into the town and said to the people,
>"Come see a man who told me everything I have done.

Could he possibly be the Christ?"
They went out of the town and came to him.
Meanwhile, the disciples urged him, "Rabbi, eat."
But he said to them,
> "I have food to eat of which you do not know."
So the disciples said to one another,
> "Could someone have brought him something to eat?"
Jesus said to them,
> "My food is to do the will of the one who sent me
> and to finish his work.

Do you not say, 'In four months the harvest will be here'?
I tell you, look up and see the fields ripe for the harvest.
The reaper is already receiving payment
> and gathering crops for eternal life,
> so that the sower and reaper can rejoice together.
For here the saying is verified that 'One sows and
> another reaps.'
I sent you to reap what you have not worked for;
> others have done the work,
> and you are sharing the fruits of their work."

[Many of the Samaritans of that town began to believe
> in him]
> because of the word of the woman who testified,
> "He told me everything I have done."
[When the Samaritans came to him,
> they invited him to stay with them;
> and he stayed there two days.
Many more began to believe in him because of his word,
> and they said to the woman,
> "We no longer believe because of your word;
> for we have heard for ourselves,
> and we know that this is truly the savior of the world."]

The Gospel of the Lord. All: Praise to you, Lord Jesus Christ.

PRAYER OVER THE OFFERINGS

Be pleased, O Lord, with these sacrificial offerings,
and grant that we who beseech pardon for our own sins,
may take care to forgive our neighbor.
Through Christ our Lord. All: **Amen.**

COMMUNION ANTIPHON (John 4:13-14)

For anyone who drinks it, says the Lord,
the water I shall give will become in him
a spring welling up to eternal life.

PRAYER AFTER COMMUNION

As we receive the pledge
of things yet hidden in heaven
and are nourished while still on earth
with the Bread that comes from on high,
we humbly entreat you, O Lord,
that what is being brought about in us in mystery
may come to true completion.
Through Christ our Lord. All: **Amen.**

# Fourth Sunday of Lent

*March 26, 2017*

*Reflection on the Gospel*

*In this gospel is the conversation-encounter of the miracle: Jesus touched, the man "went and washed." There are the conversation-encounters of relationships: the disciples and Jesus, Jesus and the blind man, the neighbors and the blind man, parents and the Pharisees, Pharisees and the blind man, Pharisees and Jesus. There are the conversation-encounters about seeing: gaining sight, resisting sight; coming to faith, resisting faith.*

*Lent invites us into the same conversation-encounters with Jesus, in
which we choose either to be drawn toward Jesus or to turn away
from him.*

* I encounter the Lord . . .

—Living Liturgy™, *Fourth Sunday of Lent 2017*

## ENTRANCE ANTIPHON (Cf. Isaiah 66:10-11)

Rejoice, Jerusalem, and all who love her.
Be joyful, all who were in mourning;
exult and be satisfied at her consoling breast.

## COLLECT

O God, who through your Word
reconcile the human race to yourself in a wonderful way,
grant, we pray,
that with prompt devotion and eager faith
the Christian people may hasten
toward the solemn celebrations to come.
Through our Lord Jesus Christ, your Son,
who lives and reigns with you in the unity of the Holy Spirit,
one God, for ever and ever. All: **Amen.**

## READING I (L 31-A) (1 Samuel 16:1b, 6-7, 10-13a)

### A reading from the first Book of Samuel

*David is anointed as king of Israel.*

**The LORD said to Samuel:**
**"Fill your horn with oil, and be on your way.**
**I am sending you to Jesse of Bethlehem,**
**for I have chosen my king from among his sons."**

**As Jesse and his sons came to the sacrifice,**
**Samuel looked at Eliab and thought,**
**"Surely the LORD's anointed is here before him."**
**But the LORD said to Samuel:**
**"Do not judge from his appearance or from his lofty**
**stature,**
**because I have rejected him.**
**Not as man sees does God see,**
**because man sees the appearance**
**but the LORD looks into the heart."**

In the same way Jesse presented seven sons before Samuel,
  but Samuel said to Jesse,
    "The LORD has not chosen any one of these."
Then Samuel asked Jesse,
  "Are these all the sons you have?"
Jesse replied,
  "There is still the youngest, who is tending the sheep."
Samuel said to Jesse,
  "Send for him;
  we will not begin the sacrificial banquet until he
      arrives here."
Jesse sent and had the young man brought to them.
He was ruddy, a youth handsome to behold
  and making a splendid appearance.
The LORD said,
  "There—anoint him, for this is the one!"
Then Samuel, with the horn of oil in hand,
  anointed David in the presence of his brothers;
  and from that day on, the spirit of the LORD rushed
      upon David.
The word of the Lord. All: Thanks be to God.

RESPONSORIAL PSALM 23

P-113

The Lord is my shep - herd; there is noth - ing I shall want.

Music: Jay F. Hunstiger, © 1990, administered by Liturgical Press. All rights reserved.

Psalm 23:1-3a, 3b-4, 5, 6

℟. (1) **The Lord is my shepherd; there is nothing I shall
    want.**

The LORD is my shepherd; I shall not want.
  In verdant pastures he gives me repose;
beside restful waters he leads me;
  he refreshes my soul. ℟.

*(continued)*

He guides me in right paths
　　for his name's sake.
Even though I walk in the dark valley
　　I fear no evil; for you are at my side
with your rod and your staff
　　that give me courage. R̸.

You spread the table before me
　　in the sight of my foes;
you anoint my head with oil;
　　my cup overflows. R̸.

Only goodness and kindness follow me
　　all the days of my life;
and I shall dwell in the house of the LORD
　　for years to come. R̸.

## READING II (Ephesians 5:8-14)

**A reading from the Letter of Saint Paul to the Ephesians**

*Arise from the dead, and Christ will give you light.*

**Brothers and sisters:**
**You were once darkness,**
　　**but now you are light in the Lord.**
**Live as children of light,**
　　**for light produces every kind of goodness**
　　**and righteousness and truth.**
**Try to learn what is pleasing to the Lord.**
**Take no part in the fruitless works of darkness;**
　　**rather expose them, for it is shameful even to mention**
　　**the things done by them in secret;**
　　**but everything exposed by the light becomes visible,**
　　**for everything that becomes visible is light.**
**Therefore, it says:**
　　**"Awake, O sleeper,**
　　**and arise from the dead,**
　　**and Christ will give you light."**

**The word of the Lord.** All: **Thanks be to God.**

GOSPEL (John 9:1-41) *or* Shorter Form [ ] (John 9:1, 6-9, 13-17, 34-38)

VERSE BEFORE THE GOSPEL (John 8:12)

℣. Praise to you, Lord Jesus Christ, King of endless glory!

℟. **Praise to you, Lord Jesus Christ, King of endless glory!**

℣. I am the light of the world, says the Lord;
whoever follows me will have the light of life. ℟.

✠ **A reading from the holy Gospel according to John**

All: **Glory to you, O Lord.**

*The man who was blind went off and washed himself and came back able to see.*

**[As Jesus passed by he saw a man blind from birth.]**
**His disciples asked him,**
**"Rabbi, who sinned, this man or his parents,**
**that he was born blind?"**
**Jesus answered,**
**"Neither he nor his parents sinned;**
**it is so that the works of God might be made visible**
**through him.**
**We have to do the works of the one who sent me while it**
**is day.**
**Night is coming when no one can work.**
**While I am in the world, I am the light of the world."**
**When he had said this, [he spat on the ground**
**and made clay with the saliva,**
**and smeared the clay on his eyes, and said to him,**
**"Go wash in the Pool of Siloam"—which means Sent—.**
**So he went and washed, and came back able to see.**

**His neighbors and those who had seen him earlier as a**
**beggar said,**
**"Isn't this the one who used to sit and beg?"**
**Some said, "It is,"**
**but others said, "No, he just looks like him."**
**He said, "I am."]**
**So they said to him, "How were your eyes opened?"**

He replied,
> "The man called Jesus made clay and anointed my eyes
> and told me, 'Go to Siloam and wash.'

So I went there and washed and was able to see."
And they said to him, "Where is he?"
He said, "I don't know."

[They brought the one who was once blind to the
>> Pharisees.

Now Jesus had made clay and opened his eyes on a
>> sabbath.
So then the Pharisees also asked him how he was able to
>> see.
He said to them,
> "He put clay on my eyes, and I washed, and now I can
> see."

So some of the Pharisees said,
> "This man is not from God,
> because he does not keep the sabbath."

But others said,
> "How can a sinful man do such signs?"

And there was a division among them.
So they said to the blind man again,
> "What do you have to say about him,
> since he opened your eyes?"

He said, "He is a prophet."]

Now the Jews did not believe
> that he had been blind and gained his sight
> until they summoned the parents of the one who had
>> gained his sight.

They asked them,
> "Is this your son, who you say was born blind?

How does he now see?"
His parents answered and said,
> "We know that this is our son and that he was born
>> blind.

We do not know how he sees now,
  nor do we know who opened his eyes.
Ask him, he is of age;
  he can speak for himself."
His parents said this because they were afraid
  of the Jews, for the Jews had already agreed
  that if anyone acknowledged him as the Christ,
  he would be expelled from the synagogue.
For this reason his parents said,
  "He is of age; question him."

So a second time they called the man who had been blind
  and said to him, "Give God the praise!
We know that this man is a sinner."
He replied,
  "If he is a sinner, I do not know.
One thing I do know is that I was blind and now I see."
So they said to him,
  "What did he do to you?
  How did he open your eyes?"
He answered them,
  "I told you already and you did not listen.
Why do you want to hear it again?
Do you want to become his disciples, too?"
They ridiculed him and said,
  "You are that man's disciple;
  we are disciples of Moses!
We know that God spoke to Moses,
  but we do not know where this one is from."
The man answered and said to them,
  "This is what is so amazing,
  that you do not know where he is from, yet he opened
    my eyes.
We know that God does not listen to sinners,
  but if one is devout and does his will, he listens to him.

It is unheard of that anyone ever opened the eyes of a
person born blind.
If this man were not from God,
he would not be able to do anything."
[They answered and said to him,
"You were born totally in sin,
and are you trying to teach us?"
Then they threw him out.

When Jesus heard that they had thrown him out,
he found him and said, "Do you believe in the Son of
Man?"
He answered and said,
"Who is he, sir, that I may believe in him?"
Jesus said to him,
"You have seen him,
and the one speaking with you is he."
He said,
"I do believe, Lord," and he worshiped him.]
Then Jesus said,
"I came into this world for judgment,
so that those who do not see might see,
and those who do see might become blind."

Some of the Pharisees who were with him heard this
and said to him, "Surely we are not also blind, are we?"
Jesus said to them,
"If you were blind, you would have no sin;
but now you are saying, 'We see,' so your sin remains."

The Gospel of the Lord. All: **Praise to you, Lord Jesus Christ.**

PRAYER OVER THE OFFERINGS
We place before you with joy these offerings,
which bring eternal remedy, O Lord,
praying that we may both faithfully revere them
and present them to you, as is fitting,
for the salvation of all the world.
Through Christ our Lord. All: **Amen.**

COMMUNION ANTIPHON (Cf. John 9:11, 38)
The Lord anointed my eyes: I went, I washed,
I saw and I believed in God.

PRAYER AFTER COMMUNION
O God, who enlighten everyone who comes into this world,
illuminate our hearts, we pray,
with the splendor of your grace,
that we may always ponder
what is worthy and pleasing to your majesty
and love you in all sincerity.
Through Christ our Lord. All: **Amen.**

# Fifth Sunday of Lent

*April 2, 2017*

---

*Reflection on the Gospel*

*Both Martha and Mary say to Jesus, "Lord, if you had been here, / my brother would not have died." Jesus purposely had delayed for two days coming to Bethany. Arriving after Lazarus was dead four days, Jesus could then reveal that death is necessary, but not the end. Out of death Jesus gives Life. Out of death Jesus reveals the deeper mystery of his own Person: "I am the resurrection and the life." Martha and Mary came "to believe." Have we?*

- *I come to believe Jesus is the resurrection and the life . . .*

—Living Liturgy™, *Fifth Sunday of Lent 2017*

ENTRANCE ANTIPHON (Cf. Psalm 43[42]:1-2)
Give me justice, O God,
and plead my cause against a nation that is faithless.
From the deceitful and cunning rescue me,
for you, O God, are my strength.

## COLLECT

By your help, we beseech you, Lord our God,
may we walk eagerly in that same charity
with which, out of love for the world,
your Son handed himself over to death.
Through our Lord Jesus Christ, your Son,
who lives and reigns with you in the unity of the Holy Spirit,
one God, for ever and ever. All: **Amen.**

## READING I (L 34-A) (Ezekiel 37:12-14)

### A reading from the Book of the Prophet Ezekiel

*I will put my spirit in you that you may live.*

**Thus says the Lord GOD:**

> **O my people, I will open your graves**
> **and have you rise from them,**
> **and bring you back to the land of Israel.**

**Then you shall know that I am the LORD,**
> **when I open your graves and have you rise from them,**
> **O my people!**

**I will put my spirit in you that you may live,**
> **and I will settle you upon your land;**
> **thus you shall know that I am the LORD.**

**I have promised, and I will do it, says the LORD.**

**The word of the Lord.** All: **Thanks be to God.**

## RESPONSORIAL PSALM 130

P-114

With the Lord there is mer-cy and full-ness of re-demp-tion.

Music: Jay F. Hunstiger, © 1990, administered by Liturgical Press. All rights reserved.

Psalm 130:1-2, 3-4, 5-6, 7-8

R̸. (7) **With the Lord there is mercy and fullness of
redemption.**

Out of the depths I cry to you, O LORD;
   LORD, hear my voice!
Let your ears be attentive
   to my voice in supplication. R̄.

If you, O LORD, mark iniquities,
   LORD, who can stand?
But with you is forgiveness,
   that you may be revered. R̄.

I trust in the LORD;
   my soul trusts in his word.
More than sentinels wait for the dawn,
   let Israel wait for the LORD. R̄.

For with the LORD is kindness
   and with him is plenteous redemption;
and he will redeem Israel
   from all their iniquities. R̄.

## READING II (Romans 8:8-11)

**A reading from the Letter of Saint Paul to the Romans**

*The Spirit of the One who raised Jesus from the dead dwells in you.*

**Brothers and sisters:**
**Those who are in the flesh cannot please God.**
**But you are not in the flesh;**
   **on the contrary, you are in the spirit,**
   **if only the Spirit of God dwells in you.**
**Whoever does not have the Spirit of Christ does not**
   **belong to him.**
**But if Christ is in you,**
   **although the body is dead because of sin,**
   **the spirit is alive because of righteousness.**
**If the Spirit of the one who raised Jesus from the dead**
   **dwells in you,**
   **the one who raised Christ from the dead**
   **will give life to your mortal bodies also,**
   **through his Spirit dwelling in you.**

**The word of the Lord.** All: **Thanks be to God.**

GOSPEL (John 11:1-45) *or* Shorter Form [ ] (John 11:3-7, 17, 20-27, 33b-45)

VERSE BEFORE THE GOSPEL (John 11:25a, 26)

℣. Praise to you, Lord Jesus Christ, King of endless glory!

℟. **Praise to you, Lord Jesus Christ, King of endless glory!**

℣. I am the resurrection and the life, says the Lord;
whoever believes in me will never die. ℟.

✠ **A reading from the holy Gospel according to John**

All: **Glory to you, O Lord.**

*I am the resurrection and the life.*

Now a man was ill, Lazarus from Bethany,
the village of Mary and her sister Martha.
Mary was the one who had anointed the Lord with
perfumed oil
and dried his feet with her hair;
it was her brother Lazarus who was ill.
So [the sisters* sent word to Jesus saying,
"Master, the one you love is ill."
When Jesus heard this he said,
"This illness is not to end in death,
but is for the glory of God,
that the Son of God may be glorified through it."
Now Jesus loved Martha and her sister and Lazarus.
So when he heard that he was ill,
he remained for two days in the place where he was.
Then after this he said to his disciples,
"Let us go back to Judea."]
The disciples said to him,
"Rabbi, the Jews were just trying to stone you,
and you want to go back there?"
Jesus answered,
"Are there not twelve hours in a day?
If one walks during the day, he does not stumble,
because he sees the light of this world.

* Shorter form: **The sisters of Lazarus**

But if one walks at night, he stumbles,
   because the light is not in him."
He said this, and then told them,
   "Our friend Lazarus is asleep,
   but I am going to awaken him."
So the disciples said to him,
   "Master, if he is asleep, he will be saved."
But Jesus was talking about his death,
   while they thought that he meant ordinary sleep.
So then Jesus said to them clearly,
   "Lazarus has died.
And I am glad for you that I was not there,
   that you may believe.
Let us go to him."
So Thomas, called Didymus, said to his fellow disciples,
   "Let us also go to die with him."

[When Jesus arrived, he found that Lazarus
   had already been in the tomb for four days.]
Now Bethany was near Jerusalem, only about two miles
      away.
And many of the Jews had come to Martha and Mary
   to comfort them about their brother.
[When Martha heard that Jesus was coming,
   she went to meet him;
   but Mary sat at home.
Martha said to Jesus,
   "Lord, if you had been here,
   my brother would not have died.
But even now I know that whatever you ask of God,
   God will give you."
Jesus said to her,
   "Your brother will rise."
Martha said to him,
   "I know he will rise,
   in the resurrection on the last day."

Jesus told her,

"I am the resurrection and the life;
whoever believes in me, even if he dies, will live,
and everyone who lives and believes in me will never
die.

Do you believe this?"
She said to him, "Yes, Lord.
I have come to believe that you are the Christ, the Son
of God,
the one who is coming into the world."]

When she had said this,
she went and called her sister Mary secretly, saying,
"The teacher is here and is asking for you."
As soon as she heard this,
she rose quickly and went to him.
For Jesus had not yet come into the village,
but was still where Martha had met him.
So when the Jews who were with her in the house
comforting her
saw Mary get up quickly and go out,
they followed her,
presuming that she was going to the tomb to weep there.
When Mary came to where Jesus was and saw him,
she fell at his feet and said to him,
"Lord, if you had been here,
my brother would not have died."
When Jesus saw her weeping and the Jews who had come
with her weeping,
[he became perturbed and deeply troubled, and said,
"Where have you laid him?"
They said to him, "Sir, come and see."
And Jesus wept.
So the Jews said, "See how he loved him."
But some of them said,
"Could not the one who opened the eyes of the blind
man

**have done something so that this man would not have
    died?"**

**So Jesus, perturbed again, came to the tomb.**

**It was a cave, and a stone lay across it.**

**Jesus said, "Take away the stone."**

**Martha, the dead man's sister, said to him,**

**    "Lord, by now there will be a stench;**

**    he has been dead for four days."**

**Jesus said to her,**

**    "Did I not tell you that if you believe**

**    you will see the glory of God?"**

**So they took away the stone.**

**And Jesus raised his eyes and said,**

**    "Father, I thank you for hearing me.**

**I know that you always hear me;**

**    but because of the crowd here I have said this,**

**    that they may believe that you sent me."**

**And when he had said this,**

**    he cried out in a loud voice,**

**    "Lazarus, come out!"**

**The dead man came out,**

**    tied hand and foot with burial bands,**

**    and his face was wrapped in a cloth.**

**So Jesus said to them,**

**    "Untie him and let him go."**

**Now many of the Jews who had come to Mary**

**    and seen what he had done began to believe in him.]**

**The Gospel of the Lord.** All: **Praise to you, Lord Jesus Christ.**

PRAYER OVER THE OFFERINGS

Hear us, almighty God,
and, having instilled in your servants
the teachings of the Christian faith,
graciously purify them
by the working of this sacrifice.
Through Christ our Lord. All: **Amen.**

Everyone who lives and believes in me
will not die for ever, says the Lord.

PRAYER AFTER COMMUNION
We pray, almighty God,
that we may always be counted among the members of Christ,
in whose Body and Blood we have communion.
Who lives and reigns for ever and ever. All: **Amen.**

# Palm Sunday of the Lord's Passion

*April 9, 2017*

*Reflection on the Gospel*

*This day—Palm Sunday—when we sing our hosannas and bow our
heads in sorrow as we hear the passion account for the first time this
year, we begin the holiest week of our Christian year. It is no ordinary
week, for we celebrate Jesus' unreserved self-giving. Holy Week brings before us the demands of self-giving. All of our daily living throughout the
year reminds us that, ultimately, like Jesus we must give ourselves over
to God so that God might give us divine Life.*

*• Today and every day we must give ourselves to God, . . .*

—*Living Liturgy™, Palm Sunday 2017*

# THE COMMEMORATION OF THE LORD'S ENTRANCE INTO JERUSALEM

## FIRST FORM: THE PROCESSION

The congregation assembles in a secondary church or chapel or in some other
suitable place distinct from the church to which the procession will move.
The faithful carry palm branches.

## Antiphon

Hosanna to the Son of David;
blessed is he who comes in the name of the Lord, the King
   of Israel.
Hosanna in the highest.

Priest: In the name of the Father, and of the Son, and of the Holy Spirit.
   All: **Amen.**

Then he greets the people in the usual way. A brief address is given, in which
the faithful are invited to participate actively and consciously in the celebration of this day, in these or similar words:

Dear brethren (brothers and sisters),
since the beginning of Lent until now
we have prepared our hearts by penance and charitable works.
Today we gather together to herald with the whole Church
the beginning of the celebration
of our Lord's Paschal Mystery,
that is to say, of his Passion and Resurrection.
For it was to accomplish this mystery
that he entered his own city of Jerusalem.
Therefore, with all faith and devotion,
let us commemorate
the Lord's entry into the city for our salvation,
following in his footsteps,
so that, being made by his grace partakers of the Cross,
we may have a share also in his Resurrection and in his life.

Let us pray.

**A**  Almighty ever-living God,
sanctify ✠ these branches with your blessing,
that we, who follow Christ the King in exultation,
may reach the eternal Jerusalem through him.
Who lives and reigns for ever and ever. All: **Amen.**

**B**  Increase the faith of those who place their hope in you, O God,
and graciously hear the prayers of those who call on you,
that we, who today hold high these branches
to hail Christ in his triumph,
may bear fruit for you by good works accomplished in him.
Who lives and reigns for ever and ever. All: **Amen.**

THE READING OF THE GOSPEL

GOSPEL (L 37-A) (Matthew 21:1-11)

✝ **A reading from the holy Gospel according to Matthew**

All: **Glory to you, O Lord.**

*Blessed is he who comes in the name of the Lord.*

**When Jesus and the disciples drew near Jerusalem**
    **and came to Bethphage on the Mount of Olives,**
    **Jesus sent two disciples, saying to them,**
    **"Go into the village opposite you,**
    **and immediately you will find an ass tethered,**
    **and a colt with her.**
**Untie them and bring them here to me.**
**And if anyone should say anything to you, reply,**
    **'The master has need of them.'**
**Then he will send them at once."**
**This happened so that what had been spoken through**
    **the prophet**
    **might be fulfilled:**
      *Say to daughter Zion,*
      *"Behold, your king comes to you,*
        *meek and riding on an ass,*
        *and on a colt, the foal of a beast of burden."*
**The disciples went and did as Jesus had ordered them.**
**They brought the ass and the colt and laid their cloaks**
    **over them,**
    **and he sat upon them.**
**The very large crowd spread their cloaks on the road,**
    **while others cut branches from the trees**
    **and strewed them on the road.**
**The crowds preceding him and those following**
    **kept crying out and saying:**
      **"Hosanna to the Son of David;**
        **blessed is he who comes in the name of the Lord;**
    **hosanna in the highest."**

And when he entered Jerusalem
  the whole city was shaken and asked, "Who is this?"
And the crowds replied,
  "This is Jesus the prophet, from Nazareth in Galilee."

**The Gospel of the Lord.** All: **Praise to you, Lord Jesus Christ.**

PROCESSION WITH THE BLESSED BRANCHES

SECOND FORM: THE SOLEMN ENTRANCE
The commemoration of the Lord's entrance may be celebrated before the
principal Mass with the solemn entrance, which takes place within the church.

THIRD FORM: THE SIMPLE ENTRANCE
The Lord's entrance is commemorated with the following simple entrance.

ENTRANCE ANTIPHON (Cf. John 12:1, 12-13; Psalm 24[23]:9-10)
Six days before the Passover,
when the Lord came into the city of Jerusalem,
the children ran to meet him;
in their hands they carried palm branches
and with a loud voice cried out:
*Hosanna in the highest!

Blessed are you, who have come in your abundant mercy!
O gates, lift high your heads;
grow higher, ancient doors.
Let him enter, the king of glory!
Who is this king of glory?
He, the Lord of hosts, he is the king of glory.
*Hosanna in the highest!

Blessed are you, who have come in your abundant mercy!

COLLECT
Almighty ever-living God,
who as an example of humility for the human race to follow
caused our Savior to take flesh and submit to the Cross,
graciously grant that we may heed his lesson of patient suffering
and so merit a share in his Resurrection.
Who lives and reigns with you in the unity of the Holy Spirit,
one God, for ever and ever. All: **Amen.**

## READING I (L 38-ABC) (Isaiah 50:4-7)

### A reading from the Book of the Prophet Isaiah

*My face I did not shield from buffets and spitting, knowing that I shall not be put to shame.*

> The Lord GOD has given me
>> a well-trained tongue,
> that I might know how to speak to the weary
>> a word that will rouse them.
> Morning after morning
>> he opens my ear that I may hear;
> and I have not rebelled,
>> have not turned back.
> I gave my back to those who beat me,
>> my cheeks to those who plucked my beard;
> my face I did not shield
>> from buffets and spitting.
> The Lord GOD is my help,
>> therefore I am not disgraced;
> I have set my face like flint,
>> knowing that I shall not be put to shame.

The word of the Lord. All: Thanks be to God.

## RESPONSORIAL PSALM 22

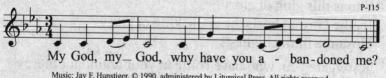

P-115

My God, my God, why have you a - ban-doned me?

Psalm 22:8-9, 17-18, 19-20, 23-24

℟. (2a) **My God, my God, why have you abandoned me?**

> All who see me scoff at me;
>> they mock me with parted lips, they wag their heads:
> "He relied on the LORD; let him deliver him,
>> let him rescue him, if he loves him." ℟.

> Indeed, many dogs surround me,
>> a pack of evildoers closes in upon me;

they have pierced my hands and my feet;
    I can count all my bones. R℞.

They divide my garments among them,
    and for my vesture they cast lots.
But you, O LORD, be not far from me;
    O my help, hasten to aid me. R℞.

I will proclaim your name to my brethren;
    in the midst of the assembly I will praise you:
"You who fear the LORD, praise him;
    all you descendants of Jacob, give glory to him;
    revere him, all you descendants of Israel!" R℞.

## READING II (Philippians 2:6-11)

**A reading from the Letter of Saint Paul to the Philippians**

*Christ humbled himself. Because of this God greatly exalted him.*

**Christ Jesus, though he was in the form of God,**
    **did not regard equality with God**
    **something to be grasped.**
**Rather, he emptied himself,**
    **taking the form of a slave,**
    **coming in human likeness;**
    **and found human in appearance,**
    **he humbled himself,**
    **becoming obedient to the point of death,**
    **even death on a cross.**
**Because of this, God greatly exalted him**
    **and bestowed on him the name**
    **which is above every name,**
    **that at the name of Jesus**
    **every knee should bend,**
    **of those in heaven and on earth and under the earth,**
    **and every tongue confess that**
    **Jesus Christ is Lord,**
    **to the glory of God the Father.**

**The word of the Lord.** All: **Thanks be to God.**

\* The message of the liturgy in proclaiming the passion narratives in full is to enable the assembly to see vividly the love of Christ for each person, despite their sins, a love that even death could not vanquish. The crimes during the Passion of Christ cannot be attributed indiscriminately to all Jews of that time, nor to Jews today. The Jewish people should not be referred to as though rejected or cursed, as if this view followed from Scripture. The Church ever keeps in mind that Jesus, his mother Mary, and the Apostles all were Jewish. As the Church has always held, Christ freely suffered his passion and death because of the sins of all, that all might be saved.

GOSPEL (Matthew 26:14—27:66) *or* Shorter Form [ ]
(Matthew 27:11-54)

VERSE BEFORE THE GOSPEL (Philippians 2:8-9)

℣. Praise to you, Lord Jesus Christ, King of endless glory!

℞. **Praise to you, Lord Jesus Christ, King of endless glory!**

℣. Christ became obedient to the point of death,
　　even death on a cross.
　　Because of this, God greatly exalted him
　　and bestowed on him the name which is above every
　　　　name. ℞.

The symbols in the following passion narrative represent:

C.　Narrator;
✛　Christ;
S.　speakers other than Christ;
SS.　groups of speakers.

**The Passion of our Lord Jesus Christ according to Matthew**

*The Passion of our Lord Jesus Christ.*

C.　**One of the Twelve, who was called Judas Iscariot,**
　　**went to the chief priests and said,**

S.　**"What are you willing to give me**
　　**if I hand him over to you?"**

C.　**They paid him thirty pieces of silver,**
　　**and from that time on he looked for an opportunity**
　　　　**to hand him over.**

　　**On the first day of the Feast of Unleavened Bread,**
　　　　**the disciples approached Jesus and said,**

SS.　**"Where do you want us to prepare**
　　　　**for you to eat the Passover?"**

C.　**He said,**

✠   "Go into the city to a certain man and tell him,
'The teacher says, "My appointed time draws near;
in your house I shall celebrate the Passover with
my disciples."'"

C.   The disciples then did as Jesus had ordered,
and prepared the Passover.

When it was evening,
he reclined at table with the Twelve.
And while they were eating, he said,

✠   "Amen, I say to you, one of you will betray me."

C.   Deeply distressed at this,
they began to say to him one after another,

S.   "Surely it is not I, Lord?"

C.   He said in reply,

✠   "He who has dipped his hand into the dish with me
is the one who will betray me.
The Son of Man indeed goes, as it is written of him,
but woe to that man by whom the Son of Man is
betrayed.
It would be better for that man if he had never been
born."

C.   Then Judas, his betrayer, said in reply,

S.   "Surely it is not I, Rabbi?"

C.   He answered,

✠   "You have said so."

C.   While they were eating,
Jesus took bread, said the blessing,
broke it, and giving it to his disciples said,
"Take and eat; this is my body."

C.   Then he took a cup, gave thanks, and gave it to them,
saying,

✠   "Drink from it, all of you,
for this is my blood of the covenant,
which will be shed on behalf of many
for the forgiveness of sins.

I tell you, from now on I shall not drink this fruit of
   the vine
      until the day when I drink it with you new
      in the kingdom of my Father."

C.   Then, after singing a hymn,
      they went out to the Mount of Olives.

Then Jesus said to them,

✝   "This night all of you will have your faith in me
      shaken,
      for it is written:

   *I will strike the shepherd,*
      *and the sheep of the flock will be dispersed;*
      but after I have been raised up,
      I shall go before you to Galilee."

C.   Peter said to him in reply,

S.   "Though all may have their faith in you shaken,
      mine will never be."

C.   Jesus said to him,

✝   "Amen, I say to you,
      this very night before the cock crows,
      you will deny me three times."

C.   Peter said to him,

S.   "Even though I should have to die with you,
      I will not deny you."

C.   And all the disciples spoke likewise.

Then Jesus came with them to a place called
         Gethsemane,
      and he said to his disciples,

✝   "Sit here while I go over there and pray."

C.   He took along Peter and the two sons of Zebedee,
      and began to feel sorrow and distress.
      Then he said to them,

✝   "My soul is sorrowful even to death.
      Remain here and keep watch with me."

C.   He advanced a little and fell prostrate in prayer,
         saying,

✝ "My Father, if it is possible,
let this cup pass from me;
yet, not as I will, but as you will."

C. When he returned to his disciples he found them
asleep.
He said to Peter,

✝ "So you could not keep watch with me for one hour?
Watch and pray that you may not undergo the test.
The spirit is willing, but the flesh is weak."

C. Withdrawing a second time, he prayed again,

✝ "My Father, if it is not possible that this cup pass
without my drinking it, your will be done!"

C. Then he returned once more and found them asleep,
for they could not keep their eyes open.
He left them and withdrew again and prayed a third
time,
saying the same thing again.
Then he returned to his disciples and said to them,

✝ "Are you still sleeping and taking your rest?
Behold, the hour is at hand
when the Son of Man is to be handed over to sinners.
Get up, let us go.
Look, my betrayer is at hand."

C. While he was still speaking,
Judas, one of the Twelve, arrived,
accompanied by a large crowd, with swords and
clubs,
who had come from the chief priests and the
elders of the people.
His betrayer had arranged a sign with them, saying,

S. "The man I shall kiss is the one; arrest him."

C. Immediately he went over to Jesus and said,

S. "Hail, Rabbi!"

C. and he kissed him.
Jesus answered him,

✝ "Friend, do what you have come for."

C.   Then stepping forward they laid hands on Jesus and
  arrested him.
 And behold, one of those who accompanied Jesus
  put his hand to his sword, drew it,
   and struck the high priest's servant, cutting off
    his ear.
 Then Jesus said to him,

✠  "Put your sword back into its sheath,
  for all who take the sword will perish by the sword.
 Do you think that I cannot call upon my Father
  and he will not provide me at this moment
   with more than twelve legions of angels?
 But then how would the Scriptures be fulfilled
  which say that it must come to pass in this way?"

C.   At that hour Jesus said to the crowds,

✠ "Have you come out as against a robber,
  with swords and clubs to seize me?
 Day after day I sat teaching in the temple area,
  yet you did not arrest me.
 But all this has come to pass
  that the writings of the prophets may be fulfilled."

C.   Then all the disciples left him and fled.

 Those who had arrested Jesus led him away
  to Caiaphas the high priest,
   where the scribes and the elders were assembled.
 Peter was following him at a distance
  as far as the high priest's courtyard,
   and going inside he sat down with the servants to
    see the outcome.
 The chief priests and the entire Sanhedrin
  kept trying to obtain false testimony against Jesus
  in order to put him to death,
  but they found none,
   though many false witnesses came forward.
 Finally two came forward who stated,

SS.  "This man said, 'I can destroy the temple of God
and within three days rebuild it.'"

C.  The high priest rose and addressed him,

S.    "Have you no answer?
What are these men testifying against you?"

C.  But Jesus was silent.
Then the high priest said to him,

S.  "I order you to tell us under oath before the living
God
whether you are the Christ, the Son of God."

C.  Jesus said to him in reply,

✝    "You have said so.
But I tell you:
From now on you will see 'the Son of Man
seated at the right hand of the Power'
and 'coming on the clouds of heaven.'"

C.  Then the high priest tore his robes and said,

S.    "He has blasphemed!
What further need have we of witnesses?
You have now heard the blasphemy;
what is your opinion?"

C.  They said in reply,

SS.  "He deserves to die!"

C.  Then they spat in his face and struck him,
while some slapped him, saying,

SS.  "Prophesy for us, Christ: who is it that struck you?"

C.  Now Peter was sitting outside in the courtyard.
One of the maids came over to him and said,

S.    "You too were with Jesus the Galilean."

C.  But he denied it in front of everyone, saying,

S.    "I do not know what you are talking about!"

C.  As he went out to the gate, another girl saw him
and said to those who were there,

S.    "This man was with Jesus the Nazorean."

C.  Again he denied it with an oath,

S.    "I do not know the man!"

C. **A little later the bystanders came over and said to Peter,**

S. **"Surely you too are one of them;
even your speech gives you away."**

C. **At that he began to curse and to swear,**

S. **"I do not know the man."**

C. **And immediately a cock crowed.
Then Peter remembered the word that Jesus had spoken:
"Before the cock crows you will deny me three times."
He went out and began to weep bitterly.**

**When it was morning,
all the chief priests and the elders of the people
took counsel against Jesus to put him to death.
They bound him, led him away,
and handed him over to Pilate, the governor.**

**Then Judas, his betrayer, seeing that Jesus had been condemned,
deeply regretted what he had done.
He returned the thirty pieces of silver
to the chief priests and elders, saying,**

S. **"I have sinned in betraying innocent blood."**

C. **They said,**

SS. **"What is that to us?
Look to it yourself."**

C. **Flinging the money into the temple,
he departed and went off and hanged himself.
The chief priests gathered up the money, but said,**

SS. **"It is not lawful to deposit this in the temple treasury,
for it is the price of blood."**

C. **After consultation, they used it to buy the potter's field
as a burial place for foreigners.
That is why that field even today is called the Field of Blood.**

Then was fulfilled what had been said through
    Jeremiah the prophet,
    *And they took the thirty pieces of silver,*
    *the value of a man with a price on his head,*
    *a price set by some of the Israelites,*
    *and they paid it out for the potter's field*
    *just as the Lord had commanded me.*

Now [Jesus stood before the governor, and he
    questioned him,

S.    "Are you the king of the Jews?"

C.  Jesus said,

✝    "You say so."

C.  And when he was accused by the chief priests and
    elders,
    he made no answer.
Then Pilate said to him,

S.    "Do you not hear how many things they are
    testifying against you?"

C.  But he did not answer him one word,
    so that the governor was greatly amazed.

Now on the occasion of the feast
    the governor was accustomed to release to the
    crowd
    one prisoner whom they wished.
And at that time they had a notorious prisoner
    called Barabbas.
So when they had assembled, Pilate said to them,

S.    "Which one do you want me to release to you,
    Barabbas, or Jesus called Christ?"

C.  For he knew that it was out of envy
    that they had handed him over.
While he was still seated on the bench,
    his wife sent him a message,
"Have nothing to do with that righteous man.
I suffered much in a dream today because of him."

The chief priests and the elders persuaded the crowds
    to ask for Barabbas but to destroy Jesus.
The governor said to them in reply,

S.    "Which of the two do you want me to release to
      you?"

C.    They answered,

SS.    "Barabbas!"

C.    Pilate said to them,

S.    "Then what shall I do with Jesus called Christ?"

C.    They all said,

SS.    "Let him be crucified!"

C.    But he said,

S.    "Why? What evil has he done?"

C.    They only shouted the louder,

SS.    "Let him be crucified!"

C.    When Pilate saw that he was not succeeding at all,
    but that a riot was breaking out instead,
      he took water and washed his hands in the sight
        of the crowd, saying,

S.    "I am innocent of this man's blood.
Look to it yourselves."

C.    And the whole people said in reply,

SS.    "His blood be upon us and upon our children."

C.    Then he released Barabbas to them,
    but after he had Jesus scourged,
    he handed him over to be crucified.

Then the soldiers of the governor took Jesus inside
    the praetorium
    and gathered the whole cohort around him.
They stripped off his clothes
    and threw a scarlet military cloak about him.
Weaving a crown out of thorns, they placed it on his
    head,
    and a reed in his right hand.
And kneeling before him, they mocked him, saying,

SS. "Hail, King of the Jews!"

C. They spat upon him and took the reed
    and kept striking him on the head.
And when they had mocked him,
    they stripped him of the cloak,
    dressed him in his own clothes,
    and led him off to crucify him.

As they were going out, they met a Cyrenian named
    Simon;
    this man they pressed into service
    to carry his cross.

And when they came to a place called Golgotha
    —which means Place of the Skull—,
    they gave Jesus wine to drink mixed with gall.
But when he had tasted it, he refused to drink.
After they had crucified him,
    they divided his garments by casting lots;
    then they sat down and kept watch over him there.
And they placed over his head the written charge
    against him:
    This is Jesus, the King of the Jews.
Two revolutionaries were crucified with him,
    one on his right and the other on his left.
Those passing by reviled him, shaking their heads
    and saying,

SS. "You who would destroy the temple and rebuild it in
    three days,
    save yourself, if you are the Son of God,
    and come down from the cross!"

C. Likewise the chief priests with the scribes and elders
    mocked him and said,

SS. "He saved others; he cannot save himself.
So he is the king of Israel!
Let him come down from the cross now,
    and we will believe in him.

He trusted in God;
let him deliver him now if he wants him.
For he said, 'I am the Son of God.'"

C.  The revolutionaries who were crucified with him
also kept abusing him in the same way.

From noon onward, darkness came over the whole
land
until three in the afternoon.
And about three o'clock Jesus cried out in a loud voice,

✛      *"Eli, Eli, lema sabachthani?"*

C.  which means,

✛      "My God, my God, why have you forsaken me?"

C.  Some of the bystanders who heard it said,

SS. "This one is calling for Elijah."

C.  Immediately one of them ran to get a sponge;
he soaked it in wine, and putting it on a reed,
gave it to him to drink.
But the rest said,

SS. "Wait, let us see if Elijah comes to save him."

C.  But Jesus cried out again in a loud voice,
and gave up his spirit.

*Here all kneel and pause for a short time.*

And behold, the veil of the sanctuary
was torn in two from top to bottom.
The earth quaked, rocks were split, tombs were opened,
and the bodies of many saints who had fallen
asleep were raised.
And coming forth from their tombs after his
resurrection,
they entered the holy city and appeared to many.
The centurion and the men with him who were
keeping watch over Jesus
feared greatly when they saw the earthquake
and all that was happening, and they said,

SS. "Truly, this was the Son of God!"]

C.   There were many women there, looking on from a
          distance,
       who had followed Jesus from Galilee, ministering
          to him.
     Among them were Mary Magdalene and Mary the
          mother of James and Joseph,
       and the mother of the sons of Zebedee.

     When it was evening,
       there came a rich man from Arimathea named
          Joseph,
       who was himself a disciple of Jesus.
     He went to Pilate and asked for the body of Jesus;
       then Pilate ordered it to be handed over.
     Taking the body, Joseph wrapped it in clean linen
       and laid it in his new tomb that he had hewn in
          the rock.
     Then he rolled a huge stone across the entrance to
          the tomb and departed.
     But Mary Magdalene and the other Mary
       remained sitting there, facing the tomb.

     The next day, the one following the day of preparation,
       the chief priests and the Pharisees
       gathered before Pilate and said,

S.   "Sir, we remember that this impostor while still
          alive said,
       'After three days I will be raised up.'
     Give orders, then, that the grave be secured until the
          third day,
       lest his disciples come and steal him and say to
          the people,
       'He has been raised from the dead.'
     This last imposture would be worse than the first."

C.   Pilate said to them,

S.   "The guard is yours;
     go, secure it as best you can."

C.    **So they went and secured the tomb
by fixing a seal to the stone and setting the guard.**

**The Gospel of the Lord.** All: **Praise to you, Lord Jesus Christ.**

PRAYER OVER THE OFFERINGS

Through the Passion of your Only Begotten Son, O Lord,
may our reconciliation with you be near at hand,
so that, though we do not merit it by our own deeds,
yet by this sacrifice made once for all,
we may feel already the effects of your mercy.
Through Christ our Lord. All: **Amen.**

COMMUNION ANTIPHON (Matthew 26:42)

Father, if this chalice cannot pass without my drinking it,
your will be done.

PRAYER AFTER COMMUNION

Nourished with these sacred gifts,
we humbly beseech you, O Lord,
that, just as through the death of your Son
you have brought us to hope for what we believe,
so by his Resurrection
you may lead us to where you call.
Through Christ our Lord. All: **Amen.**

# THE SACRED PASCHAL TRIDUUM

*Reflection on the Gospel*

*The divine love we celebrate these days is so immeasurable that it reconciles all to itself in a supreme act of self-giving. It is so immense that the divine Son's arms open wide to embrace the world from the ignominy of a cross of human making. It is so impartial that sinners and outcasts, the poor and desperate, those alienated and forgotten all can receive without cost, without judgment, without losing dignity. Divine love is nothing less than the inner Life of the Trinity.*

- *The love of God knows no limit . . .*

—Living Liturgy™, *Easter Triduum 2017*

*Holy Thursday solemnly inaugurates "the triduum during which the Lord died, was buried and rose again" (St. Augustine). To these days Jesus referred when he prophesied: "Destroy this temple and in three days I will raise it up again" (John 2:14).*

# Thursday of the Lord's Supper (Holy Thursday)

## AT THE EVENING MASS

*April 13, 2017*

*Reflection on the Gospel*

*Jesus' human life is nearing the end, and he knows it—he knows he will be betrayed and handed over. But this does not deter Jesus from loving his disciples "to the end." He showed the immeasurable depth of his love by reversing roles: the master becomes the servant who washes feet, the teacher becomes the learner who accepts that the disciples still don't*

*understand. There is nothing Jesus would not do to show his love.*
*This we "should also do."*

- *"As I have done for you, you should also do."* . . .

—Living Liturgy™, *Holy Thursday 2017*

## ENTRANCE ANTIPHON (Cf. Galatians 6:14)

We should glory in the Cross of our Lord Jesus Christ,
in whom is our salvation, life and resurrection,
through whom we are saved and delivered.

## COLLECT

O God, who have called us to participate
in this most sacred Supper,
in which your Only Begotten Son,
when about to hand himself over to death,
entrusted to the Church a sacrifice new for all eternity,
the banquet of his love,
grant, we pray,
that we may draw from so great a mystery,
the fullness of charity and of life.
Through our Lord Jesus Christ, your Son,
who lives and reigns with you in the unity of the Holy Spirit,
one God, for ever and ever. All: **Amen.**

## READING I (L 39-ABC) (Exodus 12:1-8, 11-14)

### A reading from the Book of Exodus

*The law regarding the Passover meal.*

The LORD said to Moses and Aaron in the land of Egypt,
"This month shall stand at the head of your calendar;
you shall reckon it the first month of the year.
Tell the whole community of Israel:
On the tenth of this month every one of your families
must procure for itself a lamb, one apiece for each
household.
If a family is too small for a whole lamb,
it shall join the nearest household in procuring one
and shall share in the lamb
in proportion to the number of persons who partake
of it.
The lamb must be a year-old male and without blemish.

You may take it from either the sheep or the goats.
You shall keep it until the fourteenth day of this month,
    and then, with the whole assembly of Israel present,
    it shall be slaughtered during the evening twilight.
They shall take some of its blood
    and apply it to the two doorposts and the lintel
    of every house in which they partake of the lamb.
That same night they shall eat its roasted flesh
    with unleavened bread and bitter herbs.

"This is how you are to eat it:
    with your loins girt, sandals on your feet and your
        staff in hand,
    you shall eat like those who are in flight.
It is the Passover of the LORD.
For on this same night I will go through Egypt,
    striking down every firstborn of the land, both man
        and beast,
    and executing judgment on all the gods of Egypt—
        I, the LORD!
But the blood will mark the houses where you are.
Seeing the blood, I will pass over you;
    thus, when I strike the land of Egypt,
    no destructive blow will come upon you.

"This day shall be a memorial feast for you,
    which all your generations shall celebrate
    with pilgrimage to the LORD, as a perpetual institution."

The word of the Lord. All: Thanks be to God.

RESPONSORIAL PSALM 116

P-116

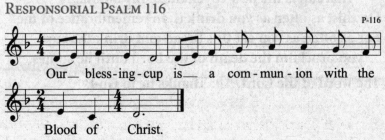

Our blessing-cup is a communion with the Blood of Christ.

Music: Jay F. Hunstiger, © 1990, administered by Liturgical Press. All rights reserved.

Psalm 116:12-13, 15-16bc, 17-18

R̷. (*See* 1 Corinthians 10:16) **Our blessing-cup is a communion with the Blood of Christ.**

How shall I make a return to the LORD
    for all the good he has done for me?
The cup of salvation I will take up,
    and I will call upon the name of the LORD. R̷.

Precious in the eyes of the LORD
    is the death of his faithful ones.
I am your servant, the son of your handmaid;
    you have loosed my bonds. R̷.

To you will I offer sacrifice of thanksgiving,
    and I will call upon the name of the LORD.
My vows to the LORD I will pay
    in the presence of all his people. R̷.

READING II (1 Corinthians 11:23-26)

**A reading from the first Letter of Saint Paul to the Corinthians**

*For as often as you eat this bread and drink the cup, you proclaim the death of the Lord.*

**Brothers and sisters:**
**I received from the Lord what I also handed on to you,**
    **that the Lord Jesus, on the night he was handed over,**
    **took bread, and, after he had given thanks,**
    **broke it and said, "This is my body that is for you.**
**Do this in remembrance of me."**
**In the same way also the cup, after supper, saying,**
    **"This cup is the new covenant in my blood.**
**Do this, as often as you drink it, in remembrance of me."**
**For as often as you eat this bread and drink the cup,**
    **you proclaim the death of the Lord until he comes.**

**The word of the Lord.** All: **Thanks be to God.**

GOSPEL (John 13:1-15)

℣. Praise to you, Lord Jesus Christ, King of endless glory!

℟. **Praise to you, Lord Jesus Christ, King of endless glory!**

℣. I give you a new commandment, says the Lord:
love one another as I have loved you. ℟.

✠ **A reading from the holy Gospel according to John**

All: **Glory to you, O Lord.**

*Jesus loved them to the end.*

**Before the feast of Passover, Jesus knew that his hour
had come
to pass from this world to the Father.
He loved his own in the world and he loved them to
the end.
The devil had already induced Judas, son of Simon the
Iscariot, to hand him over.
So, during supper,
fully aware that the Father had put everything into
his power
and that he had come from God and was returning
to God,
he rose from supper and took off his outer garments.
He took a towel and tied it around his waist.
Then he poured water into a basin
and began to wash the disciples' feet
and dry them with the towel around his waist.
He came to Simon Peter, who said to him,
"Master, are you going to wash my feet?"
Jesus answered and said to him,
"What I am doing, you do not understand now,
but you will understand later."
Peter said to him, "You will never wash my feet."
Jesus answered him,
"Unless I wash you, you will have no inheritance
with me."**

Simon Peter said to him,
"Master, then not only my feet, but my hands and
head as well."
Jesus said to him,
"Whoever has bathed has no need except to have his
feet washed,
for he is clean all over;
so you are clean, but not all."
For he knew who would betray him;
for this reason, he said, "Not all of you are clean."

So when he had washed their feet
and put his garments back on and reclined at table
again,
he said to them, "Do you realize what I have done
for you?
You call me 'teacher' and 'master,' and rightly so,
for indeed I am.
If I, therefore, the master and teacher, have washed
your feet,
you ought to wash one another's feet.
I have given you a model to follow,
so that as I have done for you, you should also do."

**The Gospel of the Lord.** All: **Praise to you, Lord Jesus Christ.**

WASHING OF FEET
Antiphons or other appropriate songs are sung.

PRAYER OVER THE OFFERINGS
Grant us, O Lord, we pray,
that we may participate worthily in these mysteries,
for whenever the memorial of this sacrifice is celebrated
the work of our redemption is accomplished.
Through Christ our Lord. All: **Amen.**

COMMUNION ANTIPHON (1 Corinthians 11:24-25)
This is the Body that will be given up for you;
this is the Chalice of the new covenant in my Blood,
says the Lord;
do this, whenever you receive it, in memory of me.

PRAYER AFTER COMMUNION
Grant, almighty God,
that, just as we are renewed
by the Supper of your Son in this present age,
so we may enjoy his banquet for all eternity.
Who lives and reigns for ever and ever. All: **Amen.**

TRANSFER OF THE MOST BLESSED SACRAMENT

# Friday of the Passion of the Lord (Good Friday)

*April 14, 2017*

*Reflection on the Gospel*

*The cross calls us to transforming self into impassioned love, obedience, and faithfulness. Jesus does not count human weakness as the last word; his last words, "It is finished," indicate that he had accomplished all that was necessary to overcome our human weakness and present us as his beloved brothers and sisters to his Father. He overcame death and turned weakness into a sweet wood that is the promise of Life. He shows us that we, too, can love passionately, courageously, and faithfully.*

• *I take up my cross and follow Jesus as I . . .*

—Living Liturgy™, *Good Friday 2017*

## THE CELEBRATION OF THE PASSION OF THE LORD

PRAYER (Let us pray is not said)
Remember your mercies, O Lord,
and with your eternal protection sanctify your servants,
for whom Christ your Son,
by the shedding of his Blood,
established the Paschal Mystery.
Who lives and reigns for ever and ever. All: **Amen.**

Or:

O God, who by the Passion of Christ your Son, our Lord,
abolished the death inherited from ancient sin
by every succeeding generation,
grant that just as, being conformed to him,
we have borne by the law of nature
the image of the man of earth,
so by the sanctification of grace
we may bear the image of the Man of heaven.
Through Christ our Lord. All: **Amen.**

## FIRST PART: LITURGY OF THE WORD

### READING I (L 40-ABC) (Isaiah 52:13—53:12)

**A reading from the Book of the Prophet Isaiah**

*He himself was wounded for our sins.*
(*Fourth oracle of the Servant of the Lord.*)

**See, my servant shall prosper,**
  **he shall be raised high and greatly exalted.**
**Even as many were amazed at him—**
  **so marred was his look beyond human semblance**
  **and his appearance beyond that of the sons of man—**
**so shall he startle many nations,**
  **because of him kings shall stand speechless;**
**for those who have not been told shall see,**
  **those who have not heard shall ponder it.**

**Who would believe what we have heard?**
  **To whom has the arm of the LORD been revealed?**
**He grew up like a sapling before him,**
  **like a shoot from the parched earth;**
**there was in him no stately bearing to make us look**
      **at him,**
  **nor appearance that would attract us to him.**
**He was spurned and avoided by people,**
  **a man of suffering, accustomed to infirmity,**
**one of those from whom people hide their faces,**
  **spurned, and we held him in no esteem.**

Yet it was our infirmities that he bore,
  our sufferings that he endured,
while we thought of him as stricken,
  as one smitten by God and afflicted.
But he was pierced for our offenses,
  crushed for our sins;
upon him was the chastisement that makes us whole,
  by his stripes we were healed.
We had all gone astray like sheep,
  each following his own way;
but the LORD laid upon him
  the guilt of us all.

Though he was harshly treated, he submitted
  and opened not his mouth;
like a lamb led to the slaughter
  or a sheep before the shearers,
  he was silent and opened not his mouth.
Oppressed and condemned, he was taken away,
  and who would have thought any more of his destiny?
When he was cut off from the land of the living,
  and smitten for the sin of his people,
a grave was assigned him among the wicked
  and a burial place with evildoers,
though he had done no wrong
  nor spoken any falsehood.
But the LORD was pleased
  to crush him in infirmity.

If he gives his life as an offering for sin,
  he shall see his descendants in a long life,
  and the will of the LORD shall be accomplished
    through him.

Because of his affliction
  he shall see the light in fullness of days;
through his suffering, my servant shall justify many,
  and their guilt he shall bear.

**Therefore I will give him his portion among the great,**
  **and he shall divide the spoils with the mighty,**
**because he surrendered himself to death**
  **and was counted among the wicked;**
**and he shall take away the sins of many,**
  **and win pardon for their offenses.**

**The word of the Lord.  All: Thanks be to God.**

## RESPONSORIAL PSALM 31

P-211

Fath-er,  into  your hands     I com-mend my spir-it.

Music: Bartholomew Sayles, O.S.B., and Cecile Gertken, O.S.B., adapt., © 1977, 1989, Order of Saint Benedict.

Psalm 31:2, 6, 12-13, 15-16, 17, 25

℟. (Luke 23:46) **Father, into your hands I commend my**
    **spirit.**

In you, O LORD, I take refuge;
  let me never be put to shame.
In your justice rescue me.
Into your hands I commend my spirit;
  you will redeem me, O LORD, O faithful God. ℟.

For all my foes I am an object of reproach,
  a laughingstock to my neighbors, and a dread to my
    friends;
  they who see me abroad flee from me.
I am forgotten like the unremembered dead;
  I am like a dish that is broken. ℟.

But my trust is in you, O LORD;
  I say, "You are my God.
In your hands is my destiny; rescue me
  from the clutches of my enemies and my persecutors." ℟.

Let your face shine upon your servant;
  save me in your kindness.
Take courage and be stouthearted,
  all you who hope in the LORD. ℟.

READING II (Hebrews 4:14-16; 5:7-9)

## A reading from the Letter to the Hebrews

*Jesus learned obedience and became the source of salvation for all who obey him.*

Brothers and sisters:

Since we have a great high priest who has passed through
    the heavens,
    Jesus, the Son of God,
    let us hold fast to our confession.

For we do not have a high priest
    who is unable to sympathize with our weaknesses,
    but one who has similarly been tested in every way,
    yet without sin.

So let us confidently approach the throne of grace
    to receive mercy and to find grace for timely help.

In the days when Christ was in the flesh,
    he offered prayers and supplications with loud cries
        and tears
    to the one who was able to save him from death,
    and he was heard because of his reverence.

Son though he was, he learned obedience from what he
    suffered;
    and when he was made perfect,
    he became the source of eternal salvation for all who
        obey him.

The word of the Lord. All: Thanks be to God.

\* *See* statement on page 170.

GOSPEL (John 18:1—19:42)

VERSE BEFORE THE GOSPEL (Philippians 2:8-9)

℣. Praise to you, Lord Jesus Christ, King of endless glory!

℟. **Praise to you, Lord Jesus Christ, King of endless glory!**

℣. Christ became obedient to the point of death,
    even death on a cross.
    Because of this, God greatly exalted him
    and bestowed on him the name which is above every
        other name. ℟.

The symbols in the following passion narrative represent:

C. Narrator;
✝ Christ;
S. speakers other than Christ;
SS. groups of speakers.

## The Passion of our Lord Jesus Christ according to John

*The Passion of our Lord Jesus Christ.*

C. **Jesus went out with his disciples across the Kidron valley**
  **to where there was a garden,**
  **into which he and his disciples entered.**
**Judas his betrayer also knew the place,**
  **because Jesus had often met there with his disciples.**
**So Judas got a band of soldiers and guards**
  **from the chief priests and the Pharisees**
  **and went there with lanterns, torches, and weapons.**
**Jesus, knowing everything that was going to happen to him,**
  **went out and said to them,**
✝ **"Whom are you looking for?"**
C. **They answered him,**
SS. **"Jesus the Nazorean."**
C. **He said to them,**
✝ **"I AM."**
C. **Judas his betrayer was also with them.**
**When he said to them, "I AM,"**
  **they turned away and fell to the ground.**
**So he again asked them,**
✝ **"Whom are you looking for?"**
C. **They said,**
SS. **"Jesus the Nazorean."**
C. **Jesus answered,**
✝ **"I told you that I AM.**
**So if you are looking for me, let these men go."**
C. **This was to fulfill what he had said,**
  **"I have not lost any of those you gave me."**

Then Simon Peter, who had a sword, drew it,
    struck the high priest's slave, and cut off his right ear.
The slave's name was Malchus.
Jesus said to Peter,

☨     "Put your sword into its scabbard.
Shall I not drink the cup that the Father gave me?"

C.   So the band of soldiers, the tribune, and the Jewish
           guards seized Jesus,
    bound him, and brought him to Annas first.
He was the father-in-law of Caiaphas,
    who was high priest that year.
It was Caiaphas who had counseled the Jews
    that it was better that one man should die rather
           than the people.

Simon Peter and another disciple followed Jesus.
Now the other disciple was known to the high priest,
    and he entered the courtyard of the high priest
           with Jesus.
But Peter stood at the gate outside.
So the other disciple, the acquaintance of the high
           priest,
    went out and spoke to the gatekeeper and brought
           Peter in.
Then the maid who was the gatekeeper said to Peter,

S.     "You are not one of this man's disciples, are you?"
C.   He said,
S.     "I am not."
C.   Now the slaves and the guards were standing around
           a charcoal fire
    that they had made, because it was cold,
    and were warming themselves.
Peter was also standing there keeping warm.

The high priest questioned Jesus
    about his disciples and about his doctrine.
Jesus answered him,

✠      "I have spoken publicly to the world.
I have always taught in a synagogue
    or in the temple area where all the Jews gather,
    and in secret I have said nothing. Why ask me?
Ask those who heard me what I said to them.
They know what I said."

C.  When he had said this,
    one of the temple guards standing there struck
       Jesus and said,

S.    "Is this the way you answer the high priest?"

C.  Jesus answered him,

✠      "If I have spoken wrongly, testify to the wrong;
but if I have spoken rightly, why do you strike me?"

C.  Then Annas sent him bound to Caiaphas the high
    priest.

Now Simon Peter was standing there keeping warm.
And they said to him,

S.    "You are not one of his disciples, are you?"

C.  He denied it and said,

S.    "I am not."

C.  One of the slaves of the high priest,
    a relative of the one whose ear Peter had cut off,
      said,

S.    "Didn't I see you in the garden with him?"

C.  Again Peter denied it.
And immediately the cock crowed.

Then they brought Jesus from Caiaphas to the
    praetorium.
It was morning.
And they themselves did not enter the praetorium,
    in order not to be defiled so that they could eat
      the Passover.
So Pilate came out to them and said,

S.    "What charge do you bring against this man?"

C.  They answered and said to him,

SS.   "If he were not a criminal,
       we would not have handed him over to you."

C.    At this, Pilate said to them,

S.    "Take him yourselves, and judge him according
             to your law."

C.    The Jews answered him,

SS.   "We do not have the right to execute anyone,"

C.    in order that the word of Jesus might be fulfilled
       that he said indicating the kind of death he would
             die.
       So Pilate went back into the praetorium
       and summoned Jesus and said to him,

S.    "Are you the King of the Jews?"

C.    Jesus answered,

✝     "Do you say this on your own
       or have others told you about me?"

C.    Pilate answered,

S.    "I am not a Jew, am I?
       Your own nation and the chief priests handed you
             over to me.
       What have you done?"

C.    Jesus answered,

✝     "My kingdom does not belong to this world.
       If my kingdom did belong to this world,
             my attendants would be fighting
             to keep me from being handed over to the Jews.
       But as it is, my kingdom is not here."

C.    So Pilate said to him,

S.    "Then you are a king?"

C.    Jesus answered,

✝     "You say I am a king.
       For this I was born and for this I came into the world,
             to testify to the truth.
       Everyone who belongs to the truth listens to my voice."

C.    Pilate said to him,

S.    "What is truth?"

C.   **When he had said this,**
     **he again went out to the Jews and said to them,**

S.      **"I find no guilt in him.**
     **But you have a custom that I release one prisoner to**
     **you at Passover.**
     **Do you want me to release to you the King of the Jews?"**

C.   **They cried out again,**

SS.     **"Not this one but Barabbas!"**

C.   **Now Barabbas was a revolutionary.**

     **Then Pilate took Jesus and had him scourged.**
     **And the soldiers wove a crown out of thorns and**
     **placed it on his head,**
     **and clothed him in a purple cloak,**
     **and they came to him and said,**

SS.     **"Hail, King of the Jews!"**

C.   **And they struck him repeatedly.**
     **Once more Pilate went out and said to them,**

S.      **"Look, I am bringing him out to you,**
     **so that you may know that I find no guilt in him."**

C.   **So Jesus came out,**
     **wearing the crown of thorns and the purple cloak.**
     **And Pilate said to them,**

S.      **"Behold, the man!"**

C.   **When the chief priests and the guards saw him they**
     **cried out,**

SS.     **"Crucify him, crucify him!"**

C.   **Pilate said to them,**

S.      **"Take him yourselves and crucify him.**
     **I find no guilt in him."**

C.   **The Jews answered,**

SS.     **"We have a law, and according to that law he ought**
     **to die,**
     **because he made himself the Son of God."**

C.   **Now when Pilate heard this statement,**
     **he became even more afraid,**
     **and went back into the praetorium and said to Jesus,**

S.　　"Where are you from?"

C.　Jesus did not answer him.
　　So Pilate said to him,

S.　　"Do you not speak to me?
　　Do you not know that I have power to release you
　　　and I have power to crucify you?"

C.　Jesus answered him,

✝　　"You would have no power over me
　　　if it had not been given to you from above.
　　For this reason the one who handed me over to you
　　　has the greater sin."

C.　Consequently, Pilate tried to release him; but the
　　　Jews cried out,

SS.　　"If you release him, you are not a Friend of Caesar.
　　Everyone who makes himself a king opposes Caesar."

C.　When Pilate heard these words he brought Jesus out
　　　and seated him on the judge's bench
　　　in the place called Stone Pavement, in Hebrew,
　　　　Gabbatha.
　　It was preparation day for Passover, and it was
　　　about noon.
　　And he said to the Jews,

S.　　"Behold, your king!"

C.　They cried out,

SS.　　"Take him away, take him away! Crucify him!"

C.　Pilate said to them,

S.　　"Shall I crucify your king?"

C.　The chief priests answered,

SS.　　"We have no king but Caesar."

C.　Then he handed him over to them to be crucified.

　　So they took Jesus, and, carrying the cross himself,
　　　he went out to what is called the Place of the Skull,
　　　in Hebrew, Golgotha.
　　There they crucified him, and with him two others,
　　　one on either side, with Jesus in the middle.

Pilate also had an inscription written and put on the
    cross.
It read,
    "Jesus the Nazorean, the King of the Jews."
Now many of the Jews read this inscription,
    because the place where Jesus was crucified was
        near the city;
    and it was written in Hebrew, Latin, and Greek.
So the chief priests of the Jews said to Pilate,

SS.    "Do not write 'The King of the Jews,'
    but that he said, 'I am the King of the Jews.'"

C.    Pilate answered,

S.    "What I have written, I have written."

C.    When the soldiers had crucified Jesus,
    they took his clothes and divided them into four
        shares,
    a share for each soldier.
They also took his tunic, but the tunic was seamless,
    woven in one piece from the top down.
So they said to one another,

SS.    "Let's not tear it, but cast lots for it to see whose it
    will be,"

C.    in order that the passage of Scripture might be
        fulfilled that says:
    *They divided my garments among them,*
       *and for my vesture they cast lots.*
This is what the soldiers did.
Standing by the cross of Jesus were his mother
    and his mother's sister, Mary the wife of Clopas,
    and Mary of Magdala.
When Jesus saw his mother and the disciple there
    whom he loved he said to his mother,

✠    "Woman, behold, your son."

C.    Then he said to the disciple,

✠    "Behold, your mother."

C. And from that hour the disciple took her into his home.

After this, aware that everything was now finished,
in order that the Scripture might be fulfilled,
Jesus said,

✝ "I thirst."

C. There was a vessel filled with common wine.
So they put a sponge soaked in wine on a sprig of hyssop
and put it up to his mouth.
When Jesus had taken the wine, he said,

✝ "It is finished."

C. And bowing his head, he handed over the spirit.

*Here all kneel and pause for a short time.*

Now since it was preparation day,
in order that the bodies might not remain
on the cross on the sabbath,
for the sabbath day of that week was a solemn one,
the Jews asked Pilate that their legs be broken
and that they be taken down.
So the soldiers came and broke the legs of the first
and then of the other one who was crucified with Jesus.
But when they came to Jesus and saw that he was already dead,
they did not break his legs,
but one soldier thrust his lance into his side,
and immediately blood and water flowed out.
An eyewitness has testified, and his testimony is true;
he knows that he is speaking the truth,
so that you also may come to believe.
For this happened so that the Scripture passage might be fulfilled:
*Not a bone of it will be broken.*
And again another passage says:
*They will look upon him whom they have pierced.*

After this, Joseph of Arimathea,
  secretly a disciple of Jesus for fear of the Jews,
  asked Pilate if he could remove the body of Jesus.
And Pilate permitted it.
So he came and took his body.
Nicodemus, the one who had first come to him at
    night,
  also came bringing a mixture of myrrh and aloes
  weighing about one hundred pounds.
They took the body of Jesus
  and bound it with burial cloths along with the
      spices,
  according to the Jewish burial custom.
Now in the place where he had been crucified there
    was a garden,
  and in the garden a new tomb, in which no one
      had yet been buried.
So they laid Jesus there because of the Jewish
    preparation day;
  for the tomb was close by.

**The Gospel of the Lord.** All: **Praise to you, Lord Jesus Christ.**

## The Solemn Intercessions

### I. For Holy Church

Let us pray, dearly beloved, for the holy Church of God,
that our God and Lord be pleased to give her peace,
to guard her and to unite her throughout the whole world
and grant that, leading our life in tranquility and quiet,
we may glorify God the Father almighty.

Prayer in silence. Then the Priest sings or says:

Almighty ever-living God,
who in Christ revealed your glory to all the nations,
watch over the works of your mercy,
that your Church, spread throughout all the world,
may persevere with steadfast faith in confessing your name.
Through Christ our Lord. All: **Amen.**

## II. For the Pope

Let us pray also for our most Holy Father Pope N.,
that our God and Lord,
who chose him for the Order of Bishops,
may keep him safe and unharmed for the Lord's holy Church,
to govern the holy People of God.

*Prayer in silence. Then the Priest sings or says:*

Almighty ever-living God,
by whose decree all things are founded,
look with favor on our prayers
and in your kindness protect the Pope chosen for us,
that, under him, the Christian people,
governed by you their maker,
may grow in merit by reason of their faith.
Through Christ our Lord. All: **Amen.**

## III. For All Orders and Degrees of the Faithful

Let us pray also for our Bishop N.,*
for all Bishops, Priests, and Deacons of the Church
and for the whole of the faithful people.

*Prayer in silence. Then the Priest sings or says:*

Almighty ever-living God,
by whose Spirit the whole body of the Church
is sanctified and governed,
hear our humble prayer for your ministers,
that, by the gift of your grace,
all may serve you faithfully.
Through Christ our Lord. All: **Amen.**

## IV. For Catechumens

Let us pray also for (our) catechumens,
that our God and Lord
may open wide the ears of their inmost hearts
and unlock the gates of his mercy,
that, having received forgiveness of all their sins
through the waters of rebirth,
they, too, may be one with Christ Jesus our Lord.

*Prayer in silence. Then the Priest sings or says:*

Almighty ever-living God,
who make your Church ever fruitful with new offspring,

* Mention may be made here of the Coadjutor Bishop, or Auxiliary Bishops,
as noted in the *General Instruction of the Roman Missal*, no. 149.

increase the faith and understanding of (our) catechumens,
that, reborn in the font of Baptism,
they may be added to the number of your adopted children.
Through Christ our Lord. **All**: **Amen.**

## V. FOR THE UNITY OF CHRISTIANS

Let us pray also for all our brothers and sisters who believe in Christ,
that our God and Lord may be pleased,
as they live the truth,
to gather them together and keep them in his one Church.

Prayer in silence. Then the Priest sings or says:

Almighty ever-living God,
who gather what is scattered
and keep together what you have gathered,
look kindly on the flock of your Son,
that those whom one Baptism has consecrated
may be joined together by integrity of faith
and united in the bond of charity.
Through Christ our Lord. **All**: **Amen.**

## VI. FOR THE JEWISH PEOPLE

Let us pray also for the Jewish people,
to whom the Lord our God spoke first,
that he may grant them to advance in love of his name
and in faithfulness to his covenant.

Prayer in silence. Then the Priest sings or says:

Almighty ever-living God,
who bestowed your promises on Abraham and his descendants,
graciously hear the prayers of your Church,
that the people you first made your own
may attain the fullness of redemption.
Through Christ our Lord. **All**: **Amen.**

## VII. FOR THOSE WHO DO NOT BELIEVE IN CHRIST

Let us pray also for those who do not believe in Christ,
that, enlightened by the Holy Spirit,
they, too, may enter on the way of salvation.

Prayer in silence. Then the Priest sings or says:

Almighty ever-living God,
grant to those who do not confess Christ
that, by walking before you with a sincere heart,
they may find the truth
and that we ourselves, being constant in mutual love
and striving to understand more fully the mystery of your life,

may be made more perfect witnesses to your love in the world.
Through Christ our Lord. All: **Amen.**

## VIII. For Those Who Do Not Believe in God

Let us pray also for those who do not acknowledge God,
that, following what is right in sincerity of heart,
they may find the way to God himself.

Prayer in silence. Then the Priest sings or says:

Almighty ever-living God,
who created all people
to seek you always by desiring you
and, by finding you, come to rest,
grant, we pray,
that, despite every harmful obstacle,
all may recognize the signs of your fatherly love
and the witness of the good works
done by those who believe in you,
and so in gladness confess you,
the one true God and Father of our human race.
Through Christ our Lord. All: **Amen.**

## IX. For Those in Public Office

Let us pray also for those in public office,
that our God and Lord
may direct their minds and hearts according to his will
for the true peace and freedom of all.

Prayer in silence. Then the Priest sings or says:

Almighty ever-living God,
in whose hand lies every human heart
and the rights of peoples,
look with favor, we pray,
on those who govern with authority over us,
that throughout the whole world,
the prosperity of peoples,
the assurance of peace,
and freedom of religion
may through your gift be made secure.
Through Christ our Lord. All: **Amen.**

## X. For Those in Tribulation

Let us pray, dearly beloved,
to God the Father almighty,
that he may cleanse the world of all errors,
banish disease, drive out hunger,

unlock prisons, loosen fetters,
granting to travelers safety, to pilgrims return,
health to the sick, and salvation to the dying.

Prayer in silence. Then the Priest sings or says:

Almighty ever-living God,
comfort of mourners, strength of all who toil,
may the prayers of those who cry out in any tribulation
come before you,
that all may rejoice,
because in their hour of need
your mercy was at hand.
Through Christ our Lord. All: **Amen.**

## SECOND PART: THE ADORATION OF THE HOLY CROSS

### THE SHOWING OF THE HOLY CROSS

The Cross is shown to the congregation in one of two ways:

**First Form:** through the gradual uncovering with a veil in the sanctuary
**Second Form:** by means of a procession through the church

In either form, either of the following is chanted three times:

**A**    ℣. Ecce lignum Crucis.
      in quo salus mundi pependit.
    All respond: **Venite adoremus.**

**B**    ℣. Behold the wood of the Cross.
      on which hung the salvation of the world.
    All respond: **Come, let us adore.**

### THE ADORATION OF THE HOLY CROSS

The Priest, clergy, and faithful approach to venerate the cross in a kind of
procession.

## THIRD PART: HOLY COMMUNION

At the Savior's command
and formed by divine teaching,
we dare to say:

The Priest, with hands extended says, and all present continue:
**Our Father, who art in heaven,**
**hallowed be thy name;**
**thy kingdom come,**
**thy will be done**
**on earth as it is in heaven.**

**Give us this day our daily bread,
and forgive us our trespasses,
as we forgive those who trespass against us;
and lead us not into temptation,
but deliver us from evil.**

With hands extended, the Priest continues alone:
Deliver us, Lord, we pray, from every evil,
graciously grant peace in our days,
that, by the help of your mercy,
we may be always free from sin
and safe from all distress,
as we await the blessed hope
and the coming of our Savior, Jesus Christ.

He joins his hands. The people conclude the prayer, acclaiming:
**For the kingdom, the power and the glory are yours
   now and for ever.**

Then the Priest, with hands joined, says quietly:
May the receiving of your Body and Blood,
Lord Jesus Christ,
not bring me to judgment and condemnation,
but through your loving mercy
be for me protection in mind and body
and a healing remedy.

The Priest then genuflects, takes a particle, and, holding it slightly raised over
the ciborium, while facing the people, says aloud:
Behold the Lamb of God,
behold him who takes away the sins of the world.
Blessed are those called to the supper of the Lamb.

And together with the people he adds once:
**Lord, I am not worthy
that you should enter under my roof,
but only say the word
and my soul shall be healed.**

PRAYER AFTER COMMUNION
Almighty ever-living God,
who have restored us to life
by the blessed Death and Resurrection of your Christ,
preserve in us the work of your mercy,
that, by partaking of this mystery,
we may have a life unceasingly devoted to you.
Through Christ our Lord. All: **Amen.**

PRAYER OVER THE PEOPLE

May abundant blessing, O Lord, we pray,
descend upon your people,
who have honored the Death of your Son
in the hope of their resurrection:
may pardon come,
comfort be given,
holy faith increase,
and everlasting redemption be made secure.
Through Christ our Lord. All: **Amen.**

After genuflecting to the Cross, all depart in silence. The altar is stripped;
the cross remains, however, with four candles.

# HOLY SATURDAY

# The Easter Vigil in the Holy Night

*April 15, 2017*

*Reflection on the Gospel*

*Oh, how playful an image: "an angel of the Lord descended from heaven, / approached, rolled back the stone, and sat upon it." Ha! Sitting triumphantly on the stone that had closed the tomb, like the angel owned the place. Gotcha, you guards: "He is not here." The guards "were shaken with fear of him." Of course they were! They were supposed to keep that tomb sealed. And now it's open. He is risen! This night we celebrate God's immeasurable, immense, impartial, impelling, impassioned love. Alleluia!*

   • *Christ has died, Christ is risen, Christ . . .*

—Living Liturgy™, *Easter Vigil 2017*

# FIRST PART: THE SOLEMN BEGINNING OF THE VIGIL OR LUCERNARIUM

## THE BLESSING OF THE FIRE AND PREPARATION OF THE CANDLE

Priest: In the name of the Father, and of the Son, and of the Holy Spirit.
   All: **Amen.**

Then he greets the assembled people in the usual way and briefly instructs them about the night vigil in these or similar words:

Dear brethren (brothers and sisters),
on this most sacred night,
in which our Lord Jesus Christ
passed over from death to life,
the Church calls upon her sons and daughters,
scattered throughout the world,
to come together to watch and pray.
If we keep the memorial
of the Lord's paschal solemnity in this way,
listening to his word and celebrating his mysteries,
then we shall have the sure hope
of sharing his triumph over death
and living with him in God.

Let us pray.
O God, who through your Son
bestowed upon the faithful the fire of your glory,
sanctify ✠ this new fire, we pray,
and grant that,
by these paschal celebrations,
we may be so inflamed with heavenly desires,
that with minds made pure
we may attain festivities of unending splendor.
Through Christ our Lord. All: **Amen.**

## PREPARATION OF THE CANDLE

(1) CHRIST YESTERDAY AND TODAY (he cuts a vertical line);
(2) THE BEGINNING AND THE END (he cuts a horizontal line);
(3) THE ALPHA (he cuts the letter Alpha above the vertical line);
(4) AND THE OMEGA (he cuts the letter Omega below the vertical line).
(5) ALL TIME BELONGS TO HIM (he cuts the first numeral of the current year in the upper left corner of the cross);
(6) AND ALL THE AGES (he cuts the second numeral of the current year in the upper right corner of the cross).
(7) TO HIM BE GLORY AND POWER (he cuts the third numeral of the current year in the lower left corner of the cross);

(8) **THROUGH EVERY AGE AND FOR EVER. AMEN.** (he cuts the fourth numeral of the current year in the lower right corner of the cross).

A

2 | 0

1 | N

Ω

(1) **BY HIS HOLY**                                                    1
(2) **AND GLORIOUS WOUNDS,**
(3) **MAY CHRIST THE LORD**                                    4 2 5
(4) **GUARD US**
(5) **AND PROTECT US. AMEN.**                                   3

May the light of Christ rising in glory
dispel the darkness of our hearts and minds.

**PROCESSION**

℣. The Light of Christ.     *or*     ℣. Lumen Christi.
℟. **Thanks be to God.**              ℟. **Deo Gratias.**

℣. The Light of Christ.     *or*     ℣. Lumen Christi.
℟. **Thanks be to God.**              ℟. **Deo Gratias.**

℣. The Light of Christ.     *or*     ℣. Lumen Christi.
℟. **Thanks be to God.**              ℟. **Deo Gratias.**

**THE EASTER PROCLAMATION (EXSULTET)**
Longer Form of the Easter Proclamation
[Shorter Form]

[Exult, let them exult, the hosts of heaven,
exult, let Angel ministers of God exult,
let the trumpet of salvation
sound aloud our mighty King's triumph!
Be glad, let earth be glad, as glory floods her,
ablaze with light from her eternal King,
let all corners of the earth be glad,
knowing an end to gloom and darkness.
Rejoice, let Mother Church also rejoice,
arrayed with the lightning of his glory,
let this holy building shake with joy,
filled with the mighty voices of the peoples.]

(Therefore, dearest friends,
standing in the awesome glory of this holy light,
invoke with me, I ask you,

the mercy of God almighty,
that he, who has been pleased to number me,
though unworthy, among the Levites,
may pour into me his light unshadowed,
that I may sing this candle's perfect praises).

[(℣. The Lord be with you.          *Sung only by an ordained minister.
℟. **And with your spirit.**)

℣. Lift up your hearts.          *Sung only by an ordained minister.
℟. **We lift them up to the Lord.**

℣. Let us give thanks to the Lord our God.
℟. **It is right and just.**          *Sung only by an ordained minister.

It is truly right and just,
with ardent love of mind and heart
and with devoted service of our voice,
to acclaim our God invisible, the almighty Father,
and Jesus Christ, our Lord, his Son, his Only Begotten.

Who for our sake paid Adam's debt to the eternal Father,
and, pouring out his own dear Blood,
wiped clean the record of our ancient sinfulness.

These then are the feasts of Passover,
in which is slain the Lamb, the one true Lamb,
whose Blood anoints the doorposts of believers.

This is the night,
when once you led our forebears, Israel's children,
from slavery in Egypt
and made them pass dry-shod through the Red Sea.

This is the night
that with a pillar of fire
banished the darkness of sin.

This is the night
that even now, throughout the world,
sets Christian believers apart from worldly vices
and from the gloom of sin,
leading them to grace
and joining them to his holy ones.

This is the night,
when Christ broke the prison-bars of death
and rose victorious from the underworld.]

Our birth would have been no gain,
had we not been redeemed.
[O wonder of your humble care for us!
O love, O charity beyond all telling,
to ransom a slave you gave away your Son!

O truly necessary sin of Adam,
destroyed completely by the Death of Christ!

O happy fault
that earned so great, so glorious a Redeemer!]

O truly blessed night,
worthy alone to know the time and hour
when Christ rose from the underworld!

This is the night
of which it is written:
The night shall be as bright as day,
dazzling is the night for me,
and full of gladness.

[The sanctifying power of this night
dispels wickedness, washes faults away,
restores innocence to the fallen, and joy to mourners,]
drives out hatred, fosters concord, and brings down the
    mighty.

[**On this, your night of grace, O holy Father,
accept this candle, a solemn offering,
the work of bees and of your servants' hands,
an evening sacrifice of praise,
this gift from your most holy Church.]

But now we know the praises of this pillar,
which glowing fire ignites for God's honor,
a fire into many flames divided,
yet never dimmed by sharing of its light,
for it is fed by melting wax,

drawn out by mother bees
to build a torch so precious.

[O truly blessed night,
when things of heaven are wed to those of earth,
and divine to the human.] [\*\*]

[Therefore, O Lord,
we pray you that this candle,
hallowed to the honor of your name,
may persevere undimmed,
to overcome the darkness of this night.
Receive it as a pleasing fragrance,
and let it mingle with the lights of heaven.
May this flame be found still burning
by the Morning Star:
the one Morning Star who never sets,
Christ your Son,
who, coming back from death's domain,
has shed his peaceful light on humanity,
and lives and reigns for ever and ever. All: **Amen.**]

SECOND PART: **THE LITURGY OF THE WORD**

Dear brethren (brothers and sisters),
now that we have begun our solemn Vigil,
let us listen with quiet hearts to the Word of God.
Let us meditate on how God in times past saved his people
and in these, the last days, has sent us his Son as our Redeemer.
Let us pray that our God may complete this paschal work of salvation
by the fullness of redemption.

READING I (L 41-ABC) (Genesis 1:1—2:2) *or* Shorter Form [ ]
(Genesis 1:1, 26-31a)

**A reading from the Book of Genesis**

*God looked at everything he had made, and he found it very good.*

[**In the beginning, when God created the heavens and
the earth,**]
   the earth was a formless wasteland, and darkness
      covered the abyss,
   **while a mighty wind swept over the waters.**

Then God said,
  "Let there be light," and there was light.
God saw how good the light was.
God then separated the light from the darkness.
God called the light "day," and the darkness he called
    "night."
Thus evening came, and morning followed—the first day.

Then God said,
  "Let there be a dome in the middle of the waters,
  to separate one body of water from the other."
And so it happened:
  God made the dome,
  and it separated the water above the dome from the
      water below it.
God called the dome "the sky."
Evening came, and morning followed—the second day.

Then God said,
  "Let the water under the sky be gathered into a single
      basin,
  so that the dry land may appear."
And so it happened:
  the water under the sky was gathered into its basin,
  and the dry land appeared.
God called the dry land "the earth,"
  and the basin of the water he called "the sea."
God saw how good it was.
Then God said,
  "Let the earth bring forth vegetation:
  every kind of plant that bears seed
  and every kind of fruit tree on earth
  that bears fruit with its seed in it."
And so it happened:
  the earth brought forth every kind of plant that
      bears seed

and every kind of fruit tree on earth
    that bears fruit with its seed in it.
God saw how good it was.
Evening came, and morning followed—the third day.

Then God said:
    "Let there be lights in the dome of the sky,
    to separate day from night.
Let them mark the fixed times, the days and the years,
    and serve as luminaries in the dome of the sky,
    to shed light upon the earth."
And so it happened:
    God made the two great lights,
    the greater one to govern the day,
    and the lesser one to govern the night;
    and he made the stars.
God set them in the dome of the sky,
    to shed light upon the earth,
    to govern the day and the night,
    and to separate the light from the darkness.
God saw how good it was.
Evening came, and morning followed—the fourth day.

Then God said,
    "Let the water teem with an abundance of living
        creatures,
    and on the earth let birds fly beneath the dome of
        the sky."
And so it happened:
    God created the great sea monsters
    and all kinds of swimming creatures with which the
        water teems,
    and all kinds of winged birds.
God saw how good it was, and God blessed them, saying,
    "Be fertile, multiply, and fill the water of the seas;
    and let the birds multiply on the earth."
Evening came, and morning followed—the fifth day.

Then God said,

"Let the earth bring forth all kinds of living creatures:
cattle, creeping things, and wild animals of all kinds."

And so it happened:

God made all kinds of wild animals, all kinds of cattle,
and all kinds of creeping things of the earth.

God saw how good it was.

Then [God said:

"Let us make man in our image, after our likeness.

Let them have dominion over the fish of the sea,

the birds of the air, and the cattle,

and over all the wild animals

and all the creatures that crawl on the ground."

God created man in his image;

in the image of God he created him;

male and female he created them.

God blessed them, saying:

"Be fertile and multiply;

fill the earth and subdue it.

Have dominion over the fish of the sea, the birds of the air,
and all the living things that move on the earth."

God also said:

"See, I give you every seed-bearing plant all over the
earth

and every tree that has seed-bearing fruit on it to be
your food;

and to all the animals of the land, all the birds of the air,

and all the living creatures that crawl on the ground,

I give all the green plants for food."

And so it happened.

God looked at everything he had made, and he found it
very good.]

Evening came, and morning followed—the sixth day.

Thus the heavens and the earth and all their array were
completed.

Since on the seventh day God was finished
  with the work he had been doing,
    he rested on the seventh day from all the work he had
      undertaken.

**The word of the Lord.**

RESPONSORIAL PSALM 104 or 33

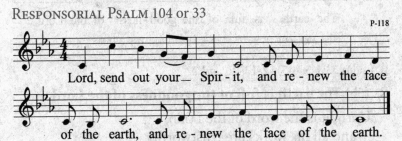

Music: Jay F. Hunstiger, © 1990, administered by Liturgical Press. All rights reserved.

A  Psalm 104:1-2, 5-6, 10, 12, 13-14, 24, 35

R̸. (30) **Lord, send out your Spirit, and renew the face of
  the earth.**

Bless the LORD, O my soul!
  O LORD, my God, you are great indeed!
You are clothed with majesty and glory,
  robed in light as with a cloak. R̸.

You fixed the earth upon its foundation,
  not to be moved forever;
with the ocean, as with a garment, you covered it;
  above the mountains the waters stood. R̸.

You send forth springs into the watercourses
  that wind among the mountains.
Beside them the birds of heaven dwell;
  from among the branches they send forth their song. R̸.

You water the mountains from your palace;
  the earth is replete with the fruit of your works.
You raise grass for the cattle,
  and vegetation for man's use,
producing bread from the earth. R̸.

How manifold are your works, O LORD!
  In wisdom you have wrought them all—  *(continued)*

the earth is full of your creatures.
Bless the LORD, O my soul! R⃰.

Or:

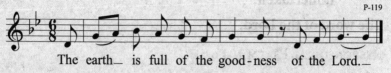

The earth_ is full of the good-ness   of the Lord._

B   Psalm 33:4-5, 6-7, 12-13, 20 and 22

R⃰. (5b) **The earth is full of the goodness of the Lord.**

Upright is the word of the LORD,
and all his works are trustworthy.
He loves justice and right;
of the kindness of the LORD the earth is full. R⃰.

By the word of the LORD the heavens were made;
by the breath of his mouth all their host.
He gathers the waters of the sea as in a flask;
in cellars he confines the deep. R⃰.

Blessed the nation whose God is the LORD,
the people he has chosen for his own inheritance.
From heaven the LORD looks down;
he sees all mankind. R⃰.

Our soul waits for the LORD,
who is our help and our shield.
May your kindness, O LORD, be upon us
who have put our hope in you. R⃰.

PRAYER
Let us pray.

Almighty ever-living God,
who are wonderful in the ordering of all your works,
may those you have redeemed understand
that there exists nothing more marvelous
than the world's creation in the beginning
except that, at the end of the ages,
Christ our Passover has been sacrificed.
Who lives and reigns for ever and ever. All: **Amen.**

Or:

On the creation of man:
O God, who wonderfully created human nature
and still more wonderfully redeemed it,
grant us, we pray,
to set our minds against the enticements of sin,
that we may merit to attain eternal joys.
Through Christ our Lord. All: **Amen.**

READING II (Genesis 22:1-18) *or* Shorter Form [ ]
(Genesis 22:1-2, 9a, 10-13, 15-18)

## A reading from the Book of Genesis

*The sacrifice of Abraham, our father in faith.*

**[God put Abraham to the test.
He called to him, "Abraham!"
"Here I am," he replied.
Then God said:**
   **"Take your son Isaac, your only one, whom you love,
      and go to the land of Moriah.
There you shall offer him up as a holocaust
      on a height that I will point out to you."]**
**Early the next morning Abraham saddled his donkey,
      took with him his son Isaac and two of his servants
            as well,
      and with the wood that he had cut for the holocaust,
      set out for the place of which God had told him.**

**On the third day Abraham got sight of the place from afar.
Then he said to his servants:**
   **"Both of you stay here with the donkey,
      while the boy and I go on over yonder.
We will worship and then come back to you."
Thereupon Abraham took the wood for the holocaust
      and laid it on his son Isaac's shoulders,
      while he himself carried the fire and the knife.
As the two walked on together, Isaac spoke to his father
            Abraham:**
   **"Father!" Isaac said.**

"Yes, son," he replied.

Isaac continued, "Here are the fire and the wood,
    but where is the sheep for the holocaust?"

"Son," Abraham answered,
    "God himself will provide the sheep for the holocaust."

Then the two continued going forward.

[When they came to the place of which God had told him,
    Abraham built an altar there and arranged the wood
        on it.]

Next he tied up his son Isaac,
    and put him on top of the wood on the altar.

[Then he reached out and took the knife to slaughter
        his son.

But the LORD's messenger called to him from heaven,
    "Abraham, Abraham!"

"Here I am!" he answered.

"Do not lay your hand on the boy," said the messenger.

"Do not do the least thing to him.

I know now how devoted you are to God,
    since you did not withhold from me your own
        beloved son."

As Abraham looked about,
    he spied a ram caught by its horns in the thicket.

So he went and took the ram
    and offered it up as a holocaust in place of his son.]

Abraham named the site Yahweh-yireh;
    hence people now say, "On the mountain the LORD
        will see."

[Again the LORD's messenger called to Abraham from
        heaven and said:

"I swear by myself, declares the LORD,
    that because you acted as you did
    in not withholding from me your beloved son,
    I will bless you abundantly
    and make your descendants as countless
    as the stars of the sky and the sands of the seashore;

your descendants shall take possession
of the gates of their enemies,
and in your descendants all the nations of the earth
    shall find blessing—
all this because you obeyed my command."]

**The word of the Lord.**

RESPONSORIAL PSALM 16

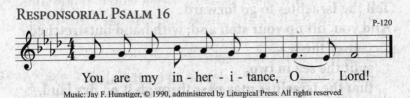

You are my in-her-i-tance, O—— Lord!

Psalm 16:5, 8, 9-10, 11

R̸. (1) **You are my inheritance, O Lord.**

O LORD, my allotted portion and my cup,
    you it is who hold fast my lot.
I set the LORD ever before me;
    with him at my right hand I shall not be disturbed. R̸.

Therefore my heart is glad and my soul rejoices,
    my body, too, abides in confidence;
because you will not abandon my soul to the netherworld,
    nor will you suffer your faithful one to undergo
        corruption. R̸.

You will show me the path to life,
    fullness of joys in your presence,
    the delights at your right hand forever. R̸.

PRAYER
Let us pray.

O God, supreme Father of the faithful,
who increase the children of your promise
by pouring out the grace of adoption
throughout the whole world
and who through the Paschal Mystery
make your servant Abraham father of nations,
as once you swore,
grant, we pray,
that your peoples may enter worthily

into the grace to which you call them.
Through Christ our Lord. All: **Amen.**

## Reading III (Exodus 14:15—15:1)

**A reading from the Book of Exodus**

*The Israelites marched on dry land through the midst of the sea.*

The Lord said to Moses, "Why are you crying out to me?
Tell the Israelites to go forward.
And you, lift up your staff and, with hand outstretched
    over the sea,
  split the sea in two,
  that the Israelites may pass through it on dry land.
But I will make the Egyptians so obstinate
  that they will go in after them.
Then I will receive glory through Pharaoh and all his army,
  his chariots and charioteers.
The Egyptians shall know that I am the Lord,
  when I receive glory through Pharaoh
  and his chariots and charioteers."

The angel of God, who had been leading Israel's camp,
  now moved and went around behind them.
The column of cloud also, leaving the front,
  took up its place behind them,
  so that it came between the camp of the Egyptians
  and that of Israel.
But the cloud now became dark, and thus the night passed
  without the rival camps coming any closer together
    all night long.
Then Moses stretched out his hand over the sea,
  and the Lord swept the sea
  with a strong east wind throughout the night
  and so turned it into dry land.
When the water was thus divided,
  the Israelites marched into the midst of the sea on
    dry land,
  with the water like a wall to their right and to their left.

The Egyptians followed in pursuit;
  all Pharaoh's horses and chariots and charioteers went
      after them
  right into the midst of the sea.
In the night watch just before dawn
  the LORD cast through the column of the fiery cloud
  upon the Egyptian force a glance that threw it into a
      panic;
  and he so clogged their chariot wheels
  that they could hardly drive.
With that the Egyptians sounded the retreat before Israel,
  because the LORD was fighting for them against the
      Egyptians.

Then the LORD told Moses, "Stretch out your hand over
    the sea,
  that the water may flow back upon the Egyptians,
  upon their chariots and their charioteers."
So Moses stretched out his hand over the sea,
  and at dawn the sea flowed back to its normal depth.
The Egyptians were fleeing head on toward the sea,
  when the LORD hurled them into its midst.
As the water flowed back,
  it covered the chariots and the charioteers of Pharaoh's
      whole army
  which had followed the Israelites into the sea.
Not a single one of them escaped.
But the Israelites had marched on dry land
  through the midst of the sea,
  with the water like a wall to their right and to their left.
Thus the LORD saved Israel on that day
  from the power of the Egyptians.
When Israel saw the Egyptians lying dead on the seashore
  and beheld the great power that the LORD
  had shown against the Egyptians,
  they feared the LORD and believed in him and in his
      servant Moses.

**Then Moses and the Israelites sang this song to the LORD:**
  **I will sing to the LORD, for he is gloriously triumphant;**
  **horse and chariot he has cast into the sea.**

**The word of the Lord.**

RESPONSORIAL PSALM (Exodus 15)

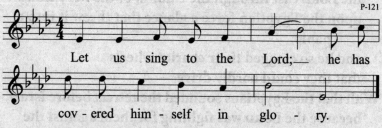

Music: Jay F. Hunstiger, © 1990, administered by Liturgical Press. All rights reserved.

Exodus 15:1-2, 3-4, 5-6, 17-18

R̸. (1b) **Let us sing to the Lord; he has covered himself in glory.**

I will sing to the LORD, for he is gloriously triumphant;
  horse and chariot he has cast into the sea.
My strength and my courage is the LORD,
  and he has been my savior.
He is my God, I praise him;
  the God of my father, I extol him. R̸.

The LORD is a warrior,
  LORD is his name!
Pharaoh's chariots and army he hurled into the sea;
  the elite of his officers were submerged in the
    Red Sea. R̸.

The flood waters covered them,
  they sank into the depths like a stone.
Your right hand, O LORD, magnificent in power,
  your right hand, O LORD, has shattered the enemy. R̸.

You brought in the people you redeemed
  and planted them on the mountain of your inheritance—
the place where you made your seat, O LORD,
  the sanctuary, LORD, which your hands established.
The LORD shall reign forever and ever. R̸.

PRAYER

Let us pray.

O God, whose ancient wonders
remain undimmed in splendor even in our day,
for what you once bestowed on a single people,
freeing them from Pharaoh's persecution
by the power of your right hand,
now you bring about as the salvation of the nations
through the waters of rebirth,
grant, we pray, that the whole world
may become children of Abraham
and inherit the dignity of Israel's birthright.
Through Christ our Lord. All: **Amen.**

Or:

O God, who by the light of the New Testament
have unlocked the meaning
of wonders worked in former times,
so that the Red Sea prefigures the sacred font
and the nation delivered from slavery
foreshadows the Christian people,
grant, we pray, that all nations,
obtaining the privilege of Israel by merit of faith,
may be reborn by partaking of your Spirit.
Through Christ our Lord. All: **Amen.**

READING IV (Isaiah 54:5-14)

**A reading from the Book of the Prophet Isaiah**

*With enduring love, the Lord your redeemer takes pity on you.*

> **The One who has become your husband is your Maker;**
> > **his name is the LORD of hosts;**
> **your redeemer is the Holy One of Israel,**
> > **called God of all the earth.**
> **The LORD calls you back,**
> > **like a wife forsaken and grieved in spirit,**
> > **a wife married in youth and then cast off,**
> > **says your God.**
> **For a brief moment I abandoned you,**
> > **but with great tenderness I will take you back.**
> **In an outburst of wrath, for a moment**
> > **I hid my face from you;**

but with enduring love I take pity on you,
 says the LORD, your redeemer.
This is for me like the days of Noah,
 when I swore that the waters of Noah
 should never again deluge the earth;
so I have sworn not to be angry with you,
 or to rebuke you.
Though the mountains leave their place
 and the hills be shaken,
my love shall never leave you
 nor my covenant of peace be shaken,
 says the LORD, who has mercy on you.
O afflicted one, storm-battered and unconsoled,
 I lay your pavements in carnelians,
 and your foundations in sapphires;
I will make your battlements of rubies,
 your gates of carbuncles,
 and all your walls of precious stones.
All your children shall be taught by the LORD,
 and great shall be the peace of your children.
In justice shall you be established,
 far from the fear of oppression,
 where destruction cannot come near you.

The word of the Lord.

## RESPONSORIAL PSALM 30

P-122

I will praise you, Lord, for you have res-cued me.

Psalm 30:2, 4, 5-6, 11-12, 13

R̥. (2a) **I will praise you, Lord, for you have rescued me.**

I will extol you, O LORD, for you drew me clear
 and did not let my enemies rejoice over me.
O LORD, you brought me up from the netherworld;

you preserved me from among those going down into
the pit. R℣.

Sing praise to the LORD, you his faithful ones,
and give thanks to his holy name.
For his anger lasts but a moment;
a lifetime, his good will.
At nightfall, weeping enters in,
but with the dawn, rejoicing. R℣.

Hear, O LORD, and have pity on me;
O LORD, be my helper.
You changed my mourning into dancing;
O LORD, my God, forever will I give you thanks. R℣.

PRAYER
Let us pray.

Almighty ever-living God,
surpass, for the honor of your name,
what you pledged to the Patriarchs by reason of their faith,
and through sacred adoption increase the children of your promise,
so that what the Saints of old never doubted would come to pass
your Church may now see in great part fulfilled.
Through Christ our Lord. All: **Amen.**

READING V (Isaiah 55:1-11)

# A reading from the Book of the Prophet Isaiah

*Come to me that you may have life. I will renew with you an
everlasting covenant.*

**Thus says the LORD:**
**All you who are thirsty,**
**come to the water!**
**You who have no money,**
**come, receive grain and eat;**
**come, without paying and without cost,**
**drink wine and milk!**
**Why spend your money for what is not bread,**
**your wages for what fails to satisfy?**
**Heed me, and you shall eat well,**
**you shall delight in rich fare.**

Come to me heedfully,
  listen, that you may have life.
I will renew with you the everlasting covenant,
  the benefits assured to David.
As I made him a witness to the peoples,
  a leader and commander of nations,
so shall you summon a nation you knew not,
  and nations that knew you not shall run to you,
because of the LORD, your God,
  the Holy One of Israel, who has glorified you.

Seek the LORD while he may be found,
  call him while he is near.
Let the scoundrel forsake his way,
  and the wicked man his thoughts;
let him turn to the LORD for mercy;
  to our God, who is generous in forgiving.
For my thoughts are not your thoughts,
  nor are your ways my ways, says the LORD.
As high as the heavens are above the earth,
  so high are my ways above your ways
  and my thoughts above your thoughts.

For just as from the heavens
  the rain and snow come down
and do not return there
  till they have watered the earth,
  making it fertile and fruitful,
giving seed to the one who sows
  and bread to the one who eats,
so shall my word be
  that goes forth from my mouth;
my word shall not return to me void,
  but shall do my will,
  achieving the end for which I sent it.

The word of the Lord.

RESPONSIVE PSALM (Isaiah 12)

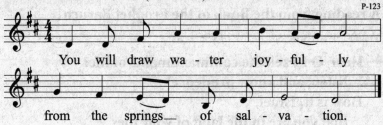

You will draw water joy-ful-ly from the springs of sal-va-tion.

Isaiah 12:2-3, 4, 5-6

R̸. (3) **You will draw water joyfully from the springs of salvation.**

God indeed is my savior;
    I am confident and unafraid.
My strength and my courage is the LORD,
    and he has been my savior.
With joy you will draw water
    at the fountain of salvation. R̸.

Give thanks to the LORD, acclaim his name;
    among the nations make known his deeds,
    proclaim how exalted is his name. R̸.

Sing praise to the LORD for his glorious achievement;
    let this be known throughout all the earth.
Shout with exultation, O city of Zion,
    for great in your midst
    is the Holy One of Israel! R̸.

PRAYER
Let us pray.

Almighty ever-living God,
sole hope of the world,
who by the preaching of your Prophets
unveiled the mysteries of this present age,
graciously increase the longing of your people,
for only at the prompting of your grace
do the faithful progress in any kind of virtue.
Through Christ our Lord. All: **Amen.**

READING VI (Baruch 3:9-15, 32—4:4)

# A reading from the Book of the Prophet Baruch

*Walk toward the splendor of the Lord.*

Hear, O Israel, the commandments of life:
   listen, and know prudence!
How is it, Israel,
   that you are in the land of your foes,
   grown old in a foreign land,
defiled with the dead,
   accounted with those destined for the netherworld?
You have forsaken the fountain of wisdom!
   Had you walked in the way of God,
   you would have dwelt in enduring peace.
Learn where prudence is,
   where strength, where understanding;
that you may know also
   where are length of days, and life,
   where light of the eyes, and peace.
Who has found the place of wisdom,
   who has entered into her treasuries?

The One who knows all things knows her;
   he has probed her by his knowledge—
the One who established the earth for all time,
   and filled it with four-footed beasts;
he who dismisses the light, and it departs,
   calls it, and it obeys him trembling;
before whom the stars at their posts
   shine and rejoice;
when he calls them, they answer, "Here we are!"
   shining with joy for their Maker.
Such is our God;
   no other is to be compared to him:
he has traced out the whole way of understanding,
   and has given her to Jacob, his servant,
   to Israel, his beloved son.

Since then she has appeared on earth,
  and moved among people.
She is the book of the precepts of God,
  the law that endures forever;
all who cling to her will live,
  but those will die who forsake her.
Turn, O Jacob, and receive her:
  walk by her light toward splendor.
Give not your glory to another,
  your privileges to an alien race.
Blessed are we, O Israel;
  for what pleases God is known to us!

**The word of the Lord.**

Responsorial Psalm 19

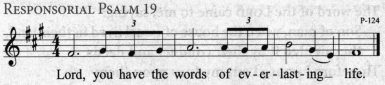

Lord, you have the words of ev-er-last-ing__ life.

Psalm 19:8, 9, 10, 11

℟. (John 6:68c) **Lord, you have the words of everlasting life.**

The law of the LORD is perfect,
  refreshing the soul;
the decree of the LORD is trustworthy,
  giving wisdom to the simple. ℟.

The precepts of the LORD are right,
  rejoicing the heart;
the command of the LORD is clear,
  enlightening the eye. ℟.

The fear of the LORD is pure,
  enduring forever;
the ordinances of the LORD are true,
  all of them just. ℟.

They are more precious than gold,
  than a heap of purest gold;

*(continued)*

sweeter also than syrup
or honey from the comb. ℟.

PRAYER

Let us pray.

O God, who constantly increase your Church
by your call to the nations,
graciously grant
to those you wash clean in the waters of Baptism
the assurance of your unfailing protection.
Through Christ our Lord. All: **Amen.**

READING VII (Ezekiel 36:16-17a, 18-28)

## A reading from the Book of the Prophet Ezekiel

*I shall sprinkle clean water upon you and I shall give you a
new heart.*

The word of the LORD came to me, saying:
Son of man, when the house of Israel lived in their land,
they defiled it by their conduct and deeds.
Therefore I poured out my fury upon them
because of the blood that they poured out on the
ground,
and because they defiled it with idols.
I scattered them among the nations,
dispersing them over foreign lands;
according to their conduct and deeds I judged them.
But when they came among the nations wherever
they came,
they served to profane my holy name,
because it was said of them: "These are the people of
the LORD,
yet they had to leave their land."
So I have relented because of my holy name
which the house of Israel profaned
among the nations where they came.
Therefore say to the house of Israel: Thus says the
Lord GOD:
Not for your sakes do I act, house of Israel,

but for the sake of my holy name,
   which you profaned among the nations to which
      you came.
I will prove the holiness of my great name, profaned
      among the nations,
   in whose midst you have profaned it.
Thus the nations shall know that I am the LORD, says the
      Lord GOD,
   when in their sight I prove my holiness through you.
For I will take you away from among the nations,
   gather you from all the foreign lands,
   and bring you back to your own land.
I will sprinkle clean water upon you
   to cleanse you from all your impurities,
   and from all your idols I will cleanse you.
I will give you a new heart and place a new spirit within
      you,
   taking from your bodies your stony hearts
   and giving you natural hearts.
I will put my spirit within you and make you live by my
      statutes,
   careful to observe my decrees.
You shall live in the land I gave your fathers;
   you shall be my people, and I will be your God.

The word of the Lord.

## RESPONSIAL PSALM

A *When baptism is celebrated*

H-291

Like the deer that longs for run-ning streams, my soul longs for you, my God.

Psalms 42:3, 5; 43:3, 4

℟. (42:2) **Like a deer that longs for running streams,
my soul longs for you, my God.**

Athirst is my soul for God, the living God.
When shall I go and behold the face of God? ℟.

I went with the throng
and led them in procession to the house of God,
amid loud cries of joy and thanksgiving,
with the multitude keeping festival. ℟.

Send forth your light and your fidelity;
they shall lead me on
and bring me to your holy mountain,
to your dwelling-place. ℟.

Then will I go in to the altar of God,
the God of my gladness and joy;
then will I give you thanks upon the harp,
O God, my God! ℟.

**B** *When baptism is not celebrated*

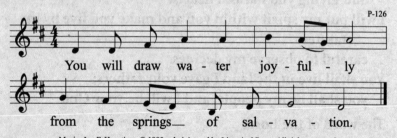

Isaiah 12:2-3, 4bcd, 5-6

℟. (3) **You will draw water joyfully from the springs of
salvation.**

God indeed is my savior;
I am confident and unafraid.
My strength and my courage is the LORD,
and he has been my savior.
With joy you will draw water
at the fountain of salvation. ℟.

Give thanks to the LORD, acclaim his name;
>among the nations make known his deeds,
>>proclaim how exalted is his name. ℟.

Sing praise to the LORD for his glorious achievement;
>let this be known throughout all the earth.
Shout with exultation, O city of Zion,
>for great in your midst
>>is the Holy One of Israel! ℟.

C *When baptism is not celebrated*

P-127

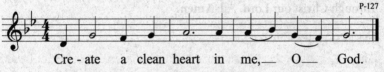

Cre - ate    a   clean  heart   in   me,___  O___  God.

Psalm 51:12-13, 14-15, 18-19

℟. (12a) **Create a clean heart in me, O God.**

A clean heart create for me, O God,
>and a steadfast spirit renew within me.
Cast me not out from your presence,
>and your Holy Spirit take not from me. ℟.

Give me back the joy of your salvation,
>and a willing spirit sustain in me.
I will teach transgressors your ways,
>and sinners shall return to you. ℟.

For you are not pleased with sacrifices;
>should I offer a holocaust, you would not accept it.
My sacrifice, O God, is a contrite spirit;
>a heart contrite and humbled, O God, you will not
>>spurn. ℟.

PRAYER
Let us pray.

O God of unchanging power and eternal light,
look with favor on the wondrous mystery of the whole Church
and serenely accomplish the work of human salvation,
which you planned from all eternity;
may the whole world know and see

that what was cast down is raised up,
what had become old is made new,
and all things are restored to integrity through Christ,
just as by him they came into being.
Who lives and reigns for ever and ever. All: **Amen.**

Or:

O God, who by the pages of both Testaments
instruct and prepare us to celebrate the Paschal Mystery,
grant that we may comprehend your mercy,
so that the gifts we receive from you this night
may confirm our hope of the gifts to come.
Through Christ our Lord. All: **Amen.**

GLORIA (*See* page 3).

COLLECT
O God, who make this most sacred night radiant
with the glory of the Lord's Resurrection,
stir up in your Church a spirit of adoption,
so that, renewed in body and mind,
we may render you undivided service.
Through our Lord Jesus Christ, your Son,
who lives and reigns with you in the unity of the Holy Spirit,
one God, for ever and ever. All: **Amen.**

EPISTLE (Romans 6:3-11)

**A reading from the Letter of Saint Paul to the Romans**

*Christ, raised from the dead, dies no more.*

**Brothers and sisters:**
**Are you unaware that we who were baptized into**
**Christ Jesus**
**were baptized into his death?**
**We were indeed buried with him through baptism into**
**death,**
**so that, just as Christ was raised from the dead**
**by the glory of the Father,**
**we too might live in newness of life.**

**For if we have grown into union with him through a**
**death like his,**
**we shall also be united with him in the resurrection.**

We know that our old self was crucified with him,
  so that our sinful body might be done away with,
  that we might no longer be in slavery to sin.
For a dead person has been absolved from sin.
If, then, we have died with Christ,
  we believe that we shall also live with him.
We know that Christ, raised from the dead, dies no more;
  death no longer has power over him.
As to his death, he died to sin once and for all;
  as to his life, he lives for God.
Consequently, you too must think of yourselves as being
    dead to sin
  and living for God in Christ Jesus.

**The word of the Lord.**

The Priest solemnly intones the Alleluia three times, raising his voice by a
step each time, with all repeating it.

### RESPONSORIAL PSALM 118

P-128

Music: Jay F. Hunstiger, © 1990, administered by Liturgical Press. All rights reserved.

Psalm 118:1-2, 16-17, 22-23

℞. **Alleluia, alleluia, alleluia.**

Give thanks to the LORD, for he is good,
  for his mercy endures forever.
Let the house of Israel say,
  "His mercy endures forever." ℞.

"The right hand of the LORD has struck with power;
  the right hand of the LORD is exalted.    *(continued)*

I shall not die, but live,
   and declare the works of the Lord." R℣.

The stone which the builders rejected
   has become the cornerstone.
By the Lord has this been done;
   it is wonderful in our eyes. R℣.

## Gospel A  (Matthew 28:1-10)

✝ **A reading from the holy Gospel according to Matthew**

All: **Glory to you, O Lord.**

*He has been raised from the dead and is going before you to Galilee.*

**After the sabbath, as the first day of the week was dawning,
   Mary Magdalene and the other Mary came to see the
      tomb.
And behold, there was a great earthquake;
   for an angel of the Lord descended from heaven,
   approached, rolled back the stone, and sat upon it.
His appearance was like lightning
   and his clothing was white as snow.
The guards were shaken with fear of him
   and became like dead men.
Then the angel said to the women in reply,
   "Do not be afraid!
I know that you are seeking Jesus the crucified.
He is not here, for he has been raised just as he said.
Come and see the place where he lay.
Then go quickly and tell his disciples,
   'He has been raised from the dead,
   and he is going before you to Galilee;
   there you will see him.'
   Behold, I have told you."
Then they went away quickly from the tomb,
   fearful yet overjoyed,
   and ran to announce this to his disciples.
And behold, Jesus met them on their way and greeted
      them.**

They approached, embraced his feet, and did him homage.
Then Jesus said to them, "Do not be afraid.
Go tell my brothers to go to Galilee,
    and there they will see me."

The Gospel of the Lord. All: **Praise to you, Lord Jesus Christ.**

## THIRD PART: BAPTISMAL LITURGY

If there are candidates to be baptized:

Dearly beloved,
with one heart and one soul, let us by our prayers
come to the aid of these our brothers and sisters in their blessed hope,
so that, as they approach the font of rebirth,
the almighty Father may bestow on them
all his merciful help.

If the font is to be blessed, but there is no one to be baptized:

Dearly beloved,
let us humbly invoke upon this font
the grace of God the almighty Father,
that those who from it are born anew
may be numbered among the children of adoption in Christ.

The Litany is sung by two cantors, with all standing (because it is Easter Time)
and responding.

### THE LITANY OF THE SAINTS

If there are candidates to be baptized, the Priest says the following prayer:

Almighty ever-living God,
be present by the mysteries of your great love
and send forth the spirit of adoption
to create the new peoples
brought to birth for you in the font of Baptism,
so that what is to be carried out by our humble service
may be brought to fulfillment by your mighty power.
Through Christ our Lord. All: **Amen.**

### BLESSING OF BAPTISMAL WATER

O God, who by invisible power
accomplish a wondrous effect
through sacramental signs
and who in many ways have prepared water, your creation,
to show forth the grace of Baptism;

O God, whose Spirit
in the first moments of the world's creation
hovered over the waters,
so that the very substance of water
would even then take to itself the power to sanctify;

O God, who by the outpouring of the flood
foreshadowed regeneration,
so that from the mystery of one and the same element of water
would come an end to vice and a beginning of virtue;

O God, who caused the children of Abraham
to pass dry-shod through the Red Sea,
so that the chosen people,
set free from slavery to Pharaoh,
would prefigure the people of the baptized;

O God, whose Son,
baptized by John in the waters of the Jordan,
was anointed with the Holy Spirit,
and, as he hung upon the Cross,
gave forth water from his side along with blood,
and after his Resurrection, commanded his disciples:
"Go forth, teach all nations, baptizing them
in the name of the Father and of the Son and of the Holy Spirit,"
look now, we pray, upon the face of your Church
and graciously unseal for her the fountain of Baptism.

May this water receive by the Holy Spirit
the grace of your Only Begotten Son,
so that human nature, created in your image
and washed clean through the Sacrament of Baptism
from all the squalor of the life of old,
may be found worthy to rise to the life of newborn children
through water and the Holy Spirit.

May the power of the Holy Spirit,
O Lord, we pray,
come down through your Son
into the fullness of this font,
so that all who have been buried with Christ
by Baptism into death
may rise again to life with him.
Who lives and reigns with you in the unity of the Holy Spirit,
one God, for ever and ever. **All: Amen.**

# CELEBRATION OF BAPTISM

## RENUNCIATION OF SIN AND PROFESSION OF FAITH

The celebrant in a series of questions to which the candidates and the parents and godparents reply **I DO**, asks the candidates and parents and godparents to renounce sin and profess their faith.

## BAPTISM OF ADULTS

Celebrant: Is it your will to be baptized in the faith of the Church, which we have all professed with you?

Candidate: **It is.**

He baptizes the candidate, saying:

## N., I baptize you in the name of the Father,

He immerses the candidate or pours water upon him.

## and of the Son,

He immerses the candidate or pours water upon him a second time.

## and of the Holy Spirit.

He immerses the candidate or pours water upon him a third time. He asks the same question and performs the same action for each candidate.

After each baptism it is appropriate for the people to sing a short acclamation:

**This is the fountain of life,**
**water made holy by the suffering of Christ, washing all the world.**
**You who are washed in this water have hope of heaven's kingdom.**

## BAPTISM OF CHILDREN

Celebrant: Is it your will that N. should be baptized in the faith of the Church, which we have all professed with you?

Parents and godparents: **It is.**

He baptizes the child, saying:

## N., I baptize you in the name of the Father,

He immerses the child or pours water upon it.

## and of the Son,

He immerses the child or pours water upon it a second time.

## and of the Holy Spirit.

He immerses the child or pours water upon it a third time. He asks the same question and performs the same action for each child.

After each baptism it is appropriate for the people to sing a short acclamation:

**This is the fountain of life,**
**water made holy by the suffering of Christ, washing all the world.**
**You who are washed in this water have hope of heaven's kingdom.**

## ANOINTING WITH CHRISM

God the Father of our Lord Jesus Christ has freed you from sin, given you a new birth by water and the Holy Spirit, and welcomed you into his holy people. He now anoints you with the chrism of salvation. As Christ was anointed Priest, Prophet, and King, so may you live always as members of his body, sharing everlasting life. All: **Amen.**

## CLOTHING WITH THE WHITE GARMENT

(N., N.,) you have become a new creation, and have clothed yourselves in Christ. See in this white garment the outward sign of your Christian dignity. With your family and friends to help you by word and example, bring that dignity unstained into the everlasting life of heaven. All: **Amen.**

## CELEBRATION OF CONFIRMATION *

If the bishop has conferred baptism, he should now also confer confirmation. If the bishop is not present, the priest who conferred baptism and received the candidates into full communion is authorized to confirm. The infants who were baptized during this celebration are not confirmed. However, the newly baptized children who have gone through the RCIA process are confirmed.

## INVITATION

My dear friends, let us pray to God our Father, that he will pour out the Holy Spirit on these candidates for confirmation to strengthen them with his gifts and anoint them to be more like Christ, the Son of God.

## LAYING ON OF HANDS

Almighty God, Father of our Lord Jesus Christ,
who brought these your servants to new birth
by water and the Holy Spirit,
freeing them from sin:
send upon them, O Lord, the Holy Spirit, the Paraclete;
give them the spirit of wisdom and understanding,
the spirit of counsel and fortitude,
the spirit of knowledge and piety;
fill them with the spirit of the fear of the Lord.
Through Christ our Lord. All: **Amen.**

## ANOINTING WITH CHRISM

N., be sealed with the Gift of the Holy Spirit.
Newly confirmed: **Amen.**

The minister of the sacrament adds: **Peace be with you.**
Newly confirmed: **And with your Spirit.**

*From the RCIA, nos. 232–235.

## THE BLESSING OF WATER

*If no one is to be baptized and the font is not to be blessed, the priest blesses the water with the following prayer:*

Dear brothers and sisters,
let us humbly beseech the Lord our God
to bless this water he has created,
which will be sprinkled upon us
as a memorial of our Baptism.
May he graciously renew us,
that we may remain faithful to the Spirit
whom we have received.

*And after a brief pause in silence, he proclaims the following prayer, with hands extended:*

Lord our God,
in your mercy be present to your people
who keep vigil on this most sacred night,
and, for us who recall the wondrous work of our creation
and the still greater work of our redemption,
graciously bless this water.
For you created water to make the fields fruitful
and to refresh and cleanse our bodies.
You also made water the instrument of your mercy:
for through water you freed your people from slavery
and quenched their thirst in the desert;
through water the Prophets proclaimed the new covenant
you were to enter upon with the human race;
and last of all,
through water, which Christ made holy in the Jordan,
you have renewed our corrupted nature
in the bath of regeneration.
Therefore, may this water be for us
a memorial of the Baptism we have received,
and grant that we may share
in the gladness of our brothers and sisters,
who at Easter have received their Baptism.
Through Christ our Lord. All: **Amen.**

## THE RENEWAL OF BAPTISMAL PROMISES

Dear brethren (brothers and sisters), through the Paschal Mystery
we have been buried with Christ in Baptism,
so that we may walk with him in newness of life.
And so, now that our Lenten observance is concluded,
let us renew the promises of Holy Baptism,

by which we once renounced Satan and his works
and promised to serve God in the holy Catholic Church.

And so I ask you:

**A**   Priest: Do you renounce Satan?   All: **I do.**
      Priest: And all his works?   All: **I do.**
      Priest: And all his empty show?   All: **I do.**

Or:

**B**   Priest: Do you renounce sin,
            so as to live in the freedom of the children of God?
         All: **I do.**

      Priest: Do you renounce the lure of evil,
            so that sin may have no mastery over you?
         All: **I do.**

      Priest: Do you renounce Satan,
            the author and prince of sin?
         All: **I do.**

Then the priest continues:

Priest: Do you believe in God,
         the Father almighty,
         Creator of heaven and earth?
   All: **I do.**

Priest: Do you believe in Jesus Christ, his only Son, our Lord,
         who was born of the Virgin Mary,
         suffered death and was buried,
         rose again from the dead,
         and is seated at the right hand of the Father?
   All: **I do.**

Priest: Do you believe in the Holy Spirit,
         the holy Catholic Church,
         the communion of saints,
         the forgiveness of sins,
         the resurrection of the body,
         and life everlasting?
   All: **I do.**

And may almighty God, the Father of our Lord Jesus Christ,
who has given us new birth by water and the Holy Spirit
and bestowed on us forgiveness of our sins,
keep us by his grace,
in Christ Jesus our Lord,
for eternal life. All: **Amen.**

The Priest sprinkles the people with the blessed water, while all sing:

Ant. I saw water flowing from the Temple,
from its right-hand side, alleluia;
and all to whom this water came were saved
and shall say: Alleluia, alleluia.

### PRAYER OF THE FAITHFUL

## FOURTH PART: THE LITURGY OF THE EUCHARIST

### PRAYER OVER THE OFFERINGS

Accept, we ask, O Lord,
the prayers of your people
with the sacrificial offerings,
that what has begun in the paschal mysteries
may, by the working of your power,
bring us to the healing of eternity.
Through Christ our Lord. All: **Amen.**

### COMMUNION ANTIPHON (1 Corinthians 5:7-8)

Christ our Passover has been sacrificed;
therefore let us keep the feast
with the unleavened bread of purity and truth, alleluia.

### PRAYER AFTER COMMUNION

Pour out on us, O Lord, the Spirit of your love,
and in your kindness make those you have nourished
by this paschal Sacrament
one in mind and heart.
Through Christ our Lord. All: **Amen.**

### DISMISSAL

To dismiss the people the Deacon or, if there is no Deacon, the Priest himself
sings or says:

Go forth, the Mass is ended, alleluia, alleluia.

Or:

Go in peace, alleluia, alleluia.

All reply: **Thanks be to God, alleluia, alleluia.**

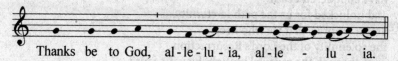

Thanks be to God, al-le-lu-ia, al-le - lu - ia.

This practice is observed throughout the Octave of Easter.

# Easter Sunday

## THE RESURRECTION OF THE LORD

## MASS DURING THE DAY

*April 16, 2017*

*Reflection on the Gospel*

*Jesus is Savior—the one who sacrificed his all out of sheer divine love for us. Eternity is eternal light; eternity is everlasting love; eternity is risen Life unceasing. Jesus had to rise from the dead so that we might come to believe that our human existence is not all there is. Our everyday Gospel living leads us on a path toward the light of wisdom, the steadfastness of love, and the eternity of Life that awaits those who accept Jesus' call to be disciples who see and believe.*

- *Christ is risen . . . the eternity of Life . . .*

—*Living Liturgy*™, *Easter Sunday 2017*

ENTRANCE ANTIPHON (Cf. Psalm 139[138]:18, 5-6)
I have risen, and I am with you still, alleluia.
You have laid your hand upon me, alleluia.
Too wonderful for me, this knowledge, alleluia, alleluia.

Or:

(Luke 24:34; cf. Revelation 1:6)
The Lord is truly risen, alleluia.
To him be glory and power
for all the ages of eternity, alleluia, alleluia.

COLLECT
O God, who on this day,
through your Only Begotten Son,
have conquered death
and unlocked for us the path to eternity,
grant, we pray, that we who keep
the solemnity of the Lord's Resurrection
may, through the renewal brought by your Spirit,
rise up in the light of life.

Through our Lord Jesus Christ, your Son,
who lives and reigns with you in the unity of the Holy Spirit,
one God, for ever and ever. All: **Amen.**

READING I (L 42) (Acts of the Apostles 10:34a, 37-43)

## A reading from the Acts of the Apostles

*We ate and drank with him after he rose from the dead.*

**Peter proceeded to speak and said:**
  "You know what has happened all over Judea,
  beginning in Galilee after the baptism
  that John preached,
  how God anointed Jesus of Nazareth
  with the Holy Spirit and power.
He went about doing good
  and healing all those oppressed by the devil,
  for God was with him.
We are witnesses of all that he did
  both in the country of the Jews and in Jerusalem.
They put him to death by hanging him on a tree.
This man God raised on the third day and granted that
      he be visible,
  not to all the people, but to us,
  the witnesses chosen by God in advance,
  who ate and drank with him after he rose from the dead.
He commissioned us to preach to the people
  and testify that he is the one appointed by God
  as judge of the living and the dead.
To him all the prophets bear witness,
  that everyone who believes in him
  will receive forgiveness of sins through his name."

**The word of the Lord.** All: **Thanks be to God.**

RESPONSORIAL PSALM 118

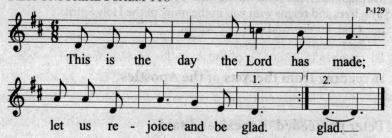

Psalm 118:1-2, 16-17, 22-23

R̂. (24) **This is the day the Lord has made; let us rejoice
and be glad.** *or:* R̂. **Alleluia.**

Give thanks to the LORD, for he is good,
for his mercy endures forever.
Let the house of Israel say,
"His mercy endures forever." R̂.

"The right hand of the LORD has struck with power;
the right hand of the LORD is exalted.
I shall not die, but live,
and declare the works of the LORD." R̂.

The stone which the builders rejected
has become the cornerstone.
By the LORD has this been done;
it is wonderful in our eyes. R̂.

READING II

A (Colossians 3:1-4)

**A reading from the Letter of Saint Paul to the Colossians**

*Seek what is above, where Christ is.*

**Brothers and sisters:**
**If then you were raised with Christ, seek what is above,**
**where Christ is seated at the right hand of God.**
**Think of what is above, not of what is on earth.**
**For you have died, and your life is hidden with Christ**
**in God.**

When Christ your life appears,
> then you too will appear with him in glory.

The word of the Lord. All: Thanks be to God.

Or:

*B* (1 Corinthians 5:6b-8)

**A reading from the first Letter of Saint Paul to the Corinthians**

*Clear out the old yeast, so that you may become a fresh batch of dough.*

**Brothers and sisters:**
**Do you not know that a little yeast leavens all the dough?**
**Clear out the old yeast,**
> **so that you may become a fresh batch of dough,**
> **inasmuch as you are unleavened.**

**For our paschal lamb, Christ, has been sacrificed.**
**Therefore, let us celebrate the feast,**
> **not with the old yeast, the yeast of malice and**
> > **wickedness,**
> **but with the unleavened bread of sincerity and truth.**

The word of the Lord. All: Thanks be to God.

SEQUENCE
*Victimae paschali laudes*

**Christians, to the Paschal Victim**
> **Offer your thankful praises!**
**A Lamb the sheep redeems;**
> **Christ, who only is sinless,**
> **Reconciles sinners to the Father.**
**Death and life have contended in that combat stupendous:**
> **The Prince of life, who died, reigns immortal.**
**Speak, Mary, declaring**
> **What you saw, wayfaring.**
**"The tomb of Christ, who is living,**
> **The glory of Jesus' resurrection;**

Bright angels attesting,
  The shroud and napkin resting.
Yes, Christ my hope is arisen;
  To Galilee he goes before you."
Christ indeed from death is risen, our new life obtaining.
  Have mercy, victor King, ever reigning!
  Amen. Alleluia.

GOSPEL
(John 20:1-9) or (Matthew 28:1-10) or afternoon (Luke 24:13-35)
ALLELUIA (*See* 1 Corinthians 5:7b-8a)

℣. Alleluia, alleluia.  ℟. **Alleluia, alleluia.**
℣. Christ, our paschal lamb, has been sacrificed;
  let us then feast with joy in the Lord. ℟.

✠ **A reading from the holy Gospel according to John**

All: **Glory to you, O Lord.**

*He had to rise from the dead.*

On the first day of the week,
  Mary of Magdala came to the tomb early in the
    morning,
  while it was still dark,
  and saw the stone removed from the tomb.
So she ran and went to Simon Peter
  and to the other disciple whom Jesus loved, and
    told them,
  "They have taken the Lord from the tomb,
  and we don't know where they put him."
So Peter and the other disciple went out and came to
  the tomb.
They both ran, but the other disciple ran faster than Peter
  and arrived at the tomb first;
  he bent down and saw the burial cloths there, but did
    not go in.
When Simon Peter arrived after him,
  he went into the tomb and saw the burial cloths there,
  and the cloth that had covered his head,

**not with the burial cloths but rolled up in a separate place.**

**Then the other disciple also went in,**
**the one who had arrived at the tomb first,**
**and he saw and believed.**

**For they did not yet understand the Scripture**
**that he had to rise from the dead.**

**The Gospel of the Lord.** All: **Praise to you, Lord Jesus Christ.**

RENEWAL OF BAPTISMAL PROMISES
The renewal of baptismal promises may take place at all Masses today. The form followed is the same as at the Easter Vigil, page 243.

PRAYER OVER THE OFFERINGS
Exultant with paschal gladness, O Lord,
we offer the sacrifice
by which your Church
is wondrously reborn and nourished.
Through Christ our Lord. All: **Amen.**

COMMUNION ANTIPHON (1 Corinthians 5:7-8)
Christ our Passover has been sacrificed, alleluia;
therefore let us keep the feast with the unleavened bread
of purity and truth, alleluia, alleluia.

PRAYER AFTER COMMUNION
Look upon your Church, O God,
with unfailing love and favor,
so that, renewed by the paschal mysteries,
she may come to the glory of the resurrection.
Through Christ our Lord. All: **Amen.**

DISMISSAL (*See* page 245)

# Second Sunday of Easter

## (or SUNDAY OF DIVINE MERCY)

*April 23, 2017*

*Reflection on the Gospel*

*From this gospel we can tease out myriad shifts:
mourning to joy, fear to peace, sinfulness to
forgiveness, being behind locked doors to being sent
out, inertia to empowerment by the Holy Spirit,
not seeing to seeing, obstinate disbelief to acclamation of faith, life before
Jesus' resurrection to new "life in his name." For those who believe, Jesus'
resurrection shifts their self-understanding and their purpose in life,
enabling them to see all things as new. Do we believe?*

- *"You believe in me, Thomas, because you have seen me, says the
  Lord; blessed are they who have not seen me, but still believe!"
  I believe because . . .*

—Living Liturgy™, *Second Sunday of Easter 2017*

**ENTRANCE ANTIPHON** (1 Peter 2:2)

Like newborn infants, you must long for the pure, spiritual
  milk,
that in him you may grow to salvation, alleluia.

**Or:**

**(4 Esdras 2:36-37)**

Receive the joy of your glory, giving thanks to God,
who has called you into the heavenly kingdom, alleluia.

**COLLECT**

God of everlasting mercy,
who in the very recurrence of the paschal feast
kindle the faith of the people you have made your own,
increase, we pray, the grace you have bestowed,
that all may grasp and rightly understand
in what font they have been washed,
by whose Spirit they have been reborn,
by whose Blood they have been redeemed.
Through our Lord Jesus Christ, your Son,

who lives and reigns with you in the unity of the Holy Spirit,
one God, for ever and ever. All: **Amen.**

<small>Reading I</small> (L 43-A) (Acts of the Apostles 2:42-47)

**A reading from the Acts of the Apostles**

*All who believed were together and had all things in common.*

They devoted themselves
    to the teaching of the apostles and to the communal
        life,
    to the breaking of bread and to the prayers.
Awe came upon everyone,
    and many wonders and signs were done through the
        apostles.
All who believed were together and had all things in
        common;
    they would sell their property and possessions
    and divide them among all according to each one's
        need.
Every day they devoted themselves
    to meeting together in the temple area
    and to breaking bread in their homes.
They ate their meals with exultation and sincerity of
        heart,
    praising God and enjoying favor with all the people.
And every day the Lord added to their number those
        who were being saved.

**The word of the Lord.** All: **Thanks be to God.**

<small>Responsorial Psalm</small> 118

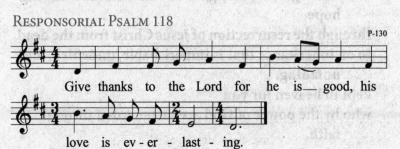

Give thanks to the Lord for he is good, his
love is ev-er-last-ing.

Psalm 118:2-4, 13-15, 22-24

R̸. (1) **Give thanks to the Lord for he is good, his love is everlasting.** *or:* R̸. **Alleluia.**

Let the house of Israel say,
"His mercy endures forever."
Let the house of Aaron say,
"His mercy endures forever."
Let those who fear the LORD say,
"His mercy endures forever." R̸.

I was hard pressed and was falling,
but the LORD helped me.
My strength and my courage is the LORD,
and he has been my savior.
The joyful shout of victory
in the tents of the just. R̸.

The stone which the builders rejected
has become the cornerstone.
By the LORD has this been done;
it is wonderful in our eyes.
This is the day the LORD has made;
let us be glad and rejoice in it. R̸.

READING II (1 Peter 1:3-9)

**A reading from the first Letter of Saint Peter**

*God has given us new birth to a living hope through the resurrection of Jesus Christ from the dead.*

**Blessed be the God and Father of our Lord Jesus Christ,**
**who in his great mercy gave us a new birth to a living**
**hope**
**through the resurrection of Jesus Christ from the dead,**
**to an inheritance that is imperishable, undefiled, and**
**unfading,**
**kept in heaven for you**
**who by the power of God are safeguarded through**
**faith,**
**to a salvation that is ready to be revealed in the final**
**time.**

In this you rejoice, although now for a little while
  you may have to suffer through various trials,
  so that the genuineness of your faith,
    more precious than gold that is perishable even
      though tested by fire,
  may prove to be for praise, glory, and honor
  at the revelation of Jesus Christ.
Although you have not seen him you love him;
  even though you do not see him now yet believe in him,
  you rejoice with an indescribable and glorious joy,
  as you attain the goal of your faith, the salvation of
    your souls.

**The word of the Lord.** All: **Thanks be to God.**

GOSPEL (John 20:19-31)
ALLELUIA (John 20:29)

℣. Alleluia, alleluia.  ℟. **Alleluia, alleluia.**
℣. You believe in me, Thomas, because you have seen me,
    says the Lord;
  blessed are they who have not seen me, but still
    believe! ℟.

✝ **A reading from the holy Gospel according to John**

All: **Glory to you, O Lord.**

*Eight days later Jesus came and stood in their midst.*

On the evening of that first day of the week,
  when the doors were locked, where the disciples were,
  for fear of the Jews,
  Jesus came and stood in their midst
  and said to them, "Peace be with you."
When he had said this, he showed them his hands and
    his side.
The disciples rejoiced when they saw the Lord.
Jesus said to them again, "Peace be with you.
As the Father has sent me, so I send you."

And when he had said this, he breathed on them and
  said to them,
  "Receive the Holy Spirit.
Whose sins you forgive are forgiven them,
  and whose sins you retain are retained."

Thomas, called Didymus, one of the Twelve,
  was not with them when Jesus came.
So the other disciples said to him, "We have seen the
  Lord."
But he said to them,
  "Unless I see the mark of the nails in his hands
  and put my finger into the nailmarks
  and put my hand into his side, I will not believe."

Now a week later his disciples were again inside
  and Thomas was with them.
Jesus came, although the doors were locked,
  and stood in their midst and said, "Peace be with you."
Then he said to Thomas, "Put your finger here and see
  my hands,
  and bring your hand and put it into my side,
  and do not be unbelieving, but believe."
Thomas answered and said to him, "My Lord and my
  God!"
Jesus said to him, "Have you come to believe because
  you have seen me?
Blessed are those who have not seen and have believed."

Now, Jesus did many other signs in the presence of his
  disciples
  that are not written in this book.
But these are written that you may come to believe
  that Jesus is the Christ, the Son of God,
  and that through this belief you may have life in his
  name.

The Gospel of the Lord. All: **Praise to you, Lord Jesus Christ.**

**PRAYER OVER THE OFFERINGS**

Accept, O Lord, we pray,
the oblations of your people
(and of those you have brought to new birth),
that, renewed by confession of your name and by Baptism,
they may attain unending happiness.
Through Christ our Lord. **All: Amen.**

**COMMUNION ANTIPHON (Cf. John 20:27)**

Bring your hand and feel the place of the nails,
and do not be unbelieving but believing, alleluia.

**PRAYER AFTER COMMUNION**

Grant, we pray, almighty God,
that our reception of this paschal Sacrament
may have a continuing effect
in our minds and hearts.
Through Christ our Lord. **All: Amen.**

# Third Sunday of Easter

*April 30, 2017*

*Reflection on the Gospel*

*The two disciples on the road to Emmaus had given up on "Jesus the Nazarene." But the risen Jesus searched them out, walked with them, broke bread with them. Their encounter led them from unbelief to belief. Further, after returning to Jerusalem, their newfound belief is confirmed by a community who attests that "The Lord has truly been raised." We must choose this same journey today, over and over again: encounter the risen Jesus, come to deeper belief, witness to others his risen Presence.*

- *As the two disciples walked with Jesus he explained to them all that had happened. . . . They recognized him in the breaking of the bread. I recognize Jesus . . .*

—*Living Liturgy*™, *Third Sunday of Easter 2017*

ENTRANCE ANTIPHON (Cf. Psalm 66[65]:1-2)
Cry out with joy to God, all the earth;
O sing to the glory of his name.
O render him glorious praise, alleluia.

COLLECT
May your people exult for ever, O God,
in renewed youthfulness of spirit,
so that, rejoicing now in the restored glory of our adoption,
we may look forward in confident hope
to the rejoicing of the day of resurrection.
Through our Lord Jesus Christ, your Son,
who lives and reigns with you in the unity of the Holy Spirit,
one God, for ever and ever. All: **Amen.**

READING I (L 46-A) (Acts of the Apostles 2:14, 22-33)

## A reading from the Acts of the Apostles

*It was impossible for Jesus to be held by death.*

Then Peter stood up with the Eleven,
 raised his voice, and proclaimed:
 "You who are Jews, indeed all of you staying in
  Jerusalem.
Let this be known to you, and listen to my words.
You who are Israelites, hear these words.
Jesus the Nazorean was a man commended to you by God
 with mighty deeds, wonders, and signs,
 which God worked through him in your midst, as you
  yourselves know.
This man, delivered up by the set plan and
  foreknowledge of God,
 you killed, using lawless men to crucify him.
But God raised him up, releasing him from the throes
  of death,
 because it was impossible for him to be held by it.
For David says of him:
 *I saw the Lord ever before me,*
  *with him at my right hand I shall not be disturbed.*

*Therefore my heart has been glad and my tongue has*
  *exulted;*
 *my flesh, too, will dwell in hope,*
*because you will not abandon my soul to the netherworld,*
 *nor will you suffer your holy one to see corruption.*
*You have made known to me the paths of life;*
 *you will fill me with joy in your presence.*

"My brothers, one can confidently say to you
 about the patriarch David that he died and was buried,
 and his tomb is in our midst to this day.
But since he was a prophet and knew that God had
  sworn an oath to him
 that he would set one of his descendants upon his
  throne,
 he foresaw and spoke of the resurrection of the Christ,
 that neither was he abandoned to the netherworld
 nor did his flesh see corruption.
God raised this Jesus;
 of this we are all witnesses.
Exalted at the right hand of God,
 he received the promise of the Holy Spirit from the
  Father
 and poured him forth, as you see and hear."

The word of the Lord. All: Thanks be to God.

RESPONSORIAL PSALM 16

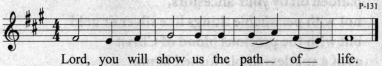

Lord, you will show us the path of life.

Music: Jay F. Hunstiger, © 1993, administered by Liturgical Press. All rights reserved.

Psalm 16:1-2, 5, 7-8, 9-10, 11

R̸. (11a) **Lord, you will show us the path of life.**
 *or:* R̸. **Alleluia.**

 Keep me, O God, for in you I take refuge;
  I say to the LORD, "My Lord are you."

*(continued)*

O Lord, my allotted portion and my cup,
 you it is who hold fast my lot. ℞.

I bless the Lord who counsels me;
 even in the night my heart exhorts me.
I set the Lord ever before me;
 with him at my right hand I shall not be disturbed. ℞.

Therefore my heart is glad and my soul rejoices,
 my body, too, abides in confidence;
because you will not abandon my soul to the netherworld,
 nor will you suffer your faithful one to undergo
  corruption. ℞.

You will show me the path to life,
 abounding joy in your presence,
 the delights at your right hand forever. ℞.

## Reading II (1 Peter 1:17-21)

**A reading from the first Letter of Saint Peter**

*You were saved with the precious Blood of Christ, as with that of*
*a spotless, unblemished lamb.*

**Beloved:**
**If you invoke as Father him who judges impartially**
 **according to each one's works,**
  **conduct yourselves with reverence during the time of**
   **your sojourning,**
  **realizing that you were ransomed from your futile**
   **conduct,**
  **handed on by your ancestors,**
  **not with perishable things like silver or gold**
  **but with the precious blood of Christ**
  **as of a spotless unblemished lamb.**

**He was known before the foundation of the world**
 **but revealed in the final time for you,**
 **who through him believe in God**
 **who raised him from the dead and gave him glory,**
 **so that your faith and hope are in God.**

**The word of the Lord.** All: **Thanks be to God.**

Gospel (Luke 24:13-35)

℣. Alleluia, alleluia.   ℟. **Alleluia, alleluia.**

℣. Lord Jesus, open the Scriptures to us;
    make our hearts burn while you speak to us. ℟.

✝ **A reading from the holy Gospel according to Luke**

All: **Glory to you, O Lord.**

*They recognized Jesus in the breaking of the bread.*

That very day, the first day of the week,
    two of Jesus' disciples were going
    to a village seven miles from Jerusalem called Emmaus,
    and they were conversing about all the things that
        had occurred.
And it happened that while they were conversing and
        debating,
    Jesus himself drew near and walked with them,
    but their eyes were prevented from recognizing him.
He asked them,
    "What are you discussing as you walk along?"
They stopped, looking downcast.
One of them, named Cleopas, said to him in reply,
    "Are you the only visitor to Jerusalem
    who does not know of the things
    that have taken place there in these days?"
And he replied to them, "What sort of things?"
They said to him,
    "The things that happened to Jesus the Nazarene,
    who was a prophet mighty in deed and word
    before God and all the people,
    how our chief priests and rulers both handed him over
    to a sentence of death and crucified him.
But we were hoping that he would be the one to redeem
        Israel;
    and besides all this,
    it is now the third day since this took place.

Some women from our group, however, have astounded
 us:
 they were at the tomb early in the morning
 and did not find his body;
 they came back and reported
 that they had indeed seen a vision of angels
 who announced that he was alive.
Then some of those with us went to the tomb
 and found things just as the women had described,
 but him they did not see."
And he said to them, "Oh, how foolish you are!
How slow of heart to believe all that the prophets spoke!
Was it not necessary that the Christ should suffer these
 things
 and enter into his glory?"
Then beginning with Moses and all the prophets,
 he interpreted to them what referred to him
 in all the Scriptures.
As they approached the village to which they were going,
 he gave the impression that he was going on farther.
But they urged him, "Stay with us,
 for it is nearly evening and the day is almost over."
So he went in to stay with them.
And it happened that, while he was with them at table,
 he took bread, said the blessing,
 broke it, and gave it to them.
With that their eyes were opened and they recognized
 him,
 but he vanished from their sight.
Then they said to each other,
 "Were not our hearts burning within us
 while he spoke to us on the way and opened the
 Scriptures to us?"
So they set out at once and returned to Jerusalem
 where they found gathered together
 the eleven and those with them who were saying,

"The Lord has truly been raised and has appeared to
   Simon!"
Then the two recounted
   what had taken place on the way
   and how he was made known to them in the breaking
      of bread.

The Gospel of the Lord. All: **Praise to you, Lord Jesus Christ.**

### PRAYER OVER THE OFFERINGS

Receive, O Lord, we pray,
these offerings of your exultant Church,
and, as you have given her cause for such great gladness,
grant also that the gifts we bring
may bear fruit in perpetual happiness.
Through Christ our Lord. All: **Amen.**

### COMMUNION ANTIPHON Year A (Luke 24:35)

The disciples recognized the Lord Jesus
in the breaking of the bread, alleluia.

### PRAYER AFTER COMMUNION

Look with kindness upon your people, O Lord,
and grant, we pray,
that those you were pleased to renew by eternal mysteries
may attain in their flesh
the incorruptible glory of the resurrection.
Through Christ our Lord. All: **Amen.**

# Fourth Sunday of Easter

*May 7, 2017*

*Reflection on the Gospel*

*There is only one true Shepherd. We know the true Shepherd from strangers or "thieves and robbers" by the sound of his voice calling each of us by name. The Pharisees refused to listen, refused to be driven to fulfill their true mission to God's people. Unlike the Pharisees, we are to heed our Shepherd's voice driving each of us out personally to continue his saving mission, his voice guiding and leading each of us personally to abundant Life.*

- *Jesus is the Good Shepherd who calls each by name. Lord, . . .*

—Living Liturgy™, *Fourth Sunday of Easter 2017*

ENTRANCE ANTIPHON (Cf. Psalm 33[32]:5-6)
The merciful love of the Lord fills the earth;
by the word of the Lord the heavens were made, alleluia.

COLLECT
Almighty ever-living God,
lead us to a share in the joys of heaven,
so that the humble flock may reach
where the brave Shepherd has gone before.
Who lives and reigns with you in the unity of the Holy Spirit,
one God, for ever and ever. All: **Amen.**

READING I (L 49-A) (Acts of the Apostles 2:14a, 36-41)

## A reading from the Acts of the Apostles

*God has made Jesus both Lord and Christ.*

**Then Peter stood up with the Eleven,
    raised his voice, and proclaimed:
"Let the whole house of Israel know for certain
    that God has made both Lord and Christ,
    this Jesus whom you crucified."**

Now when they heard this, they were cut to the heart,
and they asked Peter and the other apostles,
"What are we to do, my brothers?"
Peter said to them,
"Repent and be baptized, every one of you,
in the name of Jesus Christ for the forgiveness of your
sins;
and you will receive the gift of the Holy Spirit.
For the promise is made to you and to your children
and to all those far off,
whomever the Lord our God will call."
He testified with many other arguments, and was
exhorting them,
"Save yourselves from this corrupt generation."
Those who accepted his message were baptized,
and about three thousand persons were added that day.

The word of the Lord. All: **Thanks be to God.**

RESPONSORIAL PSALM 23

P-132

The Lord is my shep - herd; there is noth - ing I shall want.

Music: Jay F. Hunstiger, © 1990, administered by Liturgical Press. All rights reserved.

Psalm 23:1-3a, 3b-4, 5, 6

℟. (1) **The Lord is my shepherd; there is nothing I shall
want.** *or:* ℟. **Alleluia.**

The LORD is my shepherd; I shall not want.
In verdant pastures he gives me repose;
beside restful waters he leads me;
he refreshes my soul. ℟.

He guides me in right paths
for his name's sake.
Even though I walk in the dark valley
I fear no evil; for you are at my side
with your rod and your staff
that give me courage. ℟.

*(continued)*

You spread the table before me
> in the sight of my foes;
you anoint my head with oil;
> my cup overflows. ℟.

Only goodness and kindness follow me
> all the days of my life;
and I shall dwell in the house of the Lord
> for years to come. ℟.

## READING II (1 Peter 2:20b-25)

**A reading from the first Letter of Saint Peter**

*You have returned to the shepherd and guardian of your souls.*

**Beloved:**
**If you are patient when you suffer for doing what is good,**
> **this is a grace before God.**
**For to this you have been called,**
> **because Christ also suffered for you,**
> > **leaving you an example that you should follow in his**
> > > **footsteps.**

*He committed no sin, and no deceit was found in his mouth.*

**When he was insulted, he returned no insult;**
> **when he suffered, he did not threaten;**
> > **instead, he handed himself over to the one who**
> > > **judges justly.**
**He himself bore our sins in his body upon the cross,**
> **so that, free from sin, we might live for righteousness.**
**By his wounds you have been healed.**
**For you had gone astray like sheep,**
> **but you have now returned to the shepherd and**
> > **guardian of your souls.**

**The word of the Lord.** All: **Thanks be to God.**

## GOSPEL (John 10:1-10)

### ALLELUIA (John 10:14)

℣. Alleluia, alleluia.  ℟. **Alleluia, alleluia.**
℣. I am the good shepherd, says the Lord;
> I know my sheep, and mine know me. ℟.

✝ **A reading from the holy Gospel according to John**

All: **Glory to you, O Lord.**

*I am the gate for the sheep.*

**Jesus said:**
    "Amen, amen, I say to you,
    whoever does not enter a sheepfold through the gate
    but climbs over elsewhere is a thief and a robber.
But whoever enters through the gate is the shepherd of
        the sheep.
The gatekeeper opens it for him, and the sheep hear his
        voice,
    as the shepherd calls his own sheep by name and leads
        them out.
When he has driven out all his own,
    he walks ahead of them, and the sheep follow him,
    because they recognize his voice.
But they will not follow a stranger;
    they will run away from him,
    because they do not recognize the voice of strangers."
Although Jesus used this figure of speech,
    the Pharisees did not realize what he was trying to tell
        them.

So Jesus said again, "Amen, amen, I say to you,
    I am the gate for the sheep.
All who came before me are thieves and robbers,
    but the sheep did not listen to them.
I am the gate.
Whoever enters through me will be saved,
    and will come in and go out and find pasture.
A thief comes only to steal and slaughter and destroy;
    I came so that they might have life and have it more
        abundantly."

The Gospel of the Lord. All: **Praise to you, Lord Jesus Christ.**

### Prayer over the Offerings

Grant, we pray, O Lord,
that we may always find delight in these paschal mysteries,
so that the renewal constantly at work within us
may be the cause of our unending joy.
Through Christ our Lord. All: **Amen.**

### Communion Antiphon

The Good Shepherd has risen,
who laid down his life for his sheep
and willingly died for his flock, alleluia.

### Prayer after Communion

Look upon your flock, kind Shepherd,
and be pleased to settle in eternal pastures
the sheep you have redeemed
by the Precious Blood of your Son.
Who lives and reigns for ever and ever. All: **Amen.**

# Fifth Sunday of Easter

## *May 14, 2017*

*Reflection on the Gospel*

*Jesus says to Thomas, "I am the way and the truth and the life." Jesus is the way: he is the path to the Father. Jesus is the truth: he is the revelation of who God is. Jesus is the life: he is risen Life for all those who believe in him. Believing is "be-living"—surrendering ourselves to him in all we are and in all we do. Through him and with him and in him we become "the way and the truth and the life."*

> • *"I am the way, the truth and the life, says the Lord; no one comes to the Father, except through me." Lord . . .*

—*Living Liturgy*™, *Fifth Sunday of Easter 2017*

(Cf. Psalm 98[97]:1-2)

O sing a new song to the Lord,
for he has worked wonders;
in the sight of the nations
he has shown his deliverance, alleluia.

COLLECT

Almighty ever-living God,
constantly accomplish the Paschal Mystery within us,
that those you were pleased to make new in Holy Baptism
may, under your protective care, bear much fruit
and come to the joys of life eternal.
Through our Lord Jesus Christ, your Son,
who lives and reigns with you in the unity of the Holy Spirit,
one God, for ever and ever. All: **Amen.**

READING I (L 52-A) (Acts of the Apostles 6:1-7)

**A reading from the Acts of the Apostles**

*They chose seven men filled with the Spirit.*

**As the number of disciples continued to grow,**
**the Hellenists complained against the Hebrews**
**because their widows**
**were being neglected in the daily distribution.**
**So the Twelve called together the community of the**
**disciples and said,**
**"It is not right for us to neglect the word of God to**
**serve at table.**
**Brothers, select from among you seven reputable men,**
**filled with the Spirit and wisdom,**
**whom we shall appoint to this task,**
**whereas we shall devote ourselves to prayer**
**and to the ministry of the word."**
**The proposal was acceptable to the whole community,**
**so they chose Stephen, a man filled with faith and the**
**Holy Spirit,**
**also Philip, Prochorus, Nicanor, Timon, Parmenas,**
**and Nicholas of Antioch, a convert to Judaism.**
**They presented these men to the apostles**
**who prayed and laid hands on them.**

**The word of God continued to spread,
and the number of the disciples in Jerusalem
increased greatly;
even a large group of priests were becoming obedient
to the faith.**

**The word of the Lord.** All: **Thanks be to God.**

RESPONSORIAL PSALM 33

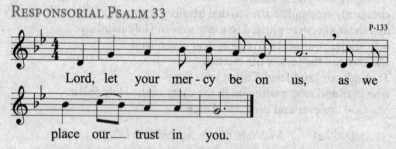

Lord, let your mer-cy be on us, as we
place our trust in you.

Psalm 33:1-2, 4-5, 18-19

R7. (22) **Lord, let your mercy be on us, as we place our
trust in you.** *or:* R7. **Alleluia.**

Exult, you just, in the LORD;
    praise from the upright is fitting.
Give thanks to the LORD on the harp;
    with the ten-stringed lyre chant his praises. R7.

Upright is the word of the LORD,
    and all his works are trustworthy.
He loves justice and right;
    of the kindness of the LORD the earth is full. R7.

See, the eyes of the LORD are upon those who fear him,
    upon those who hope for his kindness,
to deliver them from death
    and preserve them in spite of famine. R7.

READING II (1 Peter 2:4-9)

**A reading from the first Letter of Saint Peter**

*You are a chosen race, a royal priesthood.*

**Beloved:**
**Come to him, a living stone, rejected by human beings**

but chosen and precious in the sight of God,
and, like living stones,
let yourselves be built into a spiritual house
to be a holy priesthood to offer spiritual sacrifices
acceptable to God through Jesus Christ.

For it says in Scripture:
*Behold, I am laying a stone in Zion,*
*a cornerstone, chosen and precious,*
*and whoever believes in it shall not be put to shame.*

Therefore, its value is for you who have faith, but for
those without faith:
*The stone that the builders rejected*
*has become the cornerstone,*
and
*a stone that will make people stumble,*
*and a rock that will make them fall.*

They stumble by disobeying the word, as is their destiny.

You are "a chosen race, a royal priesthood,
a holy nation, a people of his own,
so that you may announce the praises" of him
who called you out of darkness into his wonderful
light.

The word of the Lord. All: Thanks be to God.

GOSPEL (John 14:1-12)
ALLELUIA (John 14:6)
℣. Alleluia, alleluia. ℟. **Alleluia, alleluia.**
℣. I am the way, the truth and the life, says the Lord;
no one comes to the Father, except through me. ℟.

✝ **A reading from the holy Gospel according to John**

All: **Glory to you, O Lord.**

*I am the way and the truth and the life.*

Jesus said to his disciples:
"Do not let your hearts be troubled.
You have faith in God; have faith also in me.

In my Father's house there are many dwelling places.
If there were not,
     would I have told you that I am going to prepare a
          place for you?
And if I go and prepare a place for you,
     I will come back again and take you to myself,
     so that where I am you also may be.
Where I am going you know the way."
Thomas said to him,
     "Master, we do not know where you are going;
     how can we know the way?"
Jesus said to him, "I am the way and the truth and the
     life.
No one comes to the Father except through me.
If you know me, then you will also know my Father.
From now on you do know him and have seen him."
Philip said to him,
     "Master, show us the Father, and that will be enough
          for us."
Jesus said to him, "Have I been with you for so long a
          time
     and you still do not know me, Philip?
Whoever has seen me has seen the Father.
How can you say, 'Show us the Father'?
Do you not believe that I am in the Father and the
          Father is in me?
The words that I speak to you I do not speak on my own.
The Father who dwells in me is doing his works.
Believe me that I am in the Father and the Father is in me,
     or else, believe because of the works themselves.
Amen, amen, I say to you,
     whoever believes in me will do the works that I do,
     and will do greater ones than these,
     because I am going to the Father."

The Gospel of the Lord. All: Praise to you, Lord Jesus Christ.

## PRAYER OVER THE OFFERINGS

O God, who by the wonderful exchange effected in this sacrifice
have made us partakers of the one supreme Godhead,
grant, we pray,
that, as we have come to know your truth,
we may make it ours by a worthy way of life.
Through Christ our Lord. All: **Amen.**

## COMMUNION ANTIPHON (Cf. John 15:1, 5)

I am the true vine and you are the branches, says the Lord.
Whoever remains in me, and I in him, bears fruit in plenty,
  alleluia.

## PRAYER AFTER COMMUNION

Graciously be present to your people, we pray, O Lord,
and lead those you have imbued with heavenly mysteries
to pass from former ways to newness of life.
Through Christ our Lord. All: **Amen.**

# Sixth Sunday of Easter

*May 21, 2017*

*Reflection on the Gospel*

*Jesus' commandments entail much more than doing this or avoiding
that. We keep Jesus' commandments by living his way of life—a life
characterized by deep care for others. His commandments are to love as
he loved, believe as he believed, live as he lived. His commandments are
the most self-engaging and challenging of all! How comforting, then,
when Jesus says, "I will not leave you orphans." No, we are not orphans:
the risen Jesus comes to us. How? In "the Spirit of truth."*

- *"I will ask the Father, and he will give you another Advocate to be
  with you always." Lord . . .*

—*Living Liturgy™, Sixth Sunday of Easter 2017*

ENTRANCE ANTIPHON (Cf. Isaiah 48:20)

Proclaim a joyful sound and let it be heard;
proclaim to the ends of the earth:
The Lord has freed his people, alleluia.

COLLECT

Grant, almighty God,
that we may celebrate with heartfelt devotion these days of joy,
which we keep in honor of the risen Lord,
and that what we relive in remembrance
we may always hold to in what we do.
Through our Lord Jesus Christ, your Son,
who lives and reigns with you in the unity of the Holy Spirit,
one God, for ever and ever. All: **Amen.**

When the Ascension of the Lord is celebrated the following Sunday,
the second reading and Gospel from the Seventh Sunday of Easter
(*See* nos. 59-61) may be read on the Sixth Sunday of Easter.

READING I (L 55-A) (Acts of the Apostles 8:5-8, 14-17)

**A reading from the Acts of the Apostles**

*Peter and John laid hands on them, and they received the
Holy Spirit.*

**Philip went down to the city of Samaria
    and proclaimed the Christ to them.
With one accord, the crowds paid attention to what was
        said by Philip
    when they heard it and saw the signs he was doing.
For unclean spirits, crying out in a loud voice,
    came out of many possessed people,
    and many paralyzed or crippled people were cured.
There was great joy in that city.**

**Now when the apostles in Jerusalem
    heard that Samaria had accepted the word of God,
    they sent them Peter and John,
    who went down and prayed for them,
    that they might receive the Holy Spirit,
    for it had not yet fallen upon any of them;
    they had only been baptized in the name of the
        Lord Jesus.**

**Then they laid hands on them
and they received the Holy Spirit.**

**The word of the Lord.** All: **Thanks be to God.**

RESPONSORIAL PSALM 66

P-134

Let all the earth cry out to God__ with__ joy: Al - le - lu - ia; cry out al - le - lu - ia!

Psalm 66:1-3, 4-5, 6-7, 16, 20

℟. (1) **Let all the earth cry out to God with joy.**
   *or:* ℟. **Alleluia.**

Shout joyfully to God, all the earth,
   sing praise to the glory of his name;
   proclaim his glorious praise.
Say to God, "How tremendous are your deeds!" ℟.

"Let all on earth worship and sing praise to you,
   sing praise to your name!"
Come and see the works of God,
   his tremendous deeds among the children of Adam. ℟.

He has changed the sea into dry land;
   through the river they passed on foot.
   Therefore let us rejoice in him.
He rules by his might forever. ℟.

Hear now, all you who fear God, while I declare
   what he has done for me.
Blessed be God who refused me not
   my prayer or his kindness! ℟.

## Reading II (1 Peter 3:15-18)

**A reading from the first Letter of Saint Peter**

*Put to death in the flesh, Christ was raised to life in the Spirit.*

Beloved:
Sanctify Christ as Lord in your hearts.
Always be ready to give an explanation
    to anyone who asks you for a reason for your hope,
    but do it with gentleness and reverence,
    keeping your conscience clear,
    so that, when you are maligned,
    those who defame your good conduct in Christ
    may themselves be put to shame.
For it is better to suffer for doing good,
    if that be the will of God, than for doing evil.
For Christ also suffered for sins once,
    the righteous for the sake of the unrighteous,
    that he might lead you to God.
Put to death in the flesh,
    he was brought to life in the Spirit.

The word of the Lord. All: **Thanks be to God.**

## Gospel (John 14:15-21)
### Alleluia (John 14:23)

℣. Alleluia, alleluia. ℟. **Alleluia, alleluia.**
℣. Whoever loves me will keep my word, says the Lord,
    and my Father will love him and we will come to him. ℟.

✝ **A reading from the holy Gospel according to John**

All: **Glory to you, O Lord.**

*I will ask the Father and he will give you another Advocate.*

Jesus said to his disciples:
    "If you love me, you will keep my commandments.
And I will ask the Father,
    and he will give you another Advocate to be with you
        always,

the Spirit of truth, whom the world cannot accept,
   because it neither sees nor knows him.
But you know him, because he remains with you,
   and will be in you.
I will not leave you orphans; I will come to you.
In a little while the world will no longer see me,
   but you will see me, because I live and you will live.
On that day you will realize that I am in my Father
   and you are in me and I in you.
Whoever has my commandments and observes them
   is the one who loves me.
And whoever loves me will be loved by my Father,
   and I will love him and reveal myself to him."

**The Gospel of the Lord.** All: **Praise to you, Lord Jesus Christ.**

PRAYER OVER THE OFFERINGS
May our prayers rise up to you, O Lord,
together with the sacrificial offerings,
so that, purified by your graciousness,
we may be conformed to the mysteries of your mighty love.
Through Christ our Lord. All: **Amen.**

COMMUNION ANTIPHON (John 14:15-16)
If you love me, keep my commandments, says the Lord,
and I will ask the Father and he will send you another
   Paraclete,
to abide with you for ever, alleluia.

PRAYER AFTER COMMUNION
Almighty ever-living God,
who restore us to eternal life in the Resurrection of Christ,
increase in us, we pray, the fruits of this paschal Sacrament
and pour into our hearts the strength of this saving food.
Through Christ our Lord. All: **Amen.**

# The Ascension of the Lord

## AT THE VIGIL MASS

### *May 24 or 27, 2017*

This Mass is used on the evening of the day
before the Solemnity, either before or after
First Vespers (Evening Prayer I) of the Ascension.

### Reflection on the Gospel

*It takes us a lifetime of following Jesus and proclaiming his Good News
to learn how gifted we are and what a gift we are to others. What the
disciples hadn't yet come fully to believe was that Jesus would always
remain with them, giving them strength. Through the Spirit. There was
a startling newness to what Jesus was doing and the message he was
conveying. Never before had someone promised the most potent
power—the Holy Spirit who is with us "until the end of the age."*

• *All power in heaven and on earth has been given to me. . . .*

—Living Liturgy™, *Ascension 2017*

ENTRANCE ANTIPHON (Psalm 68[67]:33, 35)
You kingdoms of the earth, sing to God;
praise the Lord, who ascends above the highest heavens;
his majesty and might are in the skies, alleluia.

COLLECT
O God, whose Son today ascended to the heavens
as the Apostles looked on,
grant, we pray, that, in accordance with his promise,
we may be worthy for him to live with us always on earth,
and we with him in heaven.
Who lives and reigns with you in the unity of the Holy Spirit,
one God, for ever and ever. All: **Amen.**

(Readings are those of the day.)

### Prayer over the Offerings

O God, whose Only Begotten Son, our High Priest,
is seated ever-living at your right hand to intercede for us,
grant that we may approach with confidence the throne of grace
and there obtain your mercy.
Through Christ our Lord. All: **Amen.**

### Communion Antiphon (Cf. Hebrews 10:12)

Christ, offering a single sacrifice for sins,
is seated for ever at God's right hand, alleluia.

### Prayer after Communion

May the gifts we have received from your altar, Lord,
kindle in our hearts a longing for the heavenly homeland
and cause us to press forward, following in the Savior's footsteps,
to the place where for our sake he entered before us.
Who lives and reigns for ever and ever. All: **Amen.**

*May 25 or 28*

# AT THE MASS DURING THE DAY

If the feast of the Ascension is celebrated on the Seventh Sunday of
Easter in your diocese, please turn to page 284 for the texts for today.

### Entrance Antiphon (Acts of the Apostles 1:11)

Men of Galilee, why gaze in wonder at the heavens?
This Jesus whom you saw ascending into heaven
will return as you saw him go, alleluia.

### Collect

Gladden us with holy joys, almighty God,
and make us rejoice with devout thanksgiving,
for the Ascension of Christ your Son
is our exaltation,
and, where the Head has gone before in glory,
the Body is called to follow in hope.
Through our Lord Jesus Christ, your Son,
who lives and reigns with you in the unity of the Holy Spirit,
one God, for ever and ever. All: **Amen.**

Or:

Grant, we pray, almighty God,
that we, who believe that your Only Begotten Son, our Redeemer,

ascended this day to the heavens,
may in spirit dwell already in heavenly realms.
Who lives and reigns with you in the unity of the Holy Spirit,
one God, for ever and ever. All: **Amen.**

READING I (L 58-A) (Acts of the Apostles 1:1-11)

## A reading from the beginning of the Acts of the Apostles

*As the Apostles were looking on, Jesus was lifted up.*

**In the first book, Theophilus,**
   **I dealt with all that Jesus did and taught**
   **until the day he was taken up,**
   **after giving instructions through the Holy Spirit**
   **to the apostles whom he had chosen.**
**He presented himself alive to them**
   **by many proofs after he had suffered,**
   **appearing to them during forty days**
   **and speaking about the kingdom of God.**
**While meeting with them,**
   **he enjoined them not to depart from Jerusalem,**
   **but to wait for "the promise of the Father**
   **about which you have heard me speak;**
   **for John baptized with water,**
   **but in a few days you will be baptized with the**
      **Holy Spirit."**

**When they had gathered together they asked him,**
   **"Lord, are you at this time going to restore the**
      **kingdom to Israel?"**
**He answered them, "It is not for you to know the times**
      **or seasons**
   **that the Father has established by his own authority.**
**But you will receive power when the Holy Spirit comes**
      **upon you,**
   **and you will be my witnesses in Jerusalem,**
   **throughout Judea and Samaria,**
   **and to the ends of the earth."**

**When he had said this, as they were looking on,**
**he was lifted up, and a cloud took him from their sight.**
**While they were looking intently at the sky as he was going,**
**suddenly two men dressed in white garments stood**
**beside them.**
**They said, "Men of Galilee,**
**why are you standing there looking at the sky?**
**This Jesus who has been taken up from you into heaven**
**will return in the same way as you have seen him**
**going into heaven."**

**The word of the Lord.** All: **Thanks be to God.**

God mounts his throne to shouts of joy, to shouts of joy.

Music: Jay F. Hunstiger, © 1990, administered by Liturgical Press. All rights reserved.

Psalm 47:2-3, 6-7, 8-9

R⁊. (6) **God mounts his throne to shouts of joy: a blare of**
**trumpets for the Lord.** *or:* R⁊. **Alleluia.**

All you peoples, clap your hands,
shout to God with cries of gladness,
for the LORD, the Most High, the awesome,
is the great king over all the earth. R⁊.

God mounts his throne amid shouts of joy;
the LORD, amid trumpet blasts.
Sing praise to God, sing praise;
sing praise to our king, sing praise. R⁊.

For king of all the earth is God;
sing hymns of praise.
God reigns over the nations,
God sits upon his holy throne. R⁊.

## READING II (Ephesians 1:17-23)

**A reading from the Letter of Saint Paul to the Ephesians**

*God seated Jesus at his right hand in the heavens.*

**Brothers and sisters:**

**May the God of our Lord Jesus Christ, the Father of glory,**
**give you a Spirit of wisdom and revelation**
**resulting in knowledge of him.**

**May the eyes of your hearts be enlightened,**
**that you may know what is the hope that belongs to**
**his call,**
**what are the riches of glory**
**in his inheritance among the holy ones,**
**and what is the surpassing greatness of his power**
**for us who believe,**
**in accord with the exercise of his great might,**
**which he worked in Christ,**
**raising him from the dead**
**and seating him at his right hand in the heavens,**
**far above every principality, authority, power, and**
**dominion,**
**and every name that is named**
**not only in this age but also in the one to come.**

**And he put all things beneath his feet**
**and gave him as head over all things to the church,**
**which is his body,**
**the fullness of the one who fills all things in every way.**

**The word of the Lord. All: Thanks be to God.**

## GOSPEL (Matthew 28:16-20)

ALLELUIA (Matthew 28:19a, 20b)

℣. Alleluia, alleluia. ℟. **Alleluia, alleluia.**

℣. Go and teach all nations, says the Lord;
I am with you always, until the end of the world. ℟.

✛ **A reading from the conclusion of the holy Gospel according to Matthew**

All:  **Glory to you, O Lord.**

*All power in heaven and on earth has been given to me.*

**The eleven disciples went to Galilee,**
>    **to the mountain to which Jesus had ordered them.**
**When they saw him, they worshiped, but they doubted.**
**Then Jesus approached and said to them,**
>    **"All power in heaven and on earth has been given to me.**
**Go, therefore, and make disciples of all nations,**
>    **baptizing them in the name of the Father,**
>    **and of the Son, and of the Holy Spirit,**
>    **teaching them to observe all that I have commanded**
>        **you.**
**And behold, I am with you always, until the end of the age."**

**The Gospel of the Lord.** All:  **Praise to you, Lord Jesus Christ.**

PRAYER OVER THE OFFERINGS
We offer sacrifice now in supplication, O Lord,
to honor the wondrous Ascension of your Son:
grant, we pray,
that through this most holy exchange
we, too, may rise up to the heavenly realms.
Through Christ our Lord. All:  **Amen.**

COMMUNION ANTIPHON (Matthew 28:20)
Behold, I am with you always,
even to the end of the age, alleluia.

PRAYER AFTER COMMUNION
Almighty ever-living God,
who allow those on earth to celebrate divine mysteries,
grant, we pray,
that Christian hope may draw us onward
to where our nature is united with you.
Through Christ our Lord. All:  **Amen.**

# Seventh Sunday of Easter

*May 28, 2017*

If the feast of the Ascension is celebrated on the Seventh Sunday of Easter in your diocese, please turn to page 279 for the texts for the feast of the ASCENSION.

*Reflection on the Gospel*

*This gospel is ultimately about the mutual giving between Jesus and the Father, and our being called into the same Life of mutual self-giving, into their Life of glory. We are to give ourselves to God and one another in love and service. In this is God's glory and ours. God is glorified by Jesus' work of salvation. Jesus is glorified by those who hear and accept his words, believe in him, and continue his saving mission. By our glorifying Jesus, God glorifies us and gives us "eternal life."*

- *While in the world, yet sharing in the glory of God, our mission is . . .*

—*Living Liturgy*™, *Seventh Sunday of Easter 2017*

## ENTRANCE ANTIPHON (Cf. Psalm 27[26]:7-9)

O Lord, hear my voice, for I have called to you;
of you my heart has spoken: Seek his face;
hide not your face from me, alleluia.

## COLLECT

Graciously hear our supplications, O Lord,
so that we, who believe that the Savior of the human race
is with you in your glory,
may experience, as he promised,
until the end of the world,
his abiding presence among us.
Who lives and reigns with you in the unity of the Holy Spirit,
one God, for ever and ever. All: **Amen.**

In those places where the Solemnity of the Ascension of the Lord has been transferred to the Seventh Sunday of Easter, the Mass and readings of the Ascension are used. *See* page 279.

Reading I (L 59-A) (Acts of the Apostles 1:12-14)

## A reading from the Acts of the Apostles

*All these devoted themselves with one accord to prayer.*

After Jesus had been taken up to heaven the apostles
returned to Jerusalem
from the mount called Olivet, which is near Jerusalem,
a sabbath day's journey away.

When they entered the city
they went to the upper room where they were staying,
Peter and John and James and Andrew,
Philip and Thomas, Bartholomew and Matthew,
James son of Alphaeus, Simon the Zealot,
and Judas son of James.

All these devoted themselves with one accord to prayer,
together with some women,
and Mary the mother of Jesus, and his brothers.

**The word of the Lord.** All: **Thanks be to God.**

Responsorial Psalm 27

P-136

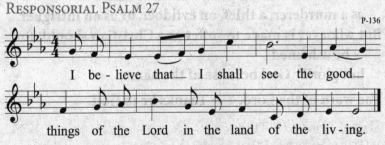

I be-lieve that I shall see the good things of the Lord in the land of the liv-ing.

Psalm 27:1, 4, 7-8

R̥. (13) **I believe that I shall see the good things of the Lord in the land of the living.** *or:* R̥. **Alleluia.**

The LORD is my light and my salvation;
whom should I fear?
The LORD is my life's refuge;
of whom should I be afraid? R̥.

One thing I ask of the LORD;
this I seek:

*(continued)*

To dwell in the house of the L&#7424;&#7424;&#7424;
    all the days of my life,
that I may gaze on the loveliness of the L&#7424;&#7424;&#7424;
    and contemplate his temple. ℟.

Hear, O L&#7424;&#7424;&#7424;, the sound of my call;
    have pity on me, and answer me.
Of you my heart speaks; you my glance seeks. ℟.

## READING II (1 Peter 4:13-16)

**A reading from the first Letter of Saint Peter**

*If you are insulted for the name of Christ, blessed are you.*

**Beloved:**
**Rejoice to the extent that you share in the sufferings of**
    **Christ,**
    **so that when his glory is revealed**
    **you may also rejoice exultantly.**
**If you are insulted for the name of Christ, blessed are you,**
    **for the Spirit of glory and of God rests upon you.**
**But let no one among you be made to suffer**
    **as a murderer, a thief, an evildoer, or as an intriguer.**
**But whoever is made to suffer as a Christian should not**
    **be ashamed**
    **but glorify God because of the name.**

**The word of the Lord.** All: **Thanks be to God.**

## GOSPEL (John 17:1-11a)

ALLELUIA (*See* John 14:18)

℣. Alleluia, alleluia. ℟. **Alleluia, alleluia.**
℣. I will not leave you orphans, says the Lord.
    I will come back to you, and your hearts will rejoice. ℟.

✠ **A reading from the holy Gospel according to John**

All: **Glory to you, O Lord.**

*Father, glorify your Son.*

**Jesus raised his eyes to heaven and said,**
    **"Father, the hour has come.**

Give glory to your son, so that your son may glorify you,
>> just as you gave him authority over all people,
>>> so that your son may give eternal life to all you gave
>>>> him.

Now this is eternal life,
>> that they should know you, the only true God,
>> and the one whom you sent, Jesus Christ.

I glorified you on earth
>> by accomplishing the work that you gave me to do.

Now glorify me, Father, with you,
>> with the glory that I had with you before the world
>>> began.

"I revealed your name to those whom you gave me out
>>> of the world.

They belonged to you, and you gave them to me,
>> and they have kept your word.

Now they know that everything you gave me is from you,
>> because the words you gave to me I have given to them,
>> and they accepted them and truly understood that I
>>> came from you,
>> and they have believed that you sent me.

I pray for them.

I do not pray for the world but for the ones you have
>>> given me,
>> because they are yours, and everything of mine is yours
>> and everything of yours is mine,
>> and I have been glorified in them.

And now I will no longer be in the world,
>> but they are in the world, while I am coming to you."

The Gospel of the Lord. All: **Praise to you, Lord Jesus Christ.**

PRAYER OVER THE OFFERINGS
Accept, O Lord, the prayers of your faithful
with the sacrificial offerings,
that through these acts of devotedness
we may pass over to the glory of heaven.
Through Christ our Lord. All: **Amen.**

Father, I pray that they may be one
as we also are one, alleluia.

PRAYER AFTER COMMUNION
Hear us, O God our Savior,
and grant us confidence,
that through these sacred mysteries
there will be accomplished in the body of the whole Church
what has already come to pass in Christ her Head.
Who lives and reigns for ever and ever. All: **Amen.**

# Pentecost Sunday

## VIGIL MASS  Simple Form

*June 3, 2017*

The Mass of the Vigil of Pentecost is used on Saturday evening in
those places where the Sunday obligation may be fulfilled on
Saturday evening.

ENTRANCE ANTIPHON (Romans 5:5; cf. 8:11)
The love of God has been poured into our hearts
through the Spirit of God dwelling within us, alleluia.

COLLECT
Almighty ever-living God,
who willed the Paschal Mystery
to be encompassed as a sign in fifty days,
grant that from out of the scattered nations
the confusion of many tongues
may be gathered by heavenly grace
into one great confession of your name.
Through our Lord Jesus Christ, your Son,
who lives and reigns with you in the unity of the Holy Spirit,
one God, for ever and ever. All: **Amen.**

Or:

Grant, we pray, almighty God,
that the splendor of your glory
may shine forth upon us
and that, by the bright rays of the Holy Spirit,
the light of your light may confirm the hearts
of those born again by your grace.
Through our Lord Jesus Christ, your Son,
who lives and reigns with you in the unity of the Holy Spirit,
one God, for ever and ever. All: **Amen.**

These readings are used at Saturday Evening Mass celebrated either
before or after Evening Prayer I of Pentecost Sunday. The first of four
options for the First Reading for this Mass is given here. Please see
the others in the lectionary: Exodus 19:3-8a, 16-20b; Ezekiel 37:1-14;
or Joel 3:1-5.

## READING I (L 62) *A* (Genesis 11:1-9)

### A reading from the Book of Genesis

*It was called Babel because there the Lord confused the speech of
all the world.*

**The whole world spoke the same language, using the
same words.
While the people were migrating in the east,
they came upon a valley in the land of Shinar and
settled there.
They said to one another,
"Come, let us mold bricks and harden them with fire."
They used bricks for stone, and bitumen for mortar.
Then they said, "Come, let us build ourselves a city
and a tower with its top in the sky,
and so make a name for ourselves;
otherwise we shall be scattered all over the earth."
The LORD came down to see the city and the tower
that the people had built.
Then the LORD said: "If now, while they are one people,
all speaking the same language,
they have started to do this,
nothing will later stop them from doing whatever they
presume to do.**

Let us then go down there and confuse their language,
  so that one will not understand what another says."
Thus the LORD scattered them from there all over the earth,
  and they stopped building the city.
That is why it was called Babel,
  because there the LORD confused the speech of all the
    world.
It was from that place that he scattered them all over the
  earth.

The word of the Lord. All: Thanks be to God.

RESPONSORIAL PSALM 104

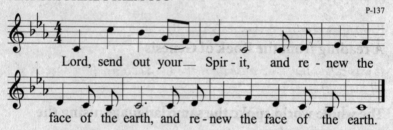

P-137

Lord, send out your Spir-it, and re-new the face of the earth, and re-new the face of the earth.

Psalm 104:1-2, 24, 35, 27-28, 29, 30

℟. (*See* 30) **Lord, send out your Spirit, and renew the face
  of the earth.** *or:* ℟. **Alleluia.**

Bless the LORD, O my soul!
  O LORD, my God, you are great indeed!
You are clothed with majesty and glory,
  robed in light as with a cloak. ℟.

How manifold are your works, O LORD!
  In wisdom you have wrought them all—
the earth is full of your creatures;
  bless the LORD, O my soul! Alleluia. ℟.

Creatures all look to you
  to give them food in due time.
When you give it to them, they gather it;
  when you open your hand, they are filled with good
    things. ℟.

If you take away their breath, they perish
and return to their dust.
When you send forth your spirit, they are created,
and you renew the face of the earth. ℟.

## READING II (Romans 8:22-27)

**A reading from the Letter of Saint Paul to the Romans**

*The Spirit intercedes with inexpressible groanings.*

**Brothers and sisters:**
**We know that all creation is groaning in labor pains**
**even until now;**
**and not only that, but we ourselves,**
**who have the firstfruits of the Spirit,**
**we also groan within ourselves**
**as we wait for adoption, the redemption of our bodies.**
**For in hope we were saved.**
**Now hope that sees is not hope.**
**For who hopes for what one sees?**
**But if we hope for what we do not see, we wait with**
**endurance.**

**In the same way, the Spirit too comes to the aid of our**
**weakness;**
**for we do not know how to pray as we ought,**
**but the Spirit himself intercedes with inexpressible**
**groanings.**
**And the one who searches hearts**
**knows what is the intention of the Spirit,**
**because he intercedes for the holy ones**
**according to God's will.**

**The word of the Lord.** All: **Thanks be to God.**

## GOSPEL (John 7:37-39)

ALLELUIA

℣. Alleluia, alleluia. ℟. **Alleluia, alleluia.**
℣. Come, Holy Spirit, fill the hearts of the faithful
and kindle in them the fire of your love. ℟.

✠ **A reading from the holy Gospel according to John**

All: **Glory to you, O Lord.**

*Rivers of living water will flow.*

**On the last and greatest day of the feast,**
　　**Jesus stood up and exclaimed,**
　　**"Let anyone who thirsts come to me and drink.**
**As Scripture says:**
　　***Rivers of living water will flow from within him* who**
　　　　**believes in me."**

**He said this in reference to the Spirit**
　　**that those who came to believe in him were to receive.**
**There was, of course, no Spirit yet,**
　　**because Jesus had not yet been glorified.**

**The Gospel of the Lord.** All: **Praise to you, Lord Jesus Christ.**

PRAYER OVER THE OFFERINGS
Pour out upon these gifts the blessing of your Spirit,
we pray, O Lord,
so that through them your Church may be imbued with such love
that the truth of your saving mystery
may shine forth for the whole world.
Through Christ our Lord. All: **Amen.**

COMMUNION ANTIPHON (John 7:37)
On the last day of the festival, Jesus stood and cried out:
If anyone is thirsty, let him come to me and drink, alleluia.

PRAYER AFTER COMMUNION
May these gifts we have consumed
benefit us, O Lord,
that we may always be aflame with the same Spirit,
whom you wondrously poured out on your Apostles.
Through Christ our Lord. All: **Amen.**

DISMISSAL
To dismiss the people the Deacon or, if there is no Deacon, the Priest himself
sings or says:

**Go forth, the Mass is ended, alleluia, alleluia.**

Or:

Go in peace, alleluia, alleluia.
All reply: **Thanks be to God, alleluia, alleluia.**

## June 4

# MASS DURING THE DAY

*Reflection on the Gospel*

*In John's gospel Pentecost takes place on Easter evening. The giving of new Life on Easter and the giving of the Spirit on Pentecost coalesce in the one Body of Christ, the church. This Body is filled with the joy of divine Presence, the grace of risen peace, the eagerness of being sent forth, the breath of new creation, the power of forgiveness. Each day when we—Christ's Body, the church—allow the Holy Spirit to work in and through us, Easter-Pentecost happens anew.*

  • *Jesus breathed on them and gave them his peace. The peace of the Lord . . .*

—Living Liturgy™, *Pentecost 2017*

ENTRANCE ANTIPHON (Wisdom 1:7)

The Spirit of the Lord has filled the whole world
and that which contains all things
understands what is said, alleluia.

Or:

(Romans 5:5; cf. 8:11)

The love of God has been poured into our hearts
through the Spirit of God dwelling within us, alleluia.

COLLECT

O God, who by the mystery of today's great feast
sanctify your whole Church in every people and nation,
pour out, we pray, the gifts of the Holy Spirit
across the face of the earth
and, with the divine grace that was at work
when the Gospel was first proclaimed,
fill now once more the hearts of believers.
Through our Lord Jesus Christ, your Son,
who lives and reigns with you in the unity of the Holy Spirit,
one God, for ever and ever. All: **Amen.**

READING I (L 63) (Acts of the Apostles 2:1-11)

## A reading from the Acts of the Apostles

*They were all filled with the Holy Spirit and began to speak.*

When the time for Pentecost was fulfilled,
  they were all in one place together.
And suddenly there came from the sky
  a noise like a strong driving wind,
  and it filled the entire house in which they were.
Then there appeared to them tongues as of fire,
  which parted and came to rest on each one of them.
And they were all filled with the Holy Spirit
  and began to speak in different tongues,
  as the Spirit enabled them to proclaim.

Now there were devout Jews from every nation under
    heaven staying in Jerusalem.
At this sound, they gathered in a large crowd,
  but they were confused
  because each one heard them speaking in his own
    language.
They were astounded, and in amazement they asked,
  "Are not all these people who are speaking Galileans?
Then how does each of us hear them in his native language?
We are Parthians, Medes, and Elamites,
  inhabitants of Mesopotamia, Judea and Cappadocia,
  Pontus and Asia, Phrygia and Pamphylia,
  Egypt and the districts of Libya near Cyrene,
  as well as travelers from Rome,
  both Jews and converts to Judaism, Cretans and Arabs,
  yet we hear them speaking in our own tongues
  of the mighty acts of God."

The word of the Lord. All: Thanks be to God.

## RESPONSORIAL PSALM 104

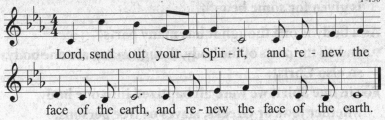

Lord, send out your Spir-it, and re-new the face of the earth, and re-new the face of the earth.

Psalm 104:1, 24, 29-30, 31, 34

℟. (*See* 30) **Lord, send out your Spirit, and renew the face of the earth.** *or:* ℟. **Alleluia.**

Bless the LORD, O my soul!
    O LORD, my God, you are great indeed!
How manifold are your works, O LORD!
    The earth is full of your creatures. ℟.

If you take away their breath, they perish
    and return to their dust.
When you send forth your spirit, they are created,
    and you renew the face of the earth. ℟.

May the glory of the LORD endure forever;
    may the LORD be glad in his works!
Pleasing to him be my theme;
    I will be glad in the LORD. ℟.

## READING II (1 Corinthians 12:3b-7, 12-13)

**A reading from the first Letter of Saint Paul to the Corinthians**

*In one Spirit we were all baptized into one body.*

**Brothers and sisters:**
**No one can say, "Jesus is Lord," except by the Holy Spirit.**

**There are different kinds of spiritual gifts but the same Spirit;**
    **there are different forms of service but the same Lord;**
    **there are different workings but the same God**
    **who produces all of them in everyone.**

To each individual the manifestation of the Spirit
   is given for some benefit.

As a body is one though it has many parts,
   and all the parts of the body, though many, are one body,
   so also Christ.
For in one Spirit we were all baptized into one body,
   whether Jews or Greeks, slaves or free persons,
   and we were all given to drink of one Spirit.

The word of the Lord. All: Thanks be to God.

## SEQUENCE
*Veni, Sancte Spiritus*

Come, Holy Spirit, come!
And from your celestial home
   Shed a ray of light divine!
Come, Father of the poor!
Come, source of all our store!
   Come, within our bosoms shine.
You, of comforters the best;
You, the soul's most welcome guest;
   Sweet refreshment here below;
In our labor, rest most sweet;
Grateful coolness in the heat;
   Solace in the midst of woe.
O most blessed Light divine,
Shine within these hearts of yours,
   And our inmost being fill!
Where you are not, we have naught,
Nothing good in deed or thought,
   Nothing free from taint of ill.
Heal our wounds, our strength renew;
On our dryness pour your dew;
   Wash the stains of guilt away:
Bend the stubborn heart and will;
Melt the frozen, warm the chill;
   Guide the steps that go astray.

On the faithful, who adore
And confess you, evermore
   In your sevenfold gift descend;
Give them virtue's sure reward;
Give them your salvation, Lord;
   Give them joys that never end. Amen.
   Alleluia.

GOSPEL (John 20:19-23)
ALLELUIA
℣. Alleluia, alleluia. ℟. **Alleluia, alleluia.**
℣. Come, Holy Spirit, fill the hearts of your faithful
   and kindle in them the fire of your love. ℟.

✠ **A reading from the holy Gospel according to John**

All: **Glory to you, O Lord.**

*As the Father sent me, so I send you. Receive the Holy Spirit.*

On the evening of that first day of the week,
   when the doors were locked, where the disciples were,
     for fear of the Jews,
   Jesus came and stood in their midst
   and said to them, "Peace be with you."
When he had said this, he showed them his hands and
     his side.
The disciples rejoiced when they saw the Lord.
Jesus said to them again, "Peace be with you.
As the Father has sent me, so I send you."
And when he had said this, he breathed on them and
     said to them,
   "Receive the Holy Spirit.
Whose sins you forgive are forgiven them,
   and whose sins you retain are retained."

The Gospel of the Lord. All: **Praise to you, Lord Jesus Christ.**

If it is customary or obligatory for the faithful to attend Mass on
the Monday or even the Tuesday after Pentecost, the readings from
the Mass of Pentecost Sunday may be repeated or the readings of the
Ritual Mass for Confirmation, nos. 764–768, may be used in its place.

PRAYER OVER THE OFFERINGS

Grant, we pray, O Lord,
that, as promised by your Son,
the Holy Spirit may reveal to us more abundantly
the hidden mystery of this sacrifice
and graciously lead us into all truth.
Through Christ our Lord. All: **Amen.**

COMMUNION ANTIPHON (Acts of the Apostles 2:4, 11)

They were all filled with the Holy Spirit
and spoke of the marvels of God, alleluia.

PRAYER AFTER COMMUNION

O God, who bestow heavenly gifts upon your Church,
safeguard, we pray, the grace you have given,
that the gift of the Holy Spirit poured out upon her
may retain all its force
and that this spiritual food
may gain her abundance of eternal redemption.
Through Christ our Lord. All: **Amen.**

DISMISSAL

To dismiss the people the Deacon or, if there is no Deacon, the Priest himself
sings or says:

Go forth, the Mass is ended, alleluia, alleluia.

Or:

Go in peace, alleluia, alleluia.
All reply: **Thanks be to God, alleluia, alleluia.**

# The Most Holy Trinity

*June 11, 2017*

*Reflection on the Gospel*

*We are destined to be with God now and forever. God chose to create and redeem humanity in an unequaled act of love. In an unparalleled act of love God sent the Son so that we might have Life. Divine Life and love extend beyond the inner intimacy of the three Persons of the Holy Trinity to us in an eternal, shared love-dance drawing us toward a fuller share in God. This is salvation: a share in God, in God's Life and love for all eternity.*

• *God sent his Son, that the world might be saved through . . .*

—Living Liturgy™, *Trinity Sunday 2017*

## Entrance Antiphon

Blest be God the Father,
and the Only Begotten Son of God,
and also the Holy Spirit,
for he has shown us his merciful love.

## Collect

God our Father, who by sending into the world
the Word of truth and the Spirit of sanctification
made known to the human race your wondrous mystery,
grant us, we pray, that in professing the true faith,
we may acknowledge the Trinity of eternal glory
and adore your Unity, powerful in majesty.
Through our Lord Jesus Christ, your Son,
who lives and reigns with you in the unity of the Holy Spirit,
one God, for ever and ever. All: **Amen.**

## Reading I (L 164-A) (Exodus 34:4b-6, 8-9)

**A reading from the Book of Exodus**

*The Lord, the Lord, a merciful and gracious God.*

Early in the morning Moses went up Mount Sinai
   as the Lord had commanded him,
   taking along the two stone tablets.

Having come down in a cloud, the Lord stood with
    Moses there
   and proclaimed his name, "Lord."
Thus the Lord passed before him and cried out,
   "The Lord, the Lord, a merciful and gracious God,
   slow to anger and rich in kindness and fidelity."
Moses at once bowed down to the ground in worship.
Then he said, "If I find favor with you, O Lord,
   do come along in our company.
This is indeed a stiff-necked people;
   yet pardon our wickedness and sins,
   and receive us as your own."

The word of the Lord. All: **Thanks be to God.**

## Responsorial Psalm (Daniel 3)

P-172

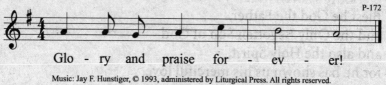

Glo - ry and praise for - ev - er!

Daniel 3:52, 53, 54, 55, 56

℟. (52b) **Glory and praise forever!**

Blessed are you, O Lord, the God of our fathers,
   praiseworthy and exalted above all forever;
and blessed is your holy and glorious name,
   praiseworthy and exalted above all for all ages. ℟.

Blessed are you in the temple of your holy glory,
   praiseworthy and glorious above all forever. ℟.

Blessed are you on the throne of your kingdom,
    praiseworthy and exalted above all forever. ℟.

Blessed are you who look into the depths
    from your throne upon the cherubim,
    praiseworthy and exalted above all forever. ℟.

READING II (2 Corinthians 13:11-13)

**A reading from the second Letter of Saint Paul to the Corinthians**

*The grace of Jesus Christ and the love of God and the fellowship of the Holy Spirit.*

**Brothers and sisters, rejoice. Mend your ways, encourage
    one another,**
    **agree with one another, live in peace,**
    **and the God of love and peace will be with you.**
**Greet one another with a holy kiss.**
**All the holy ones greet you.**

**The grace of the Lord Jesus Christ**
    **and the love of God**
    **and the fellowship of the Holy Spirit be with all of you.**

**The word of the Lord.** All: **Thanks be to God.**

GOSPEL (John 3:16-18)
ALLELUIA (*See* Revelation 1:8)
℣. Alleluia, alleluia. ℟. **Alleluia, alleluia.**
℣. Glory to the Father, the Son, and the Holy Spirit;
    to God who is, who was, and who is to come. ℟.

✢ **A reading from the holy Gospel according to John**

All: **Glory to you, O Lord.**

*God sent his Son, that the world might be saved through him.*

**God so loved the world that he gave his only Son,**
    **so that everyone who believes in him might not perish**
    **but might have eternal life.**
**For God did not send his Son into the world to condemn**
    **the world,**
    **but that the world might be saved through him.**

**Whoever believes in him will not be condemned,**
**but whoever does not believe has already been**
**condemned,**
**because he has not believed in the name of the only**
**Son of God.**

**The Gospel of the Lord.** All: **Praise to you, Lord Jesus Christ.**

PRAYER OVER THE OFFERINGS
Sanctify by the invocation of your name,
we pray, O Lord our God,
this oblation of our service,
and by it make of us an eternal offering to you.
Through Christ our Lord. All: **Amen.**

COMMUNION ANTIPHON (Galatians 4:6)
Since you are children of God,
God has sent into your hearts the Spirit of his Son,
the Spirit who cries out: Abba, Father.

PRAYER AFTER COMMUNION
May receiving this Sacrament, O Lord our God,
bring us health of body and soul,
as we confess your eternal holy Trinity and undivided Unity.
Through Christ our Lord. All: **Amen.**

# The Most Holy Body and Blood of Christ (Corpus Christi)

*June 18, 2017*

---

## Reflection on the Gospel

*Jesus giving himself as living bread is a foretaste of the Life that one day we will share eternally with him. When we eat this bread we "will live forever." Heaven is above. Forever beyond. Life is fleeting. But Life eternal is here and now in Jesus, "the living bread." We who eat his flesh and drink his blood have eternal Life now. Heaven is not above. Forever is not beyond. Life is not fleeting. Because Jesus is living bread.*

- *The bread is one, and we, though many, are one body. . . .*

—Living Liturgy™, *Body and Blood of Christ 2017*

## ENTRANCE ANTIPHON (Cf. Psalm 81[80]:17)

He fed them with the finest wheat
and satisfied them with honey from the rock.

## COLLECT

O God, who in this wonderful Sacrament
have left us a memorial of your Passion,
grant us, we pray,
so to revere the sacred mysteries of your Body and Blood
that we may always experience in ourselves
the fruits of your redemption.
Who live and reign with God the Father
in the unity of the Holy Spirit,
one God, for ever and ever. All: **Amen.**

## READING I (L 167-A) (Deuteronomy 8:2-3, 14b-16a)

### A reading from the Book of Deuteronomy

*He gave you a food unknown to you and your fathers.*

Moses said to the people:

"Remember how for forty years now the LORD,
your God,
has directed all your journeying in the desert,
so as to test you by affliction
and find out whether or not it was your intention
to keep his commandments.
He therefore let you be afflicted with hunger,
and then fed you with manna,
a food unknown to you and your fathers,
in order to show you that not by bread alone does
one live,
but by every word that comes forth from the mouth
of the LORD.

"Do not forget the Lord, your God,
who brought you out of the land of Egypt,
that place of slavery;
who guided you through the vast and terrible desert
with its saraph serpents and scorpions,
its parched and waterless ground;
who brought forth water for you from the flinty rock
and fed you in the desert with manna,
a food unknown to your fathers."

The word of the Lord. All: Thanks be to God.

RESPONSORIAL PSALM 147

P-173

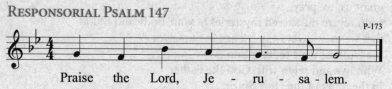

Praise    the    Lord,    Je  -  ru  -  sa - lem.

Psalm 147:12-13, 14-15, 19-20

R⁷. (12) **Praise the Lord, Jerusalem.** *or:* R⁷. **Alleluia.**

Glorify the LORD, O Jerusalem;
praise your God, O Zion.

For he has strengthened the bars of your gates;
>   he has blessed your children within you. R̸.

He has granted peace in your borders;
>   with the best of wheat he fills you.

He sends forth his command to the earth;
>   swiftly runs his word! R̸.

He has proclaimed his word to Jacob,
>   his statutes and his ordinances to Israel.

He has not done thus for any other nation;
>   his ordinances he has not made known to them.
>>   Alleluia. R̸.

## READING II (1 Corinthians 10:16-17)

**A reading from the first Letter of Saint Paul to the Corinthians**

*The bread is one, and we, though many, are one body.*

**Brothers and sisters:**

**The cup of blessing that we bless,**
>   **is it not a participation in the blood of Christ?**

**The bread that we break,**
>   **is it not a participation in the body of Christ?**

**Because the loaf of bread is one,**
>   **we, though many, are one body,**
>   **for we all partake of the one loaf.**

**The word of the Lord.** All: **Thanks be to God.**

## SEQUENCE
*Lauda Sion*

The sequence *Laud, O Zion (Lauda Sion)*, or the shorter form beginning with the verse *Lo! the angel's food is given*, may be sung optionally before the Alleluia.

**Laud, O Zion, your salvation,**
**Laud with hymns of exultation,**
>   **Christ, your king and shepherd true:**

**Bring him all the praise you know,**
**He is more than you bestow.**
>   **Never can you reach his due.**

Special theme for glad thanksgiving
Is the quick'ning and the living
   Bread today before you set:

From his hands of old partaken,
As we know, by faith unshaken,
   Where the Twelve at supper met.

Full and clear ring out your chanting,
Joy nor sweetest grace be wanting,
   From your heart let praises burst:

For today the feast is holden,
When the institution olden
   Of that supper was rehearsed.

Here the new law's new oblation,
By the new king's revelation,
   Ends the form of ancient rite:

Now the new the old effaces,
Truth away the shadow chases,
   Light dispels the gloom of night.

What he did at supper seated,
Christ ordained to be repeated,
   His memorial ne'er to cease:

And his rule for guidance taking,
Bread and wine we hallow, making
   Thus our sacrifice of peace.

This the truth each Christian learns,
Bread into his flesh he turns,
   To his precious blood the wine:

Sight has fail'd, nor thought conceives,
But a dauntless faith believes,
   Resting on a pow'r divine.

Here beneath these signs are hidden
Priceless things to sense forbidden;
   Signs, not things are all we see:

Blood is poured and flesh is broken,
Yet in either wondrous token
   Christ entire we know to be.

Whoso of this food partakes,
Does not rend the Lord nor breaks;
   Christ is whole to all that taste:

Thousands are, as one, receivers,
One, as thousands of believers,
   Eats of him who cannot waste.

Bad and good the feast are sharing,
Of what divers dooms preparing,
   Endless death, or endless life.

Life to these, to those damnation,
See how like participation
   Is with unlike issues rife.

When the sacrament is broken,
Doubt not, but believe 'tis spoken,
   That each sever'd outward token
      doth the very whole contain.

Nought the precious gift divides,
Breaking but the sign betides
   Jesus still the same abides,
      still unbroken does remain.

*The shorter form of the sequence begins here.*

Lo! the angel's food is given
To the pilgrim who has striven;
   See the children's bread from heaven,
      which on dogs may not be spent.

Truth the ancient types fulfilling,
Isaac bound, a victim willing,
   Paschal lamb, its lifeblood spilling,
      manna to the fathers sent.

Very bread, good shepherd, tend us,
Jesu, of your love befriend us,
　　You refresh us, you defend us,
　　Your eternal goodness send us
In the land of life to see.

You who all things can and know,
Who on earth such food bestow,
　　Grant us with your saints, though lowest,
　　Where the heav'nly feast you show,
Fellow heirs and guests to be. Amen. Alleluia.

GOSPEL (John 6:51-58)
ALLELUIA (John 6:51)
℣. Alleluia, alleluia.　℟. **Alleluia, alleluia.**
℣. I am the living bread that came down from heaven,
　　　　says the Lord;
　whoever eats this bread will live forever. ℟.

✛ **A reading from the holy Gospel according to John**

All: **Glory to you, O Lord.**

*My flesh is true food, and my blood is true drink.*

Jesus said to the Jewish crowds:
　　"I am the living bread that came down from heaven;
　　whoever eats this bread will live forever;
　　and the bread that I will give
　　is my flesh for the life of the world."

The Jews quarreled among themselves, saying,
　　"How can this man give us his flesh to eat?"
Jesus said to them,
　　"Amen, amen, I say to you,
　　unless you eat the flesh of the Son of Man and drink
　　　　his blood,
　　you do not have life within you.
Whoever eats my flesh and drinks my blood
　　has eternal life,
　　and I will raise him on the last day.

For my flesh is true food,
and my blood is true drink.
Whoever eats my flesh and drinks my blood
remains in me and I in him.
Just as the living Father sent me
and I have life because of the Father,
so also the one who feeds on me
will have life because of me.
This is the bread that came down from heaven.
Unlike your ancestors who ate and still died,
whoever eats this bread will live forever."

**The Gospel of the Lord.** All: **Praise to you, Lord Jesus Christ.**

PRAYER OVER THE OFFERINGS
Grant your Church, O Lord, we pray,
the gifts of unity and peace,
whose signs are to be seen in mystery
in the offerings we here present.
Through Christ our Lord. All: **Amen.**

COMMUNION ANTIPHON (John 6:57)
Whoever eats my flesh and drinks my blood
remains in me and I in him, says the Lord.

PRAYER AFTER COMMUNION
Grant, O Lord, we pray,
that we may delight for all eternity
in that share in your divine life,
which is foreshadowed in the present age
by our reception of your precious Body and Blood.
Who live and reign for ever and ever. All: **Amen.**

# Twelfth Sunday in Ordinary Time

*June 25, 2017*

*Reflection on the Gospel*

*Jesus begins with the bold statement, "Fear no one." Yet, in the next breath he tells us to "be afraid of the one who can destroy / both soul and body." Does Jesus contradict himself? No, not really. He is helping us sort out fear. We need not fear when we choose to live and "speak in the light" and acknowledge Jesus as Lord. We do need to fear when we choose infidelity and denial of Jesus in any form. Fearless or fearful? Which does our daily choosing reveal?*

• *The gift is not like the transgression. . . .*

—Living Liturgy™, *Twelfth Sunday in Ordinary Time 2017*

## ENTRANCE ANTIPHON (Cf. Psalm 28[27]:8-9)

The Lord is the strength of his people,
a saving refuge for the one he has anointed.
Save your people, Lord, and bless your heritage,
and govern them for ever.

## COLLECT

Grant, O Lord,
that we may always revere and love your holy name,
for you never deprive of your guidance
those you set firm on the foundation of your love.
Through our Lord Jesus Christ, your Son,
who lives and reigns with you in the unity of the Holy Spirit,
one God, for ever and ever. All: **Amen.**

## READING I (L 94-A) (Jeremiah 20:10-13)

### A reading from the Book of the Prophet Jeremiah

*He has rescued the life of the poor from the power of the wicked.*

**Jeremiah said:**
"**I hear the whisperings of many:**
'**Terror on every side!**
**Denounce! Let us denounce him!**'

All those who were my friends
  are on the watch for any misstep of mine.
'Perhaps he will be trapped; then we can prevail,
  and take our vengeance on him.'
But the Lord is with me, like a mighty champion:
  my persecutors will stumble, they will not triumph.
In their failure they will be put to utter shame,
  to lasting, unforgettable confusion.
O Lord of hosts, you who test the just,
  who probe mind and heart,
let me witness the vengeance you take on them,
  for to you I have entrusted my cause.
Sing to the Lord,
  praise the Lord,
for he has rescued the life of the poor
  from the power of the wicked!"

The word of the Lord. All: Thanks be to God.

## RESPONSORIAL PSALM 69

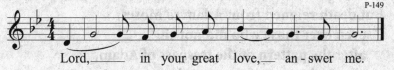

P-149

Lord,___ in your great love,___ an-swer me.

Psalm 69:8-10, 14, 17, 33-35

℟. (14c) **Lord, in your great love, answer me.**

For your sake I bear insult,
  and shame covers my face.
I have become an outcast to my brothers,
  a stranger to my children,
because zeal for your house consumes me,
  and the insults of those who blaspheme you fall
      upon me. ℟.

I pray to you, O Lord,
  for the time of your favor, O God!
In your great kindness answer me
  with your constant help. *(continued)*

Answer me, O Lord, for bounteous is your kindness;
    in your great mercy turn toward me. R⁊.

"See, you lowly ones, and be glad;
    you who seek God, may your hearts revive!
For the Lord hears the poor,
    and his own who are in bonds he spurns not.
Let the heavens and the earth praise him,
    the seas and whatever moves in them!" R⁊.

## READING II (Romans 5:12-15)

**A reading from the Letter of Saint Paul to the Romans**

*The gift is not like the transgression.*

**Brothers and sisters:**
**Through one man sin entered the world,**
    **and through sin, death,**
    **and thus death came to all men, inasmuch as all**
        **sinned—**
    **for up to the time of the law, sin was in the world,**
    **though sin is not accounted when there is no law.**
**But death reigned from Adam to Moses,**
    **even over those who did not sin**
    **after the pattern of the trespass of Adam,**
    **who is the type of the one who was to come.**

**But the gift is not like the transgression.**
**For if by the transgression of the one the many died,**
    **how much more did the grace of God**
    **and the gracious gift of the one man Jesus Christ**
    **overflow for the many.**

**The word of the Lord.** All: **Thanks be to God.**

## GOSPEL (Matthew 10:26-33)
### ALLELUIA (John 15:26b, 27a)

℣. Alleluia, alleluia. R⁊. **Alleluia, alleluia.**
℣. The Spirit of truth will testify to me, says the Lord;
    and you also will testify. R⁊.

✠ **A reading from the holy Gospel according to Matthew**

All: **Glory to you, O Lord.**

*Do not be afraid of those who kill the body.*

**Jesus said to the Twelve:**
    **"Fear no one.**
**Nothing is concealed that will not be revealed,**
    **nor secret that will not be known.**
**What I say to you in the darkness, speak in the light;**
    **what you hear whispered, proclaim on the housetops.**
**And do not be afraid of those who kill the body but**
        **cannot kill the soul;**
    **rather, be afraid of the one who can destroy**
    **both soul and body in Gehenna.**
**Are not two sparrows sold for a small coin?**
**Yet not one of them falls to the ground without your**
        **Father's knowledge.**
**Even all the hairs of your head are counted.**
**So do not be afraid; you are worth more than many**
        **sparrows.**
**Everyone who acknowledges me before others**
    **I will acknowledge before my heavenly Father.**
**But whoever denies me before others,**
    **I will deny before my heavenly Father."**

**The Gospel of the Lord.** All: **Praise to you, Lord Jesus Christ.**

PRAYER OVER THE OFFERINGS
Receive, O Lord, the sacrifice of conciliation and praise
and grant that, cleansed by its action,
we may make offering of a heart pleasing to you.
Through Christ our Lord. All: **Amen.**

COMMUNION ANTIPHON (Psalm 145[144]:15)
The eyes of all look to you, Lord,
and you give them their food in due season.

Or:

(John 10:11, 15)
I am the Good Shepherd,
and I lay down my life for my sheep, says the Lord.

### Prayer after Communion

Renewed and nourished
by the Sacred Body and Precious Blood of your Son,
we ask of your mercy, O Lord,
that what we celebrate with constant devotion
may be our sure pledge of redemption.
Through Christ our Lord. All: **Amen.**

# Thirteenth Sunday in Ordinary Time

*July 2, 2017*

*Reflection on the Gospel*

*Jesus clearly states that he is to be above everyone and everything in our lives—even family. Jesus also says that whoever receives his followers receives him. Jesus is reminding us that our relationship to him is expressed in our relationship with each other. In giving and receiving we make evident that Jesus is the center and focus of our lives. In giving and receiving we lose our lives for the sake of others. In giving and receiving we find fullness of Life—Jesus himself.*

• *Whoever does not take up his cross is not worthy of me.*

—Living Liturgy™, *Thirteenth Sunday in Ordinary Time 2017*

### Entrance Antiphon (Psalm 47[46]:2)

All peoples, clap your hands.
Cry to God with shouts of joy!

COLLECT
O God, who through the grace of adoption
chose us to be children of light,
grant, we pray,
that we may not be wrapped in the darkness of error
but always be seen to stand in the bright light of truth.
Through our Lord Jesus Christ, your Son,
who lives and reigns with you in the unity of the Holy Spirit,
one God, for ever and ever. All: **Amen.**

READING I (L 97-A) (2 Kings 4:8-11, 14-16a)
**A reading from the second Book of Kings**

*Elisha is a holy man of God, let him remain.*

**One day Elisha came to Shunem,**
**where there was a woman of influence, who urged him**
**to dine with her.**
**Afterward, whenever he passed by, he used to stop there**
**to dine.**
**So she said to her husband, "I know that Elisha is a holy**
**man of God.**
**Since he visits us often, let us arrange a little room on**
**the roof**
**and furnish it for him with a bed, table, chair, and**
**lamp,**
**so that when he comes to us he can stay there."**
**Sometime later Elisha arrived and stayed in the room**
**overnight.**

**Later Elisha asked, "Can something be done for her?"**
**His servant Gehazi answered, "Yes!**
**She has no son, and her husband is getting on in years."**
**Elisha said, "Call her."**
**When the woman had been called and stood at the door,**
**Elisha promised, "This time next year**
**you will be fondling a baby son."**

**The word of the Lord.** All: **Thanks be to God.**

RESPONSIVE PSALM 89

Psalm 89:2-3, 16-17, 18-19

℟. (2a) **Forever I will sing the goodness of the Lord.**

The promises of the LORD I will sing forever,
  through all generations my mouth shall proclaim
    your faithfulness.
For you have said, "My kindness is established forever";
  in heaven you have confirmed your faithfulness. ℟.

Blessed the people who know the joyful shout;
  in the light of your countenance, O LORD, they walk.
At your name they rejoice all the day,
  and through your justice they are exalted. ℟.

You are the splendor of their strength,
  and by your favor our horn is exalted.
For to the LORD belongs our shield,
  and to the Holy One of Israel, our king. ℟.

READING II (Romans 6:3-4, 8-11)

**A reading from the Letter of Saint Paul to the Romans**

*Buried with Christ in baptism, we shall walk in the newness
of life.*

**Brothers and sisters:**
**Are you unaware that we who were baptized into Christ**
    **Jesus**
  **were baptized into his death?**
**We were indeed buried with him through baptism into**
    **death,**
  **so that, just as Christ was raised from the dead**
  **by the glory of the Father,**
  **we too might live in newness of life.**

If, then, we have died with Christ,
  we believe that we shall also live with him.
We know that Christ, raised from the dead, dies no more;
  death no longer has power over him.
As to his death, he died to sin once and for all;
  as to his life, he lives for God.
Consequently, you too must think of yourselves as dead
    to sin
  and living for God in Christ Jesus.

The word of the Lord. All: Thanks be to God.

GOSPEL (Matthew 10:37-42)
ALLELUIA (1 Peter 2:9)
℣. Alleluia, alleluia.  ℟. **Alleluia, alleluia.**
℣. You are a chosen race, a royal priesthood, a holy nation;
  announce the praises of him who called you out of
    darkness into his wonderful light. ℟.

✠ **A reading from the holy Gospel according to Matthew**

All: **Glory to you, O Lord.**

*Whoever does not take up his cross is not worthy of me.*
*Whoever receives you, receives me.*

**Jesus said to his apostles:**
  **"Whoever loves father or mother more than me is not**
      **worthy of me,**
  **and whoever loves son or daughter more than me is**
      **not worthy of me;**
  **and whoever does not take up his cross**
  **and follow after me is not worthy of me.**
**Whoever finds his life will lose it,**
  **and whoever loses his life for my sake will find it.**
**Whoever receives you receives me,**
  **and whoever receives me receives the one who sent me.**
**Whoever receives a prophet because he is a prophet**
  **will receive a prophet's reward,**
  **and whoever receives a righteous man**

because he is a righteous man
will receive a righteous man's reward.
**And whoever gives only a cup of cold water**
to one of these little ones to drink
because the little one is a disciple–
amen, I say to you, he will surely not lose his reward."

**The Gospel of the Lord.** All: **Praise to you, Lord Jesus Christ.**

PRAYER OVER THE OFFERINGS
O God, who graciously accomplish
the effects of your mysteries,
grant, we pray,
that the deeds by which we serve you
may be worthy of these sacred gifts.
Through Christ our Lord. All: **Amen.**

COMMUNION ANTIPHON (Cf. Psalm 103[102]:1)
Bless the Lord, O my soul,
and all within me, his holy name.

Or:

(John 17:20-21)
O Father, I pray for them, that they may be one in us,
that the world may believe that you have sent me, says the
    Lord.

PRAYER AFTER COMMUNION
May this divine sacrifice we have offered and received
fill us with life, O Lord, we pray,
so that, bound to you in lasting charity,
we may bear fruit that lasts for ever.
Through Christ our Lord. All: **Amen.**

# Fourteenth Sunday in Ordinary Time

*July 9, 2017*

*Reflection on the Gospel*

*What is our greatest labor and burden? Getting to know the Father through the Son. On our own, we labor under a chafing and unwieldy yoke. However, when we come to Jesus, he shoulders our labor by teaching us, revealing his Father to us, and sharing our burden. How do we come to Jesus? By being filled with the same meekness and humility of heart he has, emptying ourselves of ourselves to be filled with him. Then our yoke becomes easy and our burden light.*

- *"Take my yoke upon you and learn from me, for I am meek and humble of heart . . .*

—Living Liturgy™, *Fourteenth Sunday in Ordinary Time 2017*

## ENTRANCE ANTIPHON (Cf. Psalm 48[47]:10-11)

Your merciful love, O God,
we have received in the midst of your temple.
Your praise, O God, like your name,
reaches the ends of the earth;
your right hand is filled with saving justice.

## COLLECT

O God, who in the abasement of your Son
have raised up a fallen world,
fill your faithful with holy joy,
for on those you have rescued from slavery to sin
you bestow eternal gladness.
Through our Lord Jesus Christ, your Son,
who lives and reigns with you in the unity of the Holy Spirit,
one God, for ever and ever. All: **Amen.**

## READING I (L 100-A) (Zechariah 9:9-10)

### A reading from the Book of the Prophet Zechariah

*See, your king comes to you humbly.*

Thus says the LORD:
Rejoice heartily, O daughter Zion,
   shout for joy, O daughter Jerusalem!
See, your king shall come to you;
   a just savior is he,
meek, and riding on an ass,
   on a colt, the foal of an ass.
He shall banish the chariot from Ephraim,
   and the horse from Jerusalem;
the warrior's bow shall be banished,
   and he shall proclaim peace to the nations.
His dominion shall be from sea to sea,
   and from the River to the ends of the earth.

The word of the Lord. All: Thanks be to God.

## RESPONSORIAL PSALM 145

P-151

I will praise your name for-ev-er, my king and my God.

Music: Jay F. Hunstiger, © 1991, administered by Liturgical Press. All rights reserved.

Psalm 145:1-2, 8-9, 10-11, 13-14

R̸. (Cf. 1) **I will praise your name forever, my king and
my God.** *or:* R̸. **Alleluia.**

I will extol you, O my God and King,
   and I will bless your name forever and ever.
Every day will I bless you,
   and I will praise your name forever and ever. R̸.

The LORD is gracious and merciful,
   slow to anger and of great kindness.
The LORD is good to all
   and compassionate toward all his works. R̸.

Let all your works give you thanks, O LORD,
   and let your faithful ones bless you.
Let them discourse of the glory of your kingdom
   and speak of your might. R̸.

The LORD is faithful in all his words
>    and holy in all his works.
The LORD lifts up all who are falling
>    and raises up all who are bowed down. R℟.

## READING II (Romans 8:9, 11-13)

**A reading from the Letter of Saint Paul to the Romans**

*If by the Spirit you put to death the deeds of the body, you will live.*

**Brothers and sisters:**
**You are not in the flesh;**
>    **on the contrary, you are in the spirit,**
>    **if only the Spirit of God dwells in you.**
**Whoever does not have the Spirit of Christ does not**
>        **belong to him.**
**If the Spirit of the one who raised Jesus from the dead**
>        **dwells in you,**
>    **the one who raised Christ from the dead**
>    **will give life to your mortal bodies also,**
>    **through his Spirit that dwells in you.**
**Consequently, brothers and sisters,**
>    **we are not debtors to the flesh,**
>    **to live according to the flesh.**
**For if you live according to the flesh, you will die,**
>    **but if by the Spirit you put to death the deeds of the**
>        **body,**
>    **you will live.**

**The word of the Lord.** All: **Thanks be to God.**

## GOSPEL (Matthew 11:25-30)

ALLELUIA (Cf. Matthew 11:25)

℣. Alleluia, alleluia.  R℟. **Alleluia, alleluia.**
℣. Blessed are you, Father, Lord of heaven and earth;
>    you have revealed to little ones the mysteries of the
>        kingdom. R℟.

## ✠ A reading from the holy Gospel according to Matthew

All: **Glory to you, O Lord.**

*I am meek and humble of heart.*

At that time Jesus exclaimed:

"I give praise to you, Father, Lord of heaven and earth,
for although you have hidden these things
from the wise and the learned
you have revealed them to little ones.
Yes, Father, such has been your gracious will.
All things have been handed over to me by my Father.
No one knows the Son except the Father,
and no one knows the Father except the Son
and anyone to whom the Son wishes to reveal him.

"Come to me, all you who labor and are burdened,
and I will give you rest.
Take my yoke upon you and learn from me,
for I am meek and humble of heart;
and you will find rest for yourselves.
For my yoke is easy, and my burden light."

The Gospel of the Lord. All: **Praise to you, Lord Jesus Christ.**

PRAYER OVER THE OFFERINGS
May this oblation dedicated to your name
purify us, O Lord,
and day by day bring our conduct
closer to the life of heaven.
Through Christ our Lord. All: **Amen.**

COMMUNION ANTIPHON (Psalm 34[33]:9)
Taste and see that the Lord is good;
blessed the man who seeks refuge in him.

Or:

(Matthew 11:28)
Come to me, all who labor and are burdened,
and I will refresh you, says the Lord.

PRAYER AFTER COMMUNION
Grant, we pray, O Lord,
that, having been replenished by such great gifts,
we may gain the prize of salvation
and never cease to praise you.
Through Christ our Lord. All: **Amen.**

# Fifteenth Sunday in Ordinary Time

*July 16, 2017*

*Reflection on the Gospel*

*Jesus tells a parable about sowing the seed-word, receptivity to the seed-word, and fruitfulness of the seed-word. To bear fruit the seed-word must take root in rich soil. We can take the parable and its interpretation one step further. The sower and seed is Jesus himself, the Word. The rich soil is our own hearts open to hearing and understanding that Word. Are our hearts open? Are we willing to listen to Jesus as a relational activity, exchanging person with Person?*

• *Creation awaits the revelation of the children of God. I . . .*

—*Living Liturgy*™, *Fifteenth Sunday in Ordinary Time 2017*

ENTRANCE ANTIPHON (Cf. Psalm 17[16]:15)

As for me, in justice I shall behold your face;
I shall be filled with the vision of your glory.

COLLECT

O God, who show the light of your truth
to those who go astray,
so that they may return to the right path,
give all who for the faith they profess
are accounted Christians
the grace to reject whatever is contrary to the name of Christ
and to strive after all that does it honor.
Through our Lord Jesus Christ, your Son,
who lives and reigns with you in the unity of the Holy Spirit,
one God, for ever and ever. All: **Amen.**

READING I (L 103-A) (Isaiah 55:10-11)

**A reading from the Book of the Prophet Isaiah**

*The rain makes the earth fruitful.*

Thus says the LORD:
Just as from the heavens
   the rain and snow come down
and do not return there
   till they have watered the earth,
   making it fertile and fruitful,
giving seed to the one who sows
   and bread to the one who eats,
so shall my word be
   that goes forth from my mouth;
my word shall not return to me void,
   but shall do my will,
   achieving the end for which I sent it.

The word of the Lord. All: Thanks be to God.

RESPONSORIAL PSALM 65

P-152

The seed that falls on good ground will
yield a fruit-ful har-vest.

Music: Jay F. Hunstiger, © 1993, administered by Liturgical Press. All rights reserved.

Psalm 65:10, 11, 12-13, 14

R℣. (Luke 8:8) **The seed that falls on good ground will
yield a fruitful harvest.**

You have visited the land and watered it;
   greatly have you enriched it.
God's watercourses are filled;
   you have prepared the grain. R℣.

Thus have you prepared the land: drenching its furrows,
   breaking up its clods,
softening it with showers,
   blessing its yield. R℣.

You have crowned the year with your bounty,
   and your paths overflow with a rich harvest;

the untilled meadows overflow with it,
and rejoicing clothes the hills. ℟.

The fields are garmented with flocks
and the valleys blanketed with grain.
They shout and sing for joy. ℟.

## READING II (Romans 8:18-23)

**A reading from the Letter of Saint Paul to the Romans**

*Creation awaits the revelation of the children of God.*

**Brothers and sisters:**
**I consider that the sufferings of this present time are as**
**nothing**
compared with the glory to be revealed for us.
**For creation awaits with eager expectation**
the revelation of the children of God;
for creation was made subject to futility,
not of its own accord but because of the one who
subjected it,
in hope that creation itself
would be set free from slavery to corruption
and share in the glorious freedom of the children of
God.
**We know that all creation is groaning in labor pains**
even until now;
and not only that, but we ourselves,
who have the firstfruits of the Spirit,
we also groan within ourselves
as we wait for adoption, the redemption of our bodies.

**The word of the Lord.** All: **Thanks be to God.**

## GOSPEL (Matthew 13:1-23) *or* Shorter Form [ ] (Matthew 13:1-9)
### ALLELUIA
℣. Alleluia, alleluia.  ℟. **Alleluia, alleluia.**
℣. The seed is the word of God, Christ is the sower.
All who come to him will have life forever. ℟.

✠ **A reading from the holy Gospel according to Matthew**

All: **Glory to you, O Lord.**

*A sower went out to sow.*

[On that day, Jesus went out of the house and sat down
    by the sea.
Such large crowds gathered around him
    that he got into a boat and sat down,
    and the whole crowd stood along the shore.
And he spoke to them at length in parables, saying:
    "A sower went out to sow.
And as he sowed, some seed fell on the path,
    and birds came and ate it up.
Some fell on rocky ground, where it had little soil.
It sprang up at once because the soil was not deep,
    and when the sun rose it was scorched,
    and it withered for lack of roots.
Some seed fell among thorns, and the thorns grew up
    and choked it.
But some seed fell on rich soil, and produced fruit,
    a hundred or sixty or thirtyfold.
Whoever has ears ought to hear."]

The disciples approached him and said,
    "Why do you speak to them in parables?"
He said to them in reply,
    "Because knowledge of the mysteries of the kingdom
        of heaven
    has been granted to you, but to them it has not been
        granted.
To anyone who has, more will be given and he will grow
        rich;
    from anyone who has not, even what he has will be
        taken away.
This is why I speak to them in parables, because
    *they look but do not see and hear but do not listen or*
        *understand.*

Isaiah's prophecy is fulfilled in them, which says:
> *You shall indeed hear but not understand,*
>> *you shall indeed look but never see.*
> *Gross is the heart of this people,*
>> *they will hardly hear with their ears,*
>> *they have closed their eyes,*
>> *lest they see with their eyes*
>> *and hear with their ears*
> *and understand with their hearts and be converted,*
>> *and I heal them.*

"But blessed are your eyes, because they see,
> and your ears, because they hear.
Amen, I say to you, many prophets and righteous people
> longed to see what you see but did not see it,
> and to hear what you hear but did not hear it.

"Hear then the parable of the sower.
The seed sown on the path is the one
> who hears the word of the kingdom without
>> understanding it,
> and the evil one comes and steals away
> what was sown in his heart.
The seed sown on rocky ground
> is the one who hears the word and receives it at once
>> with joy.
But he has no root and lasts only for a time.
When some tribulation or persecution comes because of
> the word,
> he immediately falls away.
The seed sown among thorns is the one who hears the
> word,
> but then worldly anxiety and the lure of riches choke
>> the word
> and it bears no fruit.
But the seed sown on rich soil
> is the one who hears the word and understands it,

**who indeed bears fruit and yields a hundred or sixty or thirtyfold."**

**The Gospel of the Lord.** All: **Praise to you, Lord Jesus Christ.**

PRAYER OVER THE OFFERINGS

Look upon the offerings of the Church, O Lord,
as she makes her prayer to you,
and grant that, when consumed by those who believe,
they may bring ever greater holiness.
Through Christ our Lord. All: **Amen.**

COMMUNION ANTIPHON (Cf. Psalm 84[83]:4-5)

The sparrow finds a home,
and the swallow a nest for her young:
by your altars, O Lord of hosts, my King and my God.
Blessed are they who dwell in your house,
for ever singing your praise.

Or:

(John 6:57)

Whoever eats my flesh and drinks my blood
remains in me and I in him, says the Lord.

PRAYER AFTER COMMUNION

Having consumed these gifts, we pray, O Lord,
that, by our participation in this mystery,
its saving effects upon us may grow.
Through Christ our Lord. All: **Amen.**

# Sixteenth Sunday in Ordinary Time

*July 23, 2017*

### Reflection on the Gospel

*"The kingdom of heaven is like . . ."* *Whatever parable Jesus uses to teach about the kingdom of heaven, always at issue is growth, abundance, increase. While "the enemy" may try to thwart the kingdom, in the end God will prevail and "the righteous will shine like the sun." So, "the kingdom of heaven is like" those of us who hear and live the Good News Jesus teaches. We ourselves are "the kingdom of heaven" when we live according to God's ways.*

• *Let them grow together until harvest. I would . . .*

—*Living Liturgy™, Sixteenth Sunday in Ordinary Time 2017*

## ENTRANCE ANTIPHON (Psalm 54[53]:6, 8)

See, I have God for my help.
The Lord sustains my soul.
I will sacrifice to you with willing heart,
and praise your name, O Lord, for it is good.

## COLLECT

Show favor, O Lord, to your servants
and mercifully increase the gifts of your grace,
that, made fervent in hope, faith and charity,
they may be ever watchful in keeping your commands.
Through our Lord Jesus Christ, your Son,
who lives and reigns with you in the unity of the Holy Spirit,
one God, for ever and ever. All: **Amen.**

## READING I (L 106-A) (Wisdom 12:13, 16-19)

### A reading from the Book of Wisdom

*You give repentance for sins.*

**There is no god besides you who have the care of all,
that you need show you have not unjustly
condemned.**

For your might is the source of justice;
>your mastery over all things makes you lenient to all.

For you show your might when the perfection of your
>power is disbelieved;

>and in those who know you, you rebuke temerity.

But though you are master of might, you judge with
>clemency,

>and with much lenience you govern us;

>for power, whenever you will, attends you.

And you taught your people, by these deeds,
>that those who are just must be kind;

and you gave your children good ground for hope
>that you would permit repentance for their sins.

The word of the Lord. All: Thanks be to God.

## RESPONSORIAL PSALM 86

P-153

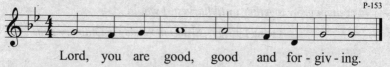

Lord, you are good, good and for - giv - ing.

Music: Jay F. Hunstiger, © 1993, administered by Liturgical Press. All rights reserved.

Psalm 86:5-6, 9-10, 15-16

R̸. (5a) **Lord, you are good and forgiving.**

You, O LORD, are good and forgiving,
>abounding in kindness to all who call upon you.

Hearken, O LORD, to my prayer
>and attend to the sound of my pleading. R̸.

All the nations you have made shall come
>and worship you, O LORD,
>and glorify your name.

For you are great, and you do wondrous deeds;
>you alone are God. R̸.

You, O LORD, are a God merciful and gracious,
>slow to anger, abounding in kindness and fidelity.

Turn toward me, and have pity on me;
>give your strength to your servant. R̸.

## READING II (Romans 8:26-27)

**A reading from the Letter of Saint Paul to the Romans**

*The Spirit intercedes with inexpressible groanings.*

**Brothers and sisters:**
**The Spirit comes to the aid of our weakness;**
>   for we do not know how to pray as we ought,
>   but the Spirit himself intercedes with inexpressible
>       groanings.

**And the one who searches hearts**
>   knows what is the intention of the Spirit,
>   because he intercedes for the holy ones
>   according to God's will.

**The word of the Lord.** All: **Thanks be to God.**

GOSPEL (Matthew 13:24-43) *or* Shorter Form [ ] (Matthew 13:24-30)

ALLELUIA (*See* Matthew 11:25)

℣. Alleluia, alleluia. ℟. **Alleluia, alleluia.**
℣. Blessed are you, Father, Lord of heaven and earth;
>   you have revealed to little ones the mysteries of the
>       kingdom. ℟.

✠ **A reading from the holy Gospel according to Matthew**

All: **Glory to you, O Lord.**

*Let them grow together until harvest.*

[Jesus proposed another parable to the crowds, saying:
**"The kingdom of heaven may be likened**
>   to a man who sowed good seed in his field.**

**While everyone was asleep his enemy came**
>   and sowed weeds all through the wheat, and then
>       went off.

**When the crop grew and bore fruit, the weeds appeared**
>   as well.

**The slaves of the householder came to him and said,**
>   'Master, did you not sow good seed in your field?

**Where have the weeds come from?'**

He answered, 'An enemy has done this.'
His slaves said to him,
   'Do you want us to go and pull them up?'
He replied, 'No, if you pull up the weeds
   you might uproot the wheat along with them.
Let them grow together until harvest;
   then at harvest time I will say to the harvesters,
   "First collect the weeds and tie them in bundles for
      burning;
   but gather the wheat into my barn."'"]

He proposed another parable to them.
"The kingdom of heaven is like a mustard seed
   that a person took and sowed in a field.
It is the smallest of all the seeds,
   yet when full-grown it is the largest of plants.
It becomes a large bush,
   and the 'birds of the sky come and dwell in its
      branches.'"

He spoke to them another parable.
"The kingdom of heaven is like yeast
   that a woman took and mixed with three measures of
      wheat flour
   until the whole batch was leavened."

All these things Jesus spoke to the crowds in parables.
He spoke to them only in parables,
   to fulfill what had been said through the prophet:
    *I will open my mouth in parables,*
      *I will announce what has lain hidden from the*
      *foundation of the world.*

Then, dismissing the crowds, he went into the house.
His disciples approached him and said,
   "Explain to us the parable of the weeds in the field."
He said in reply, "He who sows good seed is the Son of Man,
   the field is the world, the good seed the children of the
      kingdom.

The weeds are the children of the evil one,
    and the enemy who sows them is the devil.
The harvest is the end of the age, and the harvesters are
      angels.
Just as weeds are collected and burned up with fire,
    so will it be at the end of the age.
The Son of Man will send his angels,
    and they will collect out of his kingdom
    all who cause others to sin and all evildoers.
They will throw them into the fiery furnace,
    where there will be wailing and grinding of teeth.
Then the righteous will shine like the sun
    in the kingdom of their Father.
Whoever has ears ought to hear."

**The Gospel of the Lord.** All: **Praise to you, Lord Jesus Christ.**

PRAYER OVER THE OFFERINGS
O God, who in the one perfect sacrifice
brought to completion varied offerings of the law,
accept, we pray, this sacrifice from your faithful servants
and make it holy, as you blessed the gifts of Abel,
so that what each has offered to the honor of your majesty
may benefit the salvation of all.
Through Christ our Lord. All: **Amen.**

COMMUNION ANTIPHON (Psalm 111[110]:4-5)
The Lord, the gracious, the merciful,
has made a memorial of his wonders;
he gives food to those who fear him.

Or:

(Revelation 3:20)
Behold, I stand at the door and knock, says the Lord.
If anyone hears my voice and opens the door to me,
I will enter his house and dine with him, and he with me.

PRAYER AFTER COMMUNION
Graciously be present to your people, we pray, O Lord,
and lead those you have imbued with heavenly mysteries
to pass from former ways to newness of life.
Through Christ our Lord. All: **Amen.**

# Seventeenth Sunday in Ordinary Time

*July 30, 2017*

*Reflection on the Gospel*

*What "the kingdom of heaven is like" is not just a treasure, pearl, or fish net. What the "kingdom of heaven" is really like is the action-response of a person who finds a treasure, a merchant who buys a prized pearl, or a fisherman who sorts the fish he catches. The "kingdom of heaven" is present in searching for, sacrificing for, and sorting for our greatest Treasure—God's very Life. We must "sell" all that we are—empty ourselves—so the Life God gives us freely and lavishly is ours forever.*

• *God predestined us to be conformed to the image of his Son. I . . .*

—Living Liturgy™, *Seventeenth Sunday in Ordinary Time 2017*

ENTRANCE ANTIPHON (Cf. Psalm 68[67]:6-7, 36)

God is in his holy place,
God who unites those who dwell in his house;
he himself gives might and strength to his people.

COLLECT

O God, protector of those who hope in you,
without whom nothing has firm foundation, nothing is holy,
bestow in abundance your mercy upon us
and grant that, with you as our ruler and guide,
we may use the good things that pass
in such a way as to hold fast even now
to those that ever endure.
Through our Lord Jesus Christ, your Son,
who lives and reigns with you in the unity of the Holy Spirit,
one God, for ever and ever. All: **Amen.**

READING I (L 109-A) (1 Kings 3:5, 7-12)

## A reading from the first Book of Kings

*You have asked for wisdom.*

The Lord appeared to Solomon in a dream at night.
God said, "Ask something of me and I will give it to you."
Solomon answered:

"O Lord, my God, you have made me, your servant,
king
to succeed my father David;
but I am a mere youth, not knowing at all how to act.
I serve you in the midst of the people whom you have
chosen,
a people so vast that it cannot be numbered or counted.
Give your servant, therefore, an understanding heart
to judge your people and to distinguish right from
wrong.
For who is able to govern this vast people of yours?"

The Lord was pleased that Solomon made this request.
So God said to him:

"Because you have asked for this—
not for a long life for yourself,
nor for riches,
nor for the life of your enemies,
but for understanding so that you may know what is
right—
I do as you requested.
I give you a heart so wise and understanding
that there has never been anyone like you up to now,
and after you there will come no one to equal you."

The word of the Lord. All: Thanks be to God.

Responsorial Psalm 119

P-154

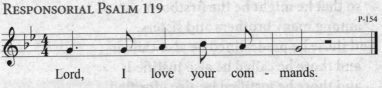

Lord, I love your com - mands.

Psalm 119:57, 72, 76-77, 127-128, 129-130

℟. (97a) **Lord, I love your commands.**

I have said, O LORD, that my part
   is to keep your words.
The law of your mouth is to me more precious
   than thousands of gold and silver pieces. ℟.

Let your kindness comfort me
   according to your promise to your servants.
Let your compassion come to me that I may live,
   for your law is my delight. ℟.

For I love your commands
   more than gold, however fine.
For in all your precepts I go forward;
   every false way I hate. ℟.

Wonderful are your decrees;
   therefore I observe them.
The revelation of your words sheds light,
   giving understanding to the simple. ℟.

## READING II (Romans 8:28-30)

**A reading from the Letter of Saint Paul to the Romans**

*God predestined us to be conformed to the image of his Son.*

**Brothers and sisters:**
**We know that all things work for good for those who**
      **love God,**
   **who are called according to his purpose.**
**For those he foreknew he also predestined**
   **to be conformed to the image of his Son,**
   **so that he might be the firstborn**
   **among many brothers and sisters.**
**And those he predestined he also called;**
   **and those he called he also justified;**
   **and those he justified he also glorified.**

**The word of the Lord.** All: **Thanks be to God.**

GOSPEL (Matthew 13:44-52) *or* Shorter Form [ ] (Matthew 13:44-46)

ALLELUIA (*See* Matthew 11:25)

℣. Alleluia, alleluia.   ℟. **Alleluia, alleluia.**

℣. Blessed are you, Father, Lord of heaven and earth;
for you have revealed to little ones the mysteries of the
kingdom. ℟.

✠ **A reading from the holy Gospel according to Matthew**

All: **Glory to you, O Lord.**

*He sells all that he has and buys the field.*

[Jesus said to his disciples:
"The kingdom of heaven is like a treasure buried in a
field,
which a person finds and hides again,
and out of joy goes and sells all that he has and buys
that field.
Again, the kingdom of heaven is like a merchant
searching for fine pearls.
When he finds a pearl of great price,
he goes and sells all that he has and buys it.]
Again, the kingdom of heaven is like a net thrown into
the sea,
which collects fish of every kind.
When it is full they haul it ashore
and sit down to put what is good into buckets.
What is bad they throw away.
Thus it will be at the end of the age.
The angels will go out and separate the wicked from the
righteous
and throw them into the fiery furnace,
where there will be wailing and grinding of teeth.

"Do you understand all these things?"
They answered, "Yes."

And he replied,

"Then every scribe who has been instructed in the
    kingdom of heaven
is like the head of a household
who brings from his storeroom both the new and the
    old."

**The Gospel of the Lord.** All: **Praise to you, Lord Jesus Christ.**

PRAYER OVER THE OFFERINGS
Accept, O Lord, we pray, the offerings
which we bring from the abundance of your gifts,
that through the powerful working of your grace
these most sacred mysteries may sanctify our present way of life
and lead us to eternal gladness.
Through Christ our Lord. All: **Amen.**

COMMUNION ANTIPHON (Psalm 103[102]:2)
Bless the Lord, O my soul,
and never forget all his benefits.

Or:

(Matthew 5:7-8)
Blessed are the merciful, for they shall receive mercy.
Blessed are the clean of heart, for they shall see God.

PRAYER AFTER COMMUNION
We have consumed, O Lord, this divine Sacrament,
the perpetual memorial of the Passion of your Son;
grant, we pray, that this gift,
which he himself gave us with love beyond all telling,
may profit us for salvation.
Through Christ our Lord. All: **Amen.**

# The Transfiguration of the Lord

*August 6, 2017*

## Reflection on the Gospel

*When the voice from the cloud tells Peter, James, and John to "listen to" Jesus, they will hear something new. They were not prepared, however, for the "new" Jesus was inaugurating: that human flesh can shine with the glory of God; that death is not the end, rising "from the dead" is. Jesus' new covenant promises us a share in his risen Life. In the transfiguration of Jesus, Peter, James, and John see their own glorification. And so do we.*

- *"Do not tell the vision to anyone until the Son of Man has been raised from the dead."*

—*Living Liturgy™, Transfiguration 2017*

## ENTRANCE ANTIPHON (Cf. Matthew 17:5)

In a resplendent cloud the Holy Spirit appeared.
The Father's voice was heard: This is my beloved Son,
with whom I am well pleased. Listen to him.

## COLLECT

O God, who in the glorious Transfiguration
of your Only Begotten Son
confirmed the mysteries of faith by the witness of the Fathers
and wonderfully prefigured our full adoption to sonship,
grant, we pray, to your servants,
that, listening to the voice of your beloved Son,
we may merit to become co-heirs with him.
Who lives and reigns with you in the unity of the Holy Spirit,
one God, for ever and ever. All: **Amen.**

## READING I (L 614) (Daniel 7:9-10, 13-14)

**A reading from the Book of the Prophet Daniel**

*His clothing was snow bright.*

**As I watched:**

> Thrones were set up
>> and the Ancient One took his throne.
>
> His clothing was snow bright,
>> and the hair on his head as white as wool;
>
> his throne was flames of fire,
>> with wheels of burning fire.
>
> A surging stream of fire
>> flowed out from where he sat;
>
> Thousands upon thousands were ministering to him,
>> and myriads upon myriads attended him.

**The court was convened and the books were opened.**

**As the visions during the night continued, I saw:**

> One like a Son of man coming,
>> on the clouds of heaven;
>
> When he reached the Ancient One
>> and was presented before him,
>
> The one like a Son of man received dominion, glory,
>> and kingship;
>
> all peoples, nations, and languages serve him.
>
> His dominion is an everlasting dominion
>> that shall not be taken away,
>> his kingship shall not be destroyed.

**The word of the Lord.** All: **Thanks be to God.**

## RESPONSORIAL PSALM 97

P-180

The Lord is king, the Most High o - ver all the earth.

Psalm 97:1-2, 5-6, 9

R℣. (1a and 9a) **The Lord is king, the Most High over all the earth.**

The LORD is king; let the earth rejoice;
   let the many islands be glad.
Clouds and darkness are round about him,
   justice and judgment are the foundation of his
         throne. R℣.

The mountains melt like wax before the LORD,
   before the LORD of all the earth.
The heavens proclaim his justice,
   and all peoples see his glory. R℣.

Because you, O LORD, are the Most High over all the
         earth,
   exalted far above all gods. R℣.

READING II (2 Peter 1:16-19)

**A reading from the second Letter of Saint Peter**

*We ourselves heard this voice come from heaven.*

**Beloved:**
**We did not follow cleverly devised myths**
   **when we made known to you**
   **the power and coming of our Lord Jesus Christ,**
   **but we had been eyewitnesses of his majesty.**
**For he received honor and glory from God the Father**
   **when that unique declaration came to him from the**
         **majestic glory,**
   **"This is my Son, my beloved, with whom I am well**
         **pleased."**
**We ourselves heard this voice come from heaven**
   **while we were with him on the holy mountain.**
**Moreover, we possess the prophetic message that is**
         **altogether reliable.**
**You will do well to be attentive to it,**
   **as to a lamp shining in a dark place,**

until day dawns and the morning star rises in your
hearts.

**The word of the Lord.** All: **Thanks be to God.**

GOSPEL (Matthew 17:1-9)
ALLELUIA (Matthew 17:5c)

℣. Alleluia, alleluia. ℟. **Alleluia, alleluia.**
℣. This is my beloved Son, with whom I am well pleased;
listen to him. ℟.

✢ **A reading from the holy Gospel according to Matthew**

All: **Glory to you, O Lord.**

*Jesus' face shone like the sun.*

**Jesus took Peter, James, and John his brother,**
**and led them up a high mountain by themselves.**
**And he was transfigured before them;**
**his face shone like the sun**
**and his clothes became white as light.**
**And behold, Moses and Elijah appeared to them,**
**conversing with him.**
**Then Peter said to Jesus in reply,**
**"Lord, it is good that we are here.**
**If you wish, I will make three tents here,**
**one for you, one for Moses, and one for Elijah."**
**While he was still speaking, behold,**
**a bright cloud cast a shadow over them,**
**then from the cloud came a voice that said,**
**"This is my beloved Son, with whom I am well pleased;**
**listen to him."**
**When the disciples heard this, they fell prostrate**
**and were very much afraid.**
**But Jesus came and touched them, saying,**
**"Rise, and do not be afraid."**
**And when the disciples raised their eyes,**
**they saw no one else but Jesus alone.**

As they were coming down from the mountain,
> Jesus charged them,
> "Do not tell the vision to anyone
> until the Son of Man has been raised from the dead."

**The Gospel of the Lord.** All: **Praise to you, Lord Jesus Christ.**

PRAYER OVER THE OFFERINGS
Sanctify, O Lord, we pray,
these offerings here made to celebrate
the glorious Transfiguration of your Only Begotten Son,
and by his radiant splendor
cleanse us from the stains of sin.
Through Christ our Lord. All: **Amen.**

COMMUNION ANTIPHON (Cf. 1 John 3:2)
When Christ appears, we shall be like him,
for we shall see him as he is.

PRAYER AFTER COMMUNION
May the heavenly nourishment we have received,
O Lord, we pray,
transform us into the likeness of your Son,
whose radiant splendor you willed to make manifest
in his glorious Transfiguration.
Who lives and reigns for ever and ever. All: **Amen.**

# Nineteenth Sunday in Ordinary Time

*August 13, 2017*

---

*Reflection on the Gospel*

*Peter brazenly tests Jesus about his identity: "Lord, if it is you . . ." Then it is that same Peter who becomes frightened and cries out to be saved when he does what Jesus commands him to do: "Come." With challenging truthfulness and saving power, Jesus responds both to Peter's brazenness and to his fright. When we act like Peter, Jesus responds to us as he did to Peter. To be certain of Jesus' challenging truthfulness and saving power, we need only to follow his command, "Come."*

- *Is my faith like that of Peter?*

—Living Liturgy™, *Nineteenth Sunday in Ordinary Time 2017*

## ENTRANCE ANTIPHON (Cf. Psalm 74[73]:20, 19, 22, 23)

Look to your covenant, O Lord,
and forget not the life of your poor ones for ever.
Arise, O God, and defend your cause,
and forget not the cries of those who seek you.

## COLLECT

Almighty ever-living God,
whom, taught by the Holy Spirit,
we dare to call our Father,
bring, we pray, to perfection in our hearts
the spirit of adoption as your sons and daughters,
that we may merit to enter into the inheritance
which you have promised.
Through our Lord Jesus Christ, your Son,
who lives and reigns with you in the unity of the Holy Spirit,
one God, for ever and ever. All: **Amen.**

## READING I (L 115-A) (1 Kings 19:9a, 11-13a)

### A reading from the first Book of Kings

*Go outside and stand on the mountain before the Lord.*

At the mountain of God, Horeb,
 Elijah came to a cave where he took shelter.
Then the LORD said to him,
 "Go outside and stand on the mountain before the
  LORD;
 the LORD will be passing by."
A strong and heavy wind was rending the mountains
 and crushing rocks before the LORD—
 but the LORD was not in the wind.
After the wind there was an earthquake—
 but the LORD was not in the earthquake.
After the earthquake there was fire—
 but the LORD was not in the fire.
After the fire there was a tiny whispering sound.
When he heard this,
 Elijah hid his face in his cloak
 and went and stood at the entrance of the cave.

The word of the Lord. All: Thanks be to God.

RESPONSORIAL PSALM 85

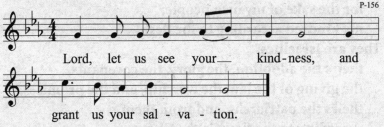

Music: Jay F. Hunstiger, © 1993, administered by Liturgical Press. All rights reserved.

Psalm 85:9, 10, 11-12, 13-14

℟. (8) **Lord, let us see your kindness, and grant us your salvation.**

I will hear what God proclaims;
 the LORD—for he proclaims peace.
Near indeed is his salvation to those who fear him,
 glory dwelling in our land. ℟.

*(continued)*

Kindness and truth shall meet;
   justice and peace shall kiss.
Truth shall spring out of the earth,
   and justice shall look down from heaven. ℟.

The LORD himself will give his benefits;
   our land shall yield its increase.
Justice shall walk before him,
   and prepare the way of his steps. ℟.

## READING II (Romans 9:1-5)

**A reading from the Letter of Saint Paul to the Romans**

*I could wish that I were accursed for the sake of my own people.*

**Brothers and sisters:**
**I speak the truth in Christ, I do not lie;**
   **my conscience joins with the Holy Spirit in bearing**
      **me witness**
   **that I have great sorrow and constant anguish in my**
      **heart.**
**For I could wish that I myself were accursed and cut off**
      **from Christ**
   **for the sake of my own people,**
   **my kindred according to the flesh.**
**They are Israelites;**
   **theirs the adoption, the glory, the covenants,**
   **the giving of the law, the worship, and the promises;**
   **theirs the patriarchs, and from them,**
   **according to the flesh, is the Christ,**
   **who is over all, God blessed forever. Amen.**

**The word of the Lord.** All: **Thanks be to God.**

## GOSPEL (Matthew 14:22-33)
### ALLELUIA (*See* Psalm 130:5)
℣. Alleluia, alleluia.   ℟. **Alleluia, alleluia.**
℣. I wait for the Lord;
   my soul waits for his word. ℟.

☩ **A reading from the holy Gospel according to Matthew**

All: **Glory to you, O Lord.**

*Command me to come to you on the water.*

**After he had fed the people, Jesus made the disciples get into a boat**
**and precede him to the other side,**
**while he dismissed the crowds.**
**After doing so, he went up on the mountain by himself to pray.**
**When it was evening he was there alone.**
**Meanwhile the boat, already a few miles offshore,**
**was being tossed about by the waves, for the wind was against it.**
**During the fourth watch of the night,**
**he came toward them walking on the sea.**
**When the disciples saw him walking on the sea they were terrified.**
**"It is a ghost," they said, and they cried out in fear.**
**At once Jesus spoke to them, "Take courage, it is I;**
**do not be afraid."**
**Peter said to him in reply,**
**"Lord, if it is you, command me to come to you on the water."**
**He said, "Come."**
**Peter got out of the boat and began to walk on the water toward Jesus.**
**But when he saw how strong the wind was he became frightened;**
**and, beginning to sink, he cried out, "Lord, save me!"**
**Immediately Jesus stretched out his hand and caught Peter,**
**and said to him, "O you of little faith, why did you doubt?"**
**After they got into the boat, the wind died down.**

**Those who were in the boat did him homage, saying,**
  **"Truly, you are the Son of God."**

**The Gospel of the Lord.** All: **Praise to you, Lord Jesus Christ.**

PRAYER OVER THE OFFERINGS
Be pleased, O Lord, to accept the offerings of your Church,
for in your mercy you have given them to be offered
and by your power you transform them
into the mystery of our salvation.
Through Christ our Lord. All: **Amen.**

COMMUNION ANTIPHON (Psalm 147:12, 14)
O Jerusalem, glorify the Lord,
who gives you your fill of finest wheat.

Or:

(Cf. John 6:51)
The bread that I will give, says the Lord,
is my flesh for the life of the world.

PRAYER AFTER COMMUNION
May the communion in your Sacrament
that we have consumed, save us, O Lord,
and confirm us in the light of your truth.
Through Christ our Lord. All: **Amen.**

# The Assumption of the Blessed Virgin Mary

## AT THE VIGIL MASS

*August 14, 2017*

The Mass of the Vigil of the Assumption is to be used at evening Masses.

*Reflection on the Gospel*

*The Holy Spirit overshadowed Mary, filling her with "the fruit of [her] womb." The Holy Spirit remained with Mary throughout her life, empowering her spirit to rejoice in God her Savior. Because of Mary's faithful response to the prompting of the Holy Spirit, she was lifted body and soul into heaven. Like Mary, all we are and are able to do as faithful disciples of the beloved Son is prompted by the Holy Spirit. Because of our faithful response, we too will be lifted up.*

- *"Blessed are you who believed that what was spoken to you by the Lord would be fulfilled."*

—*Living Liturgy™, Assumption 2017*

## ENTRANCE ANTIPHON

Glorious things are spoken of you, O Mary,
who today were exalted above the choirs of Angels
into eternal triumph with Christ.

## COLLECT

O God, who, looking on the lowliness of the Blessed Virgin Mary,
raised her to this grace,
that your Only Begotten Son was born of her according to the flesh
and that she was crowned this day with surpassing glory,
grant through her prayers,
that, saved by the mystery of your redemption,
we may merit to be exalted by you on high.
Through our Lord Jesus Christ, your Son,
who lives and reigns with you in the unity of the Holy Spirit,
one God, for ever and ever. All: **Amen.**

READING I (L 621) (1 Chronicles 15:3-4, 15-16; 16:1-2)

## A reading from the first Book of Chronicles

*They brought in the ark of God and set it within the tent which David had pitched for it.*

David assembled all Israel in Jerusalem to bring the ark
of the LORD
to the place which he had prepared for it.
David also called together the sons of Aaron and the
Levites.

The Levites bore the ark of God on their shoulders with
poles,
as Moses had ordained according to the word of the
LORD.

David commanded the chiefs of the Levites
to appoint their kinsmen as chanters,
to play on musical instruments, harps, lyres, and
cymbals,
to make a loud sound of rejoicing.

They brought in the ark of God and set it within the tent
which David had pitched for it.
Then they offered up burnt offerings and peace offerings
to God.
When David had finished offering up the burnt offerings
and peace offerings,
he blessed the people in the name of the LORD.

The word of the Lord. All: Thanks be to God.

RESPONSORIAL PSALM 132

P-181

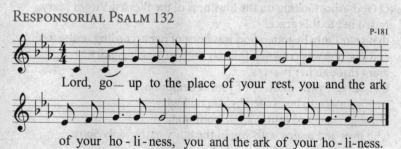

Lord, go— up to the place of your rest, you and the ark
of your ho - li - ness, you and the ark of your ho - li - ness.

Psalm 132:6-7, 9-10, 13-14

R℣. (8) **Lord, go up to the place of your rest, you and the ark of your holiness.**

Behold, we heard of it in Ephrathah;
  we found it in the fields of Jaar.
Let us enter into his dwelling,
  let us worship at his footstool. R℣.

May your priests be clothed with justice;
  let your faithful ones shout merrily for joy.
For the sake of David your servant,
  reject not the plea of your anointed. R℣.

For the LORD has chosen Zion;
  he prefers her for his dwelling.
"Zion is my resting place forever;
  in her will I dwell, for I prefer her." R℣.

READING II (1 Corinthians 15:54b-57)

**A reading from the first Letter of Saint Paul to the Corinthians**

*God gave us victory through Jesus Christ.*

**Brothers and sisters:**
**When that which is mortal clothes itself with immortality, then the word that is written shall come about:**

> *Death is swallowed up in victory.*
> *Where, O death, is your victory?*
> *Where, O death, is your sting?*

**The sting of death is sin,**
  **and the power of sin is the law.**
**But thanks be to God who gives us the victory**
  **through our Lord Jesus Christ.**

**The word of the Lord.** All: **Thanks be to God.**

## GOSPEL (Luke 11:27-28)

ALLELUIA (Luke 11:28)

℣. Alleluia, alleluia.  ℟. **Alleluia, alleluia.**

℣. Blessed are they who hear the word of God
and observe it. ℟.

✛ **A reading from the holy Gospel according to Luke**

All: **Glory to you, O Lord.**

*Blessed is the womb that carried you!*

**While Jesus was speaking,**
**a woman from the crowd called out and said to him,**
**"Blessed is the womb that carried you**
**and the breasts at which you nursed."**
**He replied,**
**"Rather, blessed are those**
**who hear the word of God and observe it."**

**The Gospel of the Lord.** All: **Praise to you, Lord Jesus Christ.**

PRAYER OVER THE OFFERINGS
Receive, we pray, O Lord,
the sacrifice of conciliation and praise,
which we celebrate on the Assumption of the holy Mother of God,
that it may lead us to your pardon
and confirm us in perpetual thanksgiving.
Through Christ our Lord. All: **Amen.**

COMMUNION ANTIPHON (Cf. Luke 11:27)
Blessed is the womb of the Virgin Mary,
which bore the Son of the eternal Father.

PRAYER AFTER COMMUNION
Having partaken of this heavenly table,
we beseech your mercy, Lord our God,
that we, who honor the Assumption of the Mother of God,
may be freed from every threat of harm.
Through Christ our Lord. All: **Amen.**

*August 15*

# AT THE MASS DURING THE DAY

ENTRANCE ANTIPHON (Cf. Revelation 12:1)
ENTRANCE ANTIPHON (Cf. Revelation 12:1)
A great sign appeared in heaven:
a woman clothed with the sun, and the moon beneath her
    feet,
and on her head a crown of twelve stars.

Or:

Let us all rejoice in the Lord,
as we celebrate the feast day in honor of the Virgin Mary,
at whose Assumption the Angels rejoice
and praise the Son of God.

COLLECT
Almighty ever-living God,
who assumed the Immaculate Virgin Mary, the Mother of your Son,
body and soul into heavenly glory,
grant, we pray,
that, always attentive to the things that are above,
we may merit to be sharers of her glory.
Through our Lord Jesus Christ, your Son,
who lives and reigns with you in the unity of the Holy Spirit,
one God, for ever and ever. All: **Amen.**

READING I (L 622) (Revelation 11:19a; 12:1-6a, 10ab)

## A reading from the Book of Revelation

*A woman clothed with the sun, with the moon beneath her feet.*

**God's temple in heaven was opened,**
    **and the ark of his covenant could be seen in the temple.**

**A great sign appeared in the sky, a woman clothed with**
    **the sun,**
    **with the moon under her feet,**
    **and on her head a crown of twelve stars.**
**She was with child and wailed aloud in pain as she**
    **labored to give birth.**
**Then another sign appeared in the sky;**

it was a huge red dragon, with seven heads and
ten horns,
and on its heads were seven diadems.
Its tail swept away a third of the stars in the sky
and hurled them down to the earth.
Then the dragon stood before the woman about to give
birth,
to devour her child when she gave birth.
She gave birth to a son, a male child,
destined to rule all the nations with an iron rod.
Her child was caught up to God and his throne.
The woman herself fled into the desert
where she had a place prepared by God.

Then I heard a loud voice in heaven say:
"Now have salvation and power come,
and the Kingdom of our God
and the authority of his Anointed One."

The word of the Lord. All: Thanks be to God.

## RESPONSORIAL PSALM 45

The queen stands at your right hand, ar-rayed in gold.

Psalm 45:10bc, 11, 12ab, 16

℟. (10bc) **The queen stands at your right hand, arrayed
in gold.**

The queen takes her place at your right hand in gold of
Ophir. ℟.

Hear, O daughter, and see; turn your ear,
forget your people and your father's house. ℟.

So shall the king desire your beauty;
for he is your lord. ℟.

They are borne in with gladness and joy;
they enter the palace of the king. ℟.

READING II (1 Corinthians 15:20-27)

**A reading from the first Letter of Saint Paul to the Corinthians**

*Christ, the firstfruits; then those who belong to him.*

**Brothers and sisters:**
**Christ has been raised from the dead,**
   **the firstfruits of those who have fallen asleep.**
**For since death came through man,**
   **the resurrection of the dead came also through man.**
**For just as in Adam all die,**
   **so too in Christ shall all be brought to life,**
   **but each one in proper order:**
   **Christ the firstfruits;**
   **then, at his coming, those who belong to Christ;**
   **then comes the end,**
   **when he hands over the Kingdom to his God and Father,**
   **when he has destroyed every sovereignty**
   **and every authority and power.**
**For he must reign until he has put all his enemies under**
      **his feet.**
**The last enemy to be destroyed is death,**
   **for "he subjected everything under his feet."**

**The word of the Lord.** All: **Thanks be to God.**

GOSPEL (Luke 1:39-56)
ALLELUIA
℣. Alleluia, alleluia.   ℟. **Alleluia, alleluia.**
℣. Mary is taken up to heaven;
   a chorus of angels exults. ℟.

☩ **A reading from the holy Gospel according to Luke**

All: **Glory to you, O Lord.**

*The Almighty has done great things for me; he has raised up the lowly.*

Mary set out
   and traveled to the hill country in haste
   to a town of Judah,
   where she entered the house of Zechariah
   and greeted Elizabeth.
When Elizabeth heard Mary's greeting,
   the infant leaped in her womb,
   and Elizabeth, filled with the Holy Spirit,
   cried out in a loud voice and said,
   "Blessed are you among women,
   and blessed is the fruit of your womb.
And how does this happen to me,
   that the mother of my Lord should come to me?
For at the moment the sound of your greeting reached
         my ears,
   the infant in my womb leaped for joy.
Blessed are you who believed
   that what was spoken to you by the Lord
   would be fulfilled."

And Mary said:
   "My soul proclaims the greatness of the Lord;
      my spirit rejoices in God my Savior
      for he has looked with favor on his lowly servant.
   From this day all generations will call me blessed:
      the Almighty has done great things for me
      and holy is his Name.
      He has mercy on those who fear him
      in every generation.
   He has shown the strength of his arm,
      and has scattered the proud in their conceit.
   He has cast down the mighty from their thrones,
      and has lifted up the lowly.
   He has filled the hungry with good things,
      and the rich he has sent away empty.

He has come to the help of his servant Israel
    for he has remembered his promise of mercy,
    the promise he made to our fathers,
    to Abraham and his children forever."

Mary remained with her about three months
    and then returned to her home.

**The Gospel of the Lord.** All: **Praise to you, Lord Jesus Christ.**

PRAYER OVER THE OFFERINGS
May this oblation, our tribute of homage,
rise up to you, O Lord,
and, through the intercession of the most Blessed Virgin Mary,
whom you assumed into heaven,
may our hearts, aflame with the fire of love,
constantly long for you.
Through Christ our Lord. All: **Amen.**

COMMUNION ANTIPHON (Luke 1:48-49)
All generations will call me blessed,
for he who is mighty has done great things for me.

PRAYER AFTER COMMUNION
Having received the Sacrament of salvation,
we ask you to grant, O Lord,
that, through the intercession of the Blessed Virgin Mary,
whom you assumed into heaven,
we may be brought to the glory of the resurrection.
Through Christ our Lord. All: **Amen.**

# Twentieth Sunday in Ordinary Time

*August 20, 2017*

*Reflection on the Gospel*

The "Canaanite woman" demonstrates the kind of faith needed to be healed by Jesus, the kind of faith needed to receive God's gift of salvation. Her faith was visible in three habits of the heart: awareness that she needed Jesus' healing intervention, persistence against all odds, and concern not only for herself but for her daughter. We too must develop and grow in the habits of the heart that make visible the great faith necessary for our healing and salvation.

- Will Jesus say to me "great is your faith!"?

—Living Liturgy™, *Twentieth Sunday in Ordinary Time 2017*

## ENTRANCE ANTIPHON (Psalm 84[83]:10-11)

Turn your eyes, O God, our shield;
and look on the face of your anointed one;
one day within your courts
is better than a thousand elsewhere.

## COLLECT

O God, who have prepared for those who love you
good things which no eye can see,
fill our hearts, we pray, with the warmth of your love,
so that, loving you in all things and above all things,
we may attain your promises,
which surpass every human desire.
Through our Lord Jesus Christ, your Son,
who lives and reigns with you in the unity of the Holy Spirit,
one God, for ever and ever. All: **Amen.**

## READING I (L 118-A) (Isaiah 56:1, 6-7)

**A reading from the Book of the Prophet Isaiah**

*I will bring foreigners to my holy mountain.*

Thus says the LORD:
Observe what is right, do what is just;
    for my salvation is about to come,
    my justice, about to be revealed.

The foreigners who join themselves to the LORD,
    ministering to him,
loving the name of the LORD,
    and becoming his servants—
all who keep the sabbath free from profanation
    and hold to my covenant,
them I will bring to my holy mountain
    and make joyful in my house of prayer;
their burnt offerings and sacrifices
    will be acceptable on my altar,
for my house shall be called
    a house of prayer for all peoples.

The word of the Lord. All: **Thanks be to God.**

RESPONSORIAL PSALM 67                                        P-157

O God, let all the na-tions praise— you!

Music: Jay F. Hunstiger, © 1991, administered by Liturgical Press. All rights reserved.

Psalm 67:2-3, 5, 6, 8

R̸. (4) **O God, let all the nations praise you!**

May God have pity on us and bless us;
    may he let his face shine upon us.
So may your way be known upon earth;
    among all nations, your salvation. R̸.

May the nations be glad and exult
    because you rule the peoples in equity;
    the nations on the earth you guide. R̸.

May the peoples praise you, O God;
    may all the peoples praise you!
May God bless us,
    and may all the ends of the earth fear him! R̸.

READING II (Romans 11:13-15, 29-32)

**A reading from the Letter of Saint Paul to the Romans**

*The gifts and the call of God for Israel are irrevocable.*

**Brothers and sisters:**
**I am speaking to you Gentiles.**
**Inasmuch as I am the apostle to the Gentiles,**
 **I glory in my ministry in order to make my race jealous**
 **and thus save some of them.**
**For if their rejection is the reconciliation of the world,**
 **what will their acceptance be but life from the dead?**

**For the gifts and the call of God are irrevocable.**
**Just as you once disobeyed God**
 **but have now received mercy because of their**
  **disobedience,**
 **so they have now disobeyed in order that,**
 **by virtue of the mercy shown to you,**
 **they too may now receive mercy.**
**For God delivered all to disobedience,**
 **that he might have mercy upon all.**

**The word of the Lord.** All: **Thanks be to God.**

GOSPEL (Matthew 15:21-28)
ALLELUIA (*See* Matthew 4:23)

℣. **Alleluia, alleluia.**  ℟. **Alleluia, alleluia.**
℣. **Jesus proclaimed the Gospel of the kingdom**
 **and cured every disease among the people.** ℟.

✠ **A reading from the holy Gospel according to Matthew**

All: **Glory to you, O Lord.**

*O woman, great is your faith!*

**At that time, Jesus withdrew to the region of Tyre and**
 **Sidon.**
**And behold, a Canaanite woman of that district came**
 **and called out,**
 **"Have pity on me, Lord, Son of David!**
**My daughter is tormented by a demon."**

But Jesus did not say a word in answer to her.
Jesus' disciples came and asked him,
   "Send her away, for she keeps calling out after us."
He said in reply,
   "I was sent only to the lost sheep of the house of Israel."
But the woman came and did Jesus homage, saying,
     "Lord, help me."
He said in reply,
   "It is not right to take the food of the children
   and throw it to the dogs."
She said, "Please, Lord, for even the dogs eat the scraps
   that fall from the table of their masters."
Then Jesus said to her in reply,
   "O woman, great is your faith!
Let it be done for you as you wish."
And the woman's daughter was healed from that hour.

The Gospel of the Lord. All: **Praise to you, Lord Jesus Christ.**

PRAYER OVER THE OFFERINGS
Receive our oblation, O Lord,
by which is brought about a glorious exchange,
that, by offering what you have given,
we may merit to receive your very self.
Through Christ our Lord. All: **Amen.**

COMMUNION ANTIPHON (Psalm 130[129]:7)
With the Lord there is mercy;
in him is plentiful redemption.

Or:

(John 6:51-52)
I am the living bread that came down from heaven,
   says the Lord.
Whoever eats of this bread will live for ever.

PRAYER AFTER COMMUNION
Made partakers of Christ through these Sacraments,
we humbly implore your mercy, Lord,
that, conformed to his image on earth,
we may merit also to be his coheirs in heaven.
Who lives and reigns for ever and ever. All: **Amen.**

# Twenty-First Sunday in Ordinary Time

### *August 27, 2017*

*Reflection on the Gospel*

*Jesus is "the Christ, the Son of the living God." Nothing short of a revelation by the "heavenly Father" could make this known to Peter. Nothing short of a revelation by the community of believers who acknowledge Jesus as "the Christ" and remain ever faithful to his saving mission could continue to make this known even to our day. The church is a fluidity of persons cemented together by the common bond of faithfully living the mystery of who Christ is.*

> • *Peter said in reply, "You are the Christ, the Son of the living God." Can I?*

—Living Liturgy™, *Twenty-first Sunday in Ordinary Time 2017*

## ENTRANCE ANTIPHON (Cf. Psalm 86[85]:1-3)

Turn your ear, O Lord, and answer me;
save the servant who trusts in you, my God.
Have mercy on me, O Lord, for I cry to you all the day long.

## COLLECT

O God, who cause the minds of the faithful
to unite in a single purpose,
grant your people to love what you command
and to desire what you promise,
that, amid the uncertainties of this world,
our hearts may be fixed on that place
where true gladness is found.
Through our Lord Jesus Christ, your Son,
who lives and reigns with you in the unity of the Holy Spirit,
one God, for ever and ever. All: **Amen.**

## Reading I (L 121-A) (Isaiah 22:19-23)

### A reading from the Book of the Prophet Isaiah

*I will place the key of the House of David upon his shoulder.*

Thus says the LORD to Shebna, master of the palace:
"I will thrust you from your office
   and pull you down from your station.
On that day I will summon my servant
   Eliakim, son of Hilkiah;
I will clothe him with your robe,
   and gird him with your sash,
   and give over to him your authority.
He shall be a father to the inhabitants of Jerusalem,
   and to the house of Judah.
I will place the key of the House of David on Eliakim's
      shoulder;
   when he opens, no one shall shut,
   when he shuts, no one shall open.
I will fix him like a peg in a sure spot,
   to be a place of honor for his family."

The word of the Lord. All: Thanks be to God.

## Responsorial Psalm 138

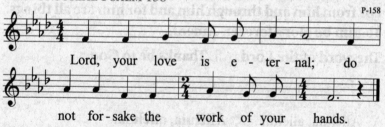

Lord, your love is e-ter-nal; do not for-sake the work of your hands.

Music: Jay F. Hunstiger, © 1993, administered by Liturgical Press. All rights reserved.

Psalm 138:1-2, 2-3, 6, 8

℟. (8bc) **Lord, your love is eternal; do not forsake the work of your hands.**

I will give thanks to you, O LORD, with all my heart,
   for you have heard the words of my mouth;

*(continued)*

in the presence of the angels I will sing your praise;
  I will worship at your holy temple. R̸.

I will give thanks to your name,
  because of your kindness and your truth:
when I called, you answered me;
  you built up strength within me. R̸.

The LORD is exalted, yet the lowly he sees,
  and the proud he knows from afar.
Your kindness, O LORD, endures forever;
  forsake not the work of your hands. R̸.

## READING II (Romans 11:33-36)

**A reading from the Letter of Saint Paul to the Romans**

*From God and through him and for him are all things.*

**Oh, the depth of the riches and wisdom and knowledge
    of God!
How inscrutable are his judgments and how
    unsearchable his ways!**
  *For who has known the mind of the Lord
    or who has been his counselor?
  Or who has given the Lord anything
    that he may be repaid?*
**For from him and through him and for him are all things.
To him be glory forever. Amen.**

**The word of the Lord.** All: **Thanks be to God.**

## GOSPEL (Matthew 16:13-20)

ALLELUIA (Matthew 16:18)

℣. Alleluia, alleluia.  R̸. **Alleluia, alleluia.**
℣. You are Peter and upon this rock I will build my Church
  and the gates of the netherworld shall not prevail
      against it. R̸.

✠ **A reading from the holy Gospel according to Matthew**

All: **Glory to you, O Lord.**

*You are Peter, and to you I will give the keys of the kingdom of
heaven.*

Jesus went into the region of Caesarea Philippi
  and he asked his disciples,
    "Who do people say that the Son of Man is?"
They replied, "Some say John the Baptist, others Elijah,
  still others Jeremiah or one of the prophets."
He said to them, "But who do you say that I am?"
Simon Peter said in reply,
  "You are the Christ, the Son of the living God."
Jesus said to him in reply,
  "Blessed are you, Simon son of Jonah.
For flesh and blood has not revealed this to you, but my
    heavenly Father.
And so I say to you, you are Peter,
  and upon this rock I will build my church,
  and the gates of the netherworld shall not prevail
    against it.
I will give you the keys to the kingdom of heaven.
Whatever you bind on earth shall be bound in heaven;
  and whatever you loose on earth shall be loosed in
    heaven."
Then he strictly ordered his disciples
  to tell no one that he was the Christ.

**The Gospel of the Lord.** All: **Praise to you, Lord Jesus Christ.**

PRAYER OVER THE OFFERINGS
O Lord, who gained for yourself a people by adoption
through the one sacrifice offered once for all,
bestow graciously on us, we pray,
the gifts of unity and peace in your Church.
Through Christ our Lord. All: **Amen.**

COMMUNION ANTIPHON (Cf. Psalm 104[103]:13-15)
The earth is replete with the fruits of your work, O Lord;
you bring forth bread from the earth
and wine to cheer the heart.

Or:

(Cf. John 6:54)

Whoever eats my flesh and drinks my blood
has eternal life, says the Lord,
and I will raise him up on the last day.

PRAYER AFTER COMMUNION
Complete within us, O Lord, we pray,
the healing work of your mercy
and graciously perfect and sustain us,
so that in all things we may please you.
Through Christ our Lord. All: **Amen.**

# Twenty-Second Sunday in Ordinary Time

*September 3, 2017*

---

*Reflection on the Gospel*

*Who wouldn't recoil, like Peter, when Jesus says that he would "suffer greatly . . . and be killed." Jesus' curt command to Peter—"Get behind me, Satan!"—points to the crux of the challenge: we are to think like God, not like humans. In God's saving plan, we must lose our life for Jesus' sake—only in this way can we share in Jesus' risen Life. No human instinctively understands or naively embraces this. God's love alone reveals this mystery and strengthens us as we surrender ourselves to it.*

- *". . . [B]e transformed by the renewal of your mind, that you may discern what is the will of God . . ."*

—*Living Liturgy™, Twenty-second Sunday in Ordinary Time 2017*

ENTRANCE ANTIPHON (Cf. Psalm 86[85]:3, 5)

Have mercy on me, O Lord, for I cry to you all the day long.
O Lord, you are good and forgiving,
full of mercy to all who call to you.

COLLECT

God of might, giver of every good gift,
put into our hearts the love of your name,
so that, by deepening our sense of reverence,
you may nurture in us what is good
and, by your watchful care,
keep safe what you have nurtured.
Through our Lord Jesus Christ, your Son,
who lives and reigns with you in the unity of the Holy Spirit,
one God, for ever and ever. All: **Amen.**

READING I (L 124-A) (Jeremiah 20:7-9)

## A reading from the Book of the Prophet Jeremiah

*The word of the Lord has brought me derision.*

You duped me, O LORD, and I let myself be duped;
  you were too strong for me, and you triumphed.
All the day I am an object of laughter;
  everyone mocks me.

Whenever I speak, I must cry out,
  violence and outrage is my message;
the word of the LORD has brought me
  derision and reproach all the day.

I say to myself, I will not mention him,
  I will speak in his name no more.
But then it becomes like fire burning in my heart,
  imprisoned in my bones;
I grow weary holding it in, I cannot endure it.

The word of the Lord. All: **Thanks be to God.**

RESPONSORIAL PSALM 63

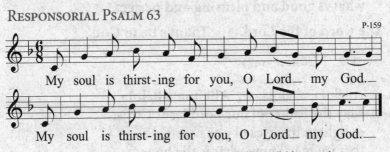

P-159

My soul is thirst-ing for you, O Lord_ my God._

My soul is thirst-ing for you, O Lord_ my God._

Psalm 63:2, 3-4, 5-6, 8-9

R̷. (2b) **My soul is thirsting for you, O Lord my God.**

O God, you are my God whom I seek;
    for you my flesh pines and my soul thirsts
    like the earth, parched, lifeless and without water. R̷.

Thus have I gazed toward you in the sanctuary
    to see your power and your glory,
for your kindness is a greater good than life;
    my lips shall glorify you. R̷.

Thus will I bless you while I live;
    lifting up my hands, I will call upon your name.
As with the riches of a banquet shall my soul be satisfied,
    and with exultant lips my mouth shall praise you. R̷.

You are my help,
    and in the shadow of your wings I shout for joy.
My soul clings fast to you;
    your right hand upholds me. R̷.

READING II (Romans 12:1-2)

**A reading from the Letter of Saint Paul to the Romans**

*Offer your bodies as a living sacrifice.*

**I urge you, brothers and sisters, by the mercies of God,**
    **to offer your bodies as a living sacrifice,**
        **holy and pleasing to God, your spiritual worship.**
**Do not conform yourselves to this age**
    **but be transformed by the renewal of your mind,**
        **that you may discern what is the will of God,**
        **what is good and pleasing and perfect.**

**The word of the Lord.** All: **Thanks be to God.**

GOSPEL (Matthew 16:21-27)

ALLELUIA (*See* Ephesians 1:17-18)

V̷. Alleluia, alleluia.   R̷. **Alleluia, alleluia.**
V̷. May the Father of our Lord Jesus Christ
    enlighten the eyes of our hearts,
    that we may know what is the hope
    that belongs to our call. R̷.

✛ **A reading from the holy Gospel according to Matthew**

All: **Glory to you, O Lord.**

*Whoever wishes to come after me must deny himself.*

Jesus began to show his disciples
    that he must go to Jerusalem and suffer greatly
    from the elders, the chief priests, and the scribes,
    and be killed and on the third day be raised.
Then Peter took Jesus aside and began to rebuke him,
    "God forbid, Lord! No such thing shall ever happen
        to you."
He turned and said to Peter,
    "Get behind me, Satan! You are an obstacle to me.
You are thinking not as God does, but as human beings
    do."

Then Jesus said to his disciples,
    "Whoever wishes to come after me must deny himself,
    take up his cross, and follow me.
For whoever wishes to save his life will lose it,
    but whoever loses his life for my sake will find it.
What profit would there be for one to gain the whole
        world
    and forfeit his life?
Or what can one give in exchange for his life?
For the Son of Man will come with his angels in his
        Father's glory,
    and then he will repay all according to his conduct."

**The Gospel of the Lord.** All: **Praise to you, Lord Jesus Christ.**

PRAYER OVER THE OFFERINGS
May this sacred offering, O Lord,
confer on us always the blessing of salvation,
that what it celebrates in mystery
it may accomplish in power.
Through Christ our Lord. All: **Amen.**

COMMUNION ANTIPHON (Psalm 31[30]:20)
How great is the goodness, Lord,
that you keep for those who fear you.

Or:

(Matthew 5:9-10)
Blessed are the peacemakers,
for they shall be called children of God.
Blessed are they who are persecuted for the sake of
    righteousness,
for theirs is the Kingdom of Heaven.

PRAYER AFTER COMMUNION
Renewed by this bread from the heavenly table,
we beseech you, Lord,
that, being the food of charity,
it may confirm our hearts
and stir us to serve you in our neighbor.
Through Christ our Lord. All: **Amen.**

# Twenty-Third Sunday in Ordinary Time

*September 10, 2017*

*Reflection on the Gospel*

*The heart of this gospel concerning reconciliation is actually about con-*
*version and the call to build up the church. To "win over" those who*
*"sin[ ] against" another in the church is to bring them to conversion of*
*life. The work of effecting reconciliation and conversion is not simply the*
*personal judgment of a single community member who has been*

*wronged. The work is always communal, informed by humble prayer,
and guided by Jesus who remains "in the midst" of his Body, the church.*

• *If your brother or sister listens to you, you have won them over.*

—Living Liturgy™, *Twenty-third Sunday in Ordinary Time 2017*

## Entrance Antiphon (Psalm 119[118]:137, 124)

You are just, O Lord, and your judgment is right;
treat your servant in accord with your merciful love.

## Collect

O God, by whom we are redeemed and receive adoption,
look graciously upon your beloved sons and daughters,
that those who believe in Christ
may receive true freedom
and an everlasting inheritance.
Through our Lord Jesus Christ, your Son,
who lives and reigns with you in the unity of the Holy Spirit,
one God, for ever and ever. All: **Amen.**

## Reading I (L 127-A) (Ezekiel 33:7-9)

### A reading from the Book of the Prophet Ezekiel

*If you do not speak out to dissuade the wicked from his way,
I will hold you responsible for his death.*

**Thus says the Lord:**
> **You, son of man, I have appointed watchman for the
> house of Israel;**
> **when you hear me say anything, you shall warn them
> for me.**
**If I tell the wicked, "O wicked one, you shall surely die,"**
> **and you do not speak out to dissuade the wicked from
> his way,**
> **the wicked shall die for his guilt,**
> **but I will hold you responsible for his death.**
**But if you warn the wicked,**
> **trying to turn him from his way,**
> **and he refuses to turn from his way,**
> **he shall die for his guilt,**
> **but you shall save yourself.**

**The word of the Lord.** All: **Thanks be to God.**

## RESPONSIONAL PSALM 95

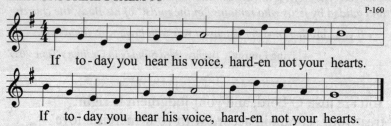

If to-day you hear his voice, hard-en not your hearts.

If to-day you hear his voice, hard-en not your hearts.

Psalm 95:1-2, 6-7, 8-9

℟. (8) **If today you hear his voice, harden not your hearts.**

Come, let us sing joyfully to the LORD;
> let us acclaim the rock of our salvation.

Let us come into his presence with thanksgiving;
> let us joyfully sing psalms to him. ℟.

Come, let us bow down in worship;
> let us kneel before the LORD who made us.

For he is our God,
> and we are the people he shepherds, the flock he
> guides. ℟.

Oh, that today you would hear his voice:
> "Harden not your hearts as at Meribah,
> as in the day of Massah in the desert,

where your fathers tempted me;
> they tested me though they had seen my works." ℟.

## READING II (Romans 13:8-10)

**A reading from the Letter of Saint Paul to the Romans**

*Love is the fulfillment of the law.*

**Brothers and sisters:**

**Owe nothing to anyone, except to love one another;**
> **for the one who loves another has fulfilled the law.**

**The commandments, "You shall not commit adultery;**
> **you shall not kill; you shall not steal; you shall not**
> **covet,"**

> **and whatever other commandment there may be,**
> **are summed up in this saying, namely,**

"You shall love your neighbor as yourself."
Love does no evil to the neighbor;
hence, love is the fulfillment of the law.

**The word of the Lord.** All: **Thanks be to God.**

GOSPEL (Matthew 18:15-20)
ALLELUIA (2 Corinthians 5:19)

℣. Alleluia, alleluia.  ℟. **Alleluia, alleluia.**
℣. God was reconciling the world to himself in Christ
and entrusting to us the message of reconciliation. ℟.

✚ **A reading from the holy Gospel according to Matthew**

All: **Glory to you, O Lord.**

*If your brother or sister listens to you, you have won them over.*

**Jesus said to his disciples:**
"If your brother sins against you,
go and tell him his fault between you and him alone.
If he listens to you, you have won over your brother.
If he does not listen,
take one or two others along with you,
so that 'every fact may be established
on the testimony of two or three witnesses.'
If he refuses to listen to them, tell the church.
If he refuses to listen even to the church,
then treat him as you would a Gentile or a tax collector.
Amen, I say to you,
whatever you bind on earth shall be bound in heaven,
and whatever you loose on earth shall be loosed in
heaven.
Again, amen, I say to you,
if two of you agree on earth
about anything for which they are to pray,
it shall be granted to them by my heavenly Father.
For where two or three are gathered together in my name,
there am I in the midst of them."

**The Gospel of the Lord.** All: **Praise to you, Lord Jesus Christ.**

PRAYER OVER THE OFFERINGS

O God, who give us the gift of true prayer and of peace,
graciously grant that, through this offering,
we may do fitting homage to your divine majesty
and, by partaking of the sacred mystery,
we may be faithfully united in mind and heart.
Through Christ our Lord. All: **Amen.**

COMMUNION ANTIPHON (Cf. Psalm 42[41]:2-3)

Like the deer that yearns for running streams,
so my soul is yearning for you, my God;
my soul is thirsting for God, the living God.

Or:

(John 8:12)

I am the light of the world, says the Lord;
whoever follows me will not walk in darkness,
but will have the light of life.

PRAYER AFTER COMMUNION

Grant that your faithful, O Lord,
whom you nourish and endow with life
through the food of your Word and heavenly Sacrament,
may so benefit from your beloved Son's great gifts
that we may merit an eternal share in his life.
Who lives and reigns for ever and ever. All: **Amen.**

# Twenty-Fourth Sunday in Ordinary Time

*September 17, 2017*

## Reflection on the Gospel

*Jesus tells a striking parable about two instances of forgiveness of debts—one lavishly given, the other miserly withheld. The implication is that God acts like the extravagant king. But not so. God's forgiveness of us is always even beyond extravagance, even beyond measure. We measure; God does not. As infinite as God's forgiveness is, to receive it is not without a substantial condition. We are to forgive one another as God forgives—from the heart, "seventy-seven times." Only forgiveness that comes from the heart is immeasurable.*

• *I am lavish with forgiveness when . . . Or I am miserly when . . .*

—Living Liturgy™, *Twenty-fourth Sunday in Ordinary Time 2017*

## ENTRANCE ANTIPHON (Cf. Sirach 36:18)

Give peace, O Lord, to those who wait for you,
that your prophets be found true.
Hear the prayers of your servant,
and of your people Israel.

## COLLECT

Look upon us, O God,
Creator and ruler of all things,
and, that we may feel the working of your mercy,
grant that we may serve you with all our heart.
Through our Lord Jesus Christ, your Son,
who lives and reigns with you in the unity of the Holy Spirit,
one God, for ever and ever. All: **Amen.**

READING I (L 130-A) (Sirach 27:30—28:7)

## A reading from the Book of Sirach

*Forgive your neighbor's injustice; then when you pray, your own sins will be forgiven.*

> Wrath and anger are hateful things,
>   yet the sinner hugs them tight.
> The vengeful will suffer the LORD's vengeance,
>   for he remembers their sins in detail.
> Forgive your neighbor's injustice;
>   then when you pray, your own sins will be forgiven.
> Could anyone nourish anger against another
>   and expect healing from the LORD?
> Could anyone refuse mercy to another like himself,
>   can he seek pardon for his own sins?
> If one who is but flesh cherishes wrath,
>   who will forgive his sins?
> Remember your last days, set enmity aside;
>   remember death and decay, and cease from sin!
> Think of the commandments, hate not your neighbor;
>   remember the Most High's covenant, and overlook
>     faults.

The word of the Lord. All: Thanks be to God.

RESPONSORIAL PSALM 103

P-161

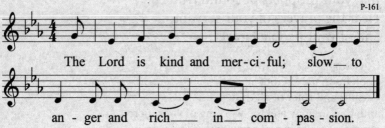

The Lord is kind and mer-ci-ful; slow to an-ger and rich in com-pas-sion.

Music: Jay F. Hunstiger, © 1993, administered by Liturgical Press. All rights reserved.

Psalm 103:1-2, 3-4, 9-10, 11-12

R̸. (8) **The Lord is kind and merciful, slow to anger, and rich in compassion.**

Bless the Lᴏʀᴅ, O my soul;
  and all my being, bless his holy name.
Bless the Lᴏʀᴅ, O my soul,
  and forget not all his benefits. ℟.

He pardons all your iniquities,
  heals all your ills,
redeems your life from destruction,
  he crowns you with kindness and compassion. ℟.

He will not always chide,
  nor does he keep his wrath forever.
Not according to our sins does he deal with us,
  nor does he requite us according to our crimes. ℟.

For as the heavens are high above the earth,
  so surpassing is his kindness toward those who fear
    him.
As far as the east is from the west,
  so far has he put our transgressions from us. ℟.

Rᴇᴀᴅɪɴɢ II (Romans 14:7-9)

**A reading from the Letter of Saint Paul to the Romans**

*Whether we live or die, we are the Lord's.*

**Brothers and sisters:**
**None of us lives for oneself, and no one dies for oneself.**
**For if we live, we live for the Lord,**
  **and if we die, we die for the Lord;**
  **so then, whether we live or die, we are the Lord's.**
**For this is why Christ died and came to life,**
  **that he might be Lord of both the dead and the living.**

**The word of the Lord.** All: **Thanks be to God.**

Gᴏsᴘᴇʟ (Matthew 18:21-35)
Aʟʟᴇʟᴜɪᴀ (John 13:34)
℣. Alleluia, alleluia. ℟. **Alleluia, alleluia.**
℣. I give you a new commandment, says the Lord;
  love one another as I have loved you. ℟.

✠ **A reading from the holy Gospel according to Matthew**

All: **Glory to you, O Lord.**

*I say to you, forgive not seven times, but seventy-seven times.*

**Peter approached Jesus and asked him,**
    **"Lord, if my brother sins against me,**
    **how often must I forgive?**
**As many as seven times?"**
**Jesus answered, "I say to you, not seven times but**
        **seventy-seven times.**
**That is why the kingdom of heaven may be likened to a**
        **king**
    **who decided to settle accounts with his servants.**
**When he began the accounting,**
    **a debtor was brought before him who owed him a**
            **huge amount.**
**Since he had no way of paying it back,**
    **his master ordered him to be sold,**
    **along with his wife, his children, and all his property,**
    **in payment of the debt.**
**At that, the servant fell down, did him homage, and said,**
    **'Be patient with me, and I will pay you back in full.'**
**Moved with compassion the master of that servant**
    **let him go and forgave him the loan.**
**When that servant had left, he found one of his fellow**
        **servants**
    **who owed him a much smaller amount.**
**He seized him and started to choke him, demanding,**
    **'Pay back what you owe.'**
**Falling to his knees, his fellow servant begged him,**
    **'Be patient with me, and I will pay you back.'**
**But he refused.**
**Instead, he had the fellow servant put in prison**
    **until he paid back the debt.**

Now when his fellow servants saw what had happened,
    they were deeply disturbed, and went to their master
    and reported the whole affair.
His master summoned him and said to him, 'You wicked
    servant!
I forgave you your entire debt because you begged me to.
Should you not have had pity on your fellow servant,
    as I had pity on you?'
Then in anger his master handed him over to the torturers
    until he should pay back the whole debt.
So will my heavenly Father do to you,
    unless each of you forgives your brother from your
        heart."

**The Gospel of the Lord.** All: **Praise to you, Lord Jesus Christ.**

PRAYER OVER THE OFFERINGS
Look with favor on our supplications, O Lord,
and in your kindness accept these, your servants' offerings,
that what each has offered to the honor of your name
may serve the salvation of all.
Through Christ our Lord. All: **Amen.**

COMMUNION ANTIPHON (Cf. Psalm 36[35]:8)
How precious is your mercy, O God!
The children of men seek shelter in the shadow of your
    wings.

Or:

(Cf. 1 Corinthians 10:16)
The chalice of blessing that we bless
is a communion in the Blood of Christ;
and the bread that we break
is a sharing in the Body of the Lord.

PRAYER AFTER COMMUNION
May the working of this heavenly gift, O Lord, we pray,
take possession of our minds and bodies,
so that its effects, and not our own desires,
may always prevail in us.
Through Christ our Lord. All: **Amen.**

# Twenty-Fifth Sunday in Ordinary Time

*September 24, 2017*

*Reflection on the Gospel*

*The workers, like the landowner, are persistent. Instead of giving up and going home, they remain in the marketplace seemingly "standing idle." Actually their idleness was not simply doing nothing—theirs was an active waiting; these workers persistently remain ready and willing to work. Of such is the "kingdom of heaven." The "kingdom of heaven" consists of those who persist in awaiting God's recurring call, and who respond willingly no matter what hour the call comes. The laborers' wage is beyond monetary expectation—it is salvation.*

  • *I am ready and willing to work for the kingdom of heaven when I,*
  . . .

—Living Liturgy™, *Twenty-fifth Sunday in Ordinary Time 2017*

## Entrance Antiphon

I am the salvation of the people, says the Lord.
Should they cry to me in any distress,
I will hear them, and I will be their Lord for ever.

## Collect

O God, who founded all the commands of your sacred Law
upon love of you and of our neighbor,
grant that, by keeping your precepts,
we may merit to attain eternal life.
Through our Lord Jesus Christ, your Son,
who lives and reigns with you in the unity of the Holy Spirit,
one God, for ever and ever. All: **Amen.**

## Reading I (L 133-A) (Isaiah 55:6-9)

**A reading from the Book of the Prophet Isaiah**

*My thoughts are not your thoughts.*

**Seek the L**ord **while he may be found,**
    **call him while he is near.**
**Let the scoundrel forsake his way,**
    **and the wicked his thoughts;**
**let him turn to the L**ord **for mercy;**
    **to our God, who is generous in forgiving.**
**For my thoughts are not your thoughts,**
    **nor are your ways my ways, says the L**ord.
**As high as the heavens are above the earth,**
    **so high are my ways above your ways**
    **and my thoughts above your thoughts.**

**The word of the Lord.** All: **Thanks be to God.**

Responsorial Psalm 145

P-162

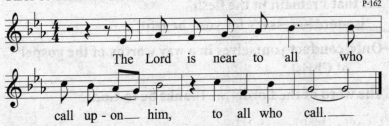

The Lord is near to all who call upon him, to all who call.

Music: Jay F. Hunstiger, © 1993, administered by Liturgical Press. All rights reserved.

Psalm 145:2-3, 8-9, 17-18

R̿. (18a) **The Lord is near to all who call upon him.**

**Every day will I bless you,**
    **and I will praise your name forever and ever.**
**Great is the L**ord **and highly to be praised;**
    **his greatness is unsearchable.** R̿.

**The L**ord **is gracious and merciful,**
    **slow to anger and of great kindness.**
**The L**ord **is good to all**
    **and compassionate toward all his works.** R̿.

**The L**ord **is just in all his ways**
    **and holy in all his works.**
**The L**ord **is near to all who call upon him,**
    **to all who call upon him in truth.** R̿.

## Reading II (Philippians 1:20c-24, 27a)

**A reading from the Letter of Saint Paul to the Philippians**

*For me to live is Christ.*

**Brothers and sisters:**
**Christ will be magnified in my body, whether by life or**
**by death.**
**For to me life is Christ, and death is gain.**
**If I go on living in the flesh,**
**that means fruitful labor for me.**
**And I do not know which I shall choose.**
**I am caught between the two.**
**I long to depart this life and be with Christ,**
**for that is far better.**
**Yet that I remain in the flesh**
**is more necessary for your benefit.**

**Only, conduct yourselves in a way worthy of the gospel**
**of Christ.**

**The word of the Lord.** All: **Thanks be to God.**

## Gospel (Matthew 20:1-16a)

Alleluia (*See* Acts of the Apostles 16:14b)

℣. Alleluia, alleluia. ℟. **Alleluia, alleluia.**
℣. Open our hearts, O Lord,
to listen to the words of your Son. ℟.

☩ **A reading from the holy Gospel according to Matthew**

All: **Glory to you, O Lord.**

*Are you envious because I am generous?*

**Jesus told his disciples this parable:**
**"The kingdom of heaven is like a landowner**
**who went out at dawn to hire laborers for his vineyard.**
**After agreeing with them for the usual daily wage,**
**he sent them into his vineyard.**
**Going out about nine o'clock,**
**the landowner saw others standing idle in the**
**marketplace,**

and he said to them, 'You too go into my vineyard,
   and I will give you what is just.'
So they went off.
And he went out again around noon,
   and around three o'clock, and did likewise.
Going out about five o'clock,
   the landowner found others standing around, and
         said to them,
   'Why do you stand here idle all day?'
They answered, 'Because no one has hired us.'
He said to them, 'You too go into my vineyard.'
When it was evening the owner of the vineyard said to
      his foreman,
   'Summon the laborers and give them their pay,
   beginning with the last and ending with the first.'
When those who had started about five o'clock came,
   each received the usual daily wage.
So when the first came, they thought that they would
      receive more,
   but each of them also got the usual wage.
And on receiving it they grumbled against the landowner,
      saying,
   'These last ones worked only one hour,
   and you have made them equal to us,
   who bore the day's burden and the heat.'
He said to one of them in reply,
   'My friend, I am not cheating you.
Did you not agree with me for the usual daily wage?
Take what is yours and go.
What if I wish to give this last one the same as you?
Or am I not free to do as I wish with my own money?
Are you envious because I am generous?'
Thus, the last will be first, and the first will be last.'"

The Gospel of the Lord. All: **Praise to you, Lord Jesus Christ.**

PRAYER OVER THE OFFERINGS
Receive with favor, O Lord, we pray,
the offerings of your people,
that what they profess with devotion and faith
may be theirs through these heavenly mysteries.
Through Christ our Lord. All: **Amen.**

COMMUNION ANTIPHON (Psalm 119[118]:4-5)
You have laid down your precepts to be carefully kept;
may my ways be firm in keeping your statutes.

Or:

(John 10:14)
I am the Good Shepherd, says the Lord;
I know my sheep, and mine know me.

PRAYER AFTER COMMUNION
Graciously raise up, O Lord,
those you renew with this Sacrament,
that we may come to possess your redemption
both in mystery and in the manner of our life.
Through Christ our Lord. All: **Amen.**

# Twenty-Sixth Sunday in Ordinary Time

*October 1, 2017*

*Reflection on the Gospel*

*Jesus pointedly indicts the "chief priests and elders of the people" by
equating them in this parable with the second son who does not do the
"father's will." Surprisingly, who does do the "father's will" are "tax
collectors and prostitutes." Their sinful lives indicated an initial no to
God, but then they came to believe, changed their minds, and repented*

*when they heard a call to "the way of righteousness." Believing is changing our way of living, walking "the way of righteousness," and doing the Father's will.*

• *To do the Father's will is to . . .*

—Living Liturgy™, *Twenty-sixth Sunday in Ordinary Time 2017*

ENTRANCE ANTIPHON (Daniel 3:31, 29, 30, 43, 42)
All that you have done to us, O Lord,
you have done with true judgment,
for we have sinned against you
and not obeyed your commandments.
But give glory to your name
and deal with us according to the bounty of your mercy.

COLLECT
O God, who manifest your almighty power
above all by pardoning and showing mercy,
bestow, we pray, your grace abundantly upon us
and make those hastening to attain your promises
heirs to the treasures of heaven.
Through our Lord Jesus Christ, your Son,
who lives and reigns with you in the unity of the Holy Spirit,
one God, for ever and ever. All: **Amen.**

READING I (L 136-A) (Ezekiel 18:25-28)

## A reading from the Book of the Prophet Ezekiel

*By turning from wickedness, a wicked person shall preserve his life.*

**Thus says the LORD:**
**You say, "The LORD's way is not fair!"**
**Hear now, house of Israel:**
  **Is it my way that is unfair, or rather, are not your ways**
    **unfair?**
**When someone virtuous turns away from virtue to**
    **commit iniquity, and dies,**
  **it is because of the iniquity he committed that he**
    **must die.**
**But if he turns from the wickedness he has committed,**
  **and does what is right and just,**
  **he shall preserve his life;**

since he has turned away from all the sins that he has
    committed,
he shall surely live, he shall not die.

**The word of the Lord.** All: **Thanks be to God.**

RESPONSORIAL PSALM 25

P-163

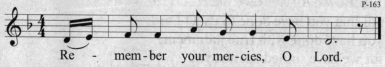

Re - mem-ber your mer-cies, O Lord.

Psalm 25:4-5, 6-7, 8-9

R℣. (6a) **Remember your mercies, O Lord.**

Your ways, O LORD, make known to me;
    teach me your paths,
guide me in your truth and teach me,
    for you are God my savior. R℣.

Remember that your compassion, O LORD,
    and your love are from of old.
The sins of my youth and my frailties remember not;
    in your kindness remember me,
    because of your goodness, O LORD. R℣.

Good and upright is the LORD;
    thus he shows sinners the way.
He guides the humble to justice,
    and teaches the humble his way. R℣.

READING II (Philippians 2:1-11) *or* Shorter Form [ ]
(Philippians 2:1-5)

**A reading from the Letter of Saint Paul to the Philippians**
*Have in you the same attitude that is also in Christ Jesus.*
[**Brothers and sisters:**
**If there is any encouragement in Christ,**
    **any solace in love,**
    **any participation in the Spirit,**
    **any compassion and mercy,**
    **complete my joy by being of the same mind, with the**
        **same love,**

united in heart, thinking one thing.
Do nothing out of selfishness or out of vainglory;
  rather, humbly regard others as more important than
      yourselves,
  each looking out not for his own interests,
  but also for those of others.

Have in you the same attitude
  that is also in Christ Jesus,]
      who, though he was in the form of God,
      did not regard equality with God
      something to be grasped.
Rather, he emptied himself,
  taking the form of a slave,
  coming in human likeness;
  and found human in appearance,
  he humbled himself,
  becoming obedient to the point of death,
  even death on a cross.
Because of this, God greatly exalted him
      and bestowed on him the name
      which is above every name,
      that at the name of Jesus
      every knee should bend,
  of those in heaven and on earth and under the
      earth,
      and every tongue confess that
      Jesus Christ is Lord,
      to the glory of God the Father.

The word of the Lord. All: Thanks be to God.

GOSPEL (Matthew 21:28-32)
ALLELUIA (John 10:27)
℣. Alleluia, alleluia. ℟. **Alleluia, alleluia.**
℣. My sheep hear my voice, says the Lord;
  I know them, and they follow me. ℟.

✠ **A reading from the holy Gospel according to Matthew**

All: **Glory to you, O Lord.**

*He changed his mind and went. Tax collectors and prostitutes are entering the kingdom of heaven before you.*

**Jesus said to the chief priests and elders of the people:**
  **"What is your opinion?**
**A man had two sons.**
**He came to the first and said,**
  **'Son, go out and work in the vineyard today.'**
**He said in reply, 'I will not,'**
  **but afterwards changed his mind and went.**
**The man came to the other son and gave the same order.**
**He said in reply, 'Yes, sir,' but did not go.**
**Which of the two did his father's will?"**
**They answered, "The first."**
**Jesus said to them, "Amen, I say to you,**
  **tax collectors and prostitutes**
  **are entering the kingdom of God before you.**
**When John came to you in the way of righteousness,**
  **you did not believe him;**
  **but tax collectors and prostitutes did.**
**Yet even when you saw that,**
  **you did not later change your minds and believe him."**

**The Gospel of the Lord.** All: **Praise to you, Lord Jesus Christ.**

PRAYER OVER THE OFFERINGS

Grant us, O merciful God,
that this our offering may find acceptance with you
and that through it the wellspring of all blessing
may be laid open before us.
Through Christ our Lord. All: **Amen.**

COMMUNION ANTIPHON (Cf. Psalm 119[118]:49-50)

Remember your word to your servant, O Lord,
by which you have given me hope.
This is my comfort when I am brought low.

Or:

(1 John 3:16)

By this we came to know the love of God:
that Christ laid down his life for us;
so we ought to lay down our lives for one another.

### Prayer after Communion

May this heavenly mystery, O Lord,
restore us in mind and body,
that we may be coheirs in glory with Christ,
to whose suffering we are united
whenever we proclaim his Death.
Who lives and reigns for ever and ever. All: **Amen.**

# Twenty-Seventh Sunday in Ordinary Time

## October 8, 2017

---

*Reflection on the Gospel*

*Jesus tells a parable about a landowner who plants, protects, and equips his vineyard, and about tenants who take progressively more violent steps to usurp what is not theirs. Jesus issues judgment against the chief priests and elders in no uncertain terms: "the kingdom of God will be taken away from you / and given to a people that will produce its fruit." The kingdom of God will be taken from anyone who acts egregiously against the norms of righteousness. It will be given to those who remain faithful to the Son, the Cornerstone. Anyone.*

- *God will lease the vineyard to other tenants . . .*

—*Living Liturgy™, Twenty-seventh Sunday in Ordinary Time 2017*

### Entrance Antiphon (Cf. Esther 4:17)

Within your will, O Lord, all things are established,
and there is none that can resist your will.

For you have made all things, the heaven and the earth,
and all that is held within the circle of heaven;
you are the Lord of all.

## COLLECT

Almighty ever-living God,
who in the abundance of your kindness
surpass the merits and the desires of those who entreat you,
pour out your mercy upon us
to pardon what conscience dreads
and to give what prayer does not dare to ask.
Through our Lord Jesus Christ, your Son,
who lives and reigns with you in the unity of the Holy Spirit,
one God, for ever and ever. All: **Amen.**

## READING I (L 139-A) (Isaiah 5:1-7)

### A reading from the Book of the Prophet Isaiah

*The vineyard of the Lord of hosts is the house of Israel.*

Let me now sing of my friend,
   my friend's song concerning his vineyard.
My friend had a vineyard
   on a fertile hillside;
he spaded it, cleared it of stones,
   and planted the choicest vines;
within it he built a watchtower,
   and hewed out a wine press.
Then he looked for the crop of grapes,
   but what it yielded was wild grapes.

Now, inhabitants of Jerusalem and people of Judah,
   judge between me and my vineyard:
What more was there to do for my vineyard
   that I had not done?
Why, when I looked for the crop of grapes,
   did it bring forth wild grapes?
Now, I will let you know
   what I mean to do with my vineyard:
take away its hedge, give it to grazing,
   break through its wall, let it be trampled!

Yes, I will make it a ruin:
   it shall not be pruned or hoed,
      but overgrown with thorns and briers;
I will command the clouds
   not to send rain upon it.
The vineyard of the LORD of hosts is the house of Israel,
   and the people of Judah are his cherished plant;
he looked for judgment, but see, bloodshed!
   for justice, but hark, the outcry!

The word of the Lord. All: Thanks be to God.

RESPONSORIAL PSALM 80

P-164

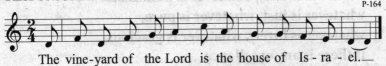

The vine-yard of the Lord is the house of Is-ra-el.

Psalm 80:9, 12, 13-14, 15-16, 19-20

R̸. (Isaiah 5:7a) **The vineyard of the Lord is the house of Israel.**

A vine from Egypt you transplanted;
   you drove away the nations and planted it.
It put forth its foliage to the Sea,
   its shoots as far as the River. R̸.

Why have you broken down its walls,
   so that every passer-by plucks its fruit,
the boar from the forest lays it waste,
   and the beasts of the field feed upon it? R̸.

Once again, O LORD of hosts,
   look down from heaven, and see;
take care of this vine,
   and protect what your right hand has planted
   the son of man whom you yourself made strong. R̸.

Then we will no more withdraw from you;
   give us new life, and we will call upon your name.
O LORD, God of hosts, restore us;
   if your face shine upon us, then we shall be saved. R̸.

## READING II (Philippians 4:6-9)

**A reading from the Letter of Saint Paul to the Philippians**

*Do these things, and the God of peace will be with you.*

**Brothers and sisters:
Have no anxiety at all, but in everything,
by prayer and petition, with thanksgiving,
make your requests known to God.
Then the peace of God that surpasses all understanding
will guard your hearts and minds in Christ Jesus.**

**Finally, brothers and sisters,
whatever is true, whatever is honorable,
whatever is just, whatever is pure,
whatever is lovely, whatever is gracious,
if there is any excellence
and if there is anything worthy of praise,
think about these things.
Keep on doing what you have learned and received
and heard and seen in me.
Then the God of peace will be with you.**

**The word of the Lord.** All: **Thanks be to God.**

## GOSPEL (Matthew 21:33-43)

ALLELUIA (*See* John 15:16)

℣. Alleluia, alleluia.  ℟. **Alleluia, alleluia.**
℣. I have chosen you from the world, says the Lord,
to go and bear fruit that will remain. ℟.

✠ **A reading from the holy Gospel according to Matthew**

All: **Glory to you, O Lord.**

*He will lease his vineyard to other tenants.*

**Jesus said to the chief priests and the elders of the people:
"Hear another parable.
There was a landowner who planted a vineyard,
put a hedge around it, dug a wine press in it, and built
a tower.
Then he leased it to tenants and went on a journey.**

When vintage time drew near,
he sent his servants to the tenants to obtain his
produce.
But the tenants seized the servants and one they beat,
another they killed, and a third they stoned.
Again he sent other servants, more numerous than the
first ones,
but they treated them in the same way.
Finally, he sent his son to them, thinking,
'They will respect my son.'
But when the tenants saw the son, they said to one
another,
'This is the heir.
Come, let us kill him and acquire his inheritance.'
They seized him, threw him out of the vineyard, and
killed him.
What will the owner of the vineyard do to those tenants
when he comes?"
They answered him,
"He will put those wretched men to a wretched death
and lease his vineyard to other tenants
who will give him the produce at the proper times."
Jesus said to them, "Did you never read in the Scriptures:
*The stone that the builders rejected*
*has become the cornerstone;*
*by the Lord has this been done,*
*and it is wonderful in our eyes?*
Therefore, I say to you,
the kingdom of God will be taken away from you
and given to a people that will produce its fruit."

The Gospel of the Lord. All: **Praise to you, Lord Jesus Christ.**

PRAYER OVER THE OFFERINGS
Accept, O Lord, we pray,
the sacrifices instituted by your commands
and, through the sacred mysteries,
which we celebrate with dutiful service,

graciously complete the sanctifying work
by which you are pleased to redeem us.
Through Christ our Lord. All: **Amen.**

**COMMUNION ANTIPHON** (Lamentations 3:25)
The Lord is good to those who hope in him,
to the soul that seeks him.

Or:

(Cf. 1 Corinthians 10:17)
Though many, we are one bread, one body,
for we all partake of the one Bread and one Chalice.

**PRAYER AFTER COMMUNION**
Grant us, almighty God,
that we may be refreshed and nourished
by the Sacrament which we have received,
so as to be transformed into what we consume.
Through Christ our Lord. All: **Amen.**

# Twenty-Eighth Sunday in Ordinary Time

## *October 15, 2017*

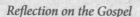

*Reflection on the Gospel*

*Jesus is relentless in the message of these parables of the last three Sundays because of what is at stake: living in the "kingdom of heaven," receiving a judgment for fullness of Life, sharing in the divine wedding feast. Actually, Jesus is purposely goading all of us—not to angry retaliation in response to his judgment, but to change our lives so that we might embrace Life itself. "Many are invited." Only those who respond appropriately "are chosen." Our very Life depends on it.*

• *I change my life and embrace Life itself when I . . .*

—Living Liturgy™, *Twenty-eighth Sunday in Ordinary Time 2017*

(Psalm 130[129]:3-4)

If you, O Lord, should mark iniquities,
Lord, who could stand?
But with you is found forgiveness,
O God of Israel.

## Collect

May your grace, O Lord, we pray,
at all times go before us and follow after
and make us always determined
to carry out good works.
Through our Lord Jesus Christ, your Son,
who lives and reigns with you in the unity of the Holy Spirit,
one God, for ever and ever. All: **Amen.**

## Reading I (L 142-A) (Isaiah 25:6-10a)

### A reading from the Book of the Prophet Isaiah

*The Lord will prepare a feast and wipe away the tears from
every face.*

> On this mountain the LORD of hosts
>     will provide for all peoples
> a feast of rich food and choice wines,
>     juicy, rich food and pure, choice wines.
> On this mountain he will destroy
>     the veil that veils all peoples,
> the web that is woven over all nations;
>     he will destroy death forever.
> The Lord GOD will wipe away
>     the tears from every face;
> the reproach of his people he will remove
>     from the whole earth; for the LORD has spoken.
>     On that day it will be said:
> "Behold our God, to whom we looked to save us!
>     This is the LORD for whom we looked;
>     let us rejoice and be glad that he has saved us!"
> For the hand of the LORD will rest on this mountain.

The word of the Lord. All: **Thanks be to God.**

## RESPONSIVE PSALM 23

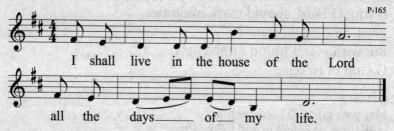

Psalm 23:1-3a, 3b-4, 5, 6

℟. (6cd) **I shall live in the house of the Lord all the days of my life.**

The LORD is my shepherd; I shall not want.
In verdant pastures he gives me repose;
beside restful waters he leads me;
he refreshes my soul. ℟.

He guides me in right paths
for his name's sake.
Even though I walk in the dark valley
I fear no evil; for you are at my side
with your rod and your staff
that give me courage. ℟.

You spread the table before me
in the sight of my foes;
you anoint my head with oil;
my cup overflows. ℟.

Only goodness and kindness follow me
all the days of my life;
and I shall dwell in the house of the LORD
for years to come. ℟.

## READING II (Philippians 4:12-14, 19-20)

**A reading from the Letter of Saint Paul to the Philippians**

*I can do all things in him who strengthens me.*

**Brothers and sisters:**
**I know how to live in humble circumstances;**
**I know also how to live with abundance.**

In every circumstance and in all things
  I have learned the secret of being well fed and of
    going hungry,
  of living in abundance and of being in need.
I can do all things in him who strengthens me.
Still, it was kind of you to share in my distress.

My God will fully supply whatever you need,
  in accord with his glorious riches in Christ Jesus.
To our God and Father, glory forever and ever. Amen.

The word of the Lord. All: Thanks be to God.

GOSPEL (Matthew 22:1-14) *or* Shorter Form [ ] (Matthew 22:1-10)

ALLELUIA (*See* Ephesians 1:17-18)

℣. Alleluia, alleluia.  ℟. **Alleluia, alleluia.**

℣. May the Father of our Lord Jesus Christ
  enlighten the eyes of our hearts,
  so that we may know what is the hope
  that belongs to our call. ℟.

✛ **A reading from the holy Gospel according to Matthew**

All: **Glory to you, O Lord.**

*Invite to the wedding feast whomever you find.*

[Jesus again in reply spoke to the chief priests and elders
    of the people
  in parables, saying,
  "The kingdom of heaven may be likened to a king
  who gave a wedding feast for his son.
He dispatched his servants
  to summon the invited guests to the feast,
  but they refused to come.
A second time he sent other servants, saying,
  'Tell those invited: "Behold, I have prepared my
    banquet,
  my calves and fattened cattle are killed,
  and everything is ready; come to the feast."'

Some ignored the invitation and went away,
  one to his farm, another to his business.
The rest laid hold of his servants,
  mistreated them, and killed them.
The king was enraged and sent his troops,
  destroyed those murderers, and burned their city.
Then he said to his servants, 'The feast is ready,
  but those who were invited were not worthy to come.
Go out, therefore, into the main roads
  and invite to the feast whomever you find.'
The servants went out into the streets
  and gathered all they found, bad and good alike,
  and the hall was filled with guests.]
But when the king came in to meet the guests,
  he saw a man there not dressed in a wedding garment.
The king said to him, 'My friend, how is it
  that you came in here without a wedding garment?'
But he was reduced to silence.
Then the king said to his attendants, 'Bind his hands and
    feet,
  and cast him into the darkness outside,
  where there will be wailing and grinding of teeth.'
Many are invited, but few are chosen."

**The Gospel of the Lord.** All: **Praise to you, Lord Jesus Christ.**

PRAYER OVER THE OFFERINGS

Accept, O Lord, the prayers of your faithful
with the sacrificial offerings,
that, through these acts of devotedness,
we may pass over to the glory of heaven.
Through Christ our Lord. All: **Amen.**

COMMUNION ANTIPHON (Cf. Psalm 34[33]:11)

The rich suffer want and go hungry,
but those who seek the Lord lack no blessing.

Or:

(1 John 3:2)

When the Lord appears, we shall be like him,
for we shall see him as he is.

**PRAYER AFTER COMMUNION**

We entreat your majesty most humbly, O Lord,
that, as you feed us with the nourishment
which comes from the most holy Body and Blood of your Son,
so you may make us sharers of his divine nature.
Who lives and reigns for ever and ever. All: **Amen.**

# Twenty-Ninth Sunday in Ordinary Time

*October 22, 2017*

(World Mission Sunday)

*Reflection on the Gospel*

*There are many deep divisions between "Caesar" and God, between earthly kingdoms and the kingdom of heaven. Jesus quickly dispatches this false divide between realms in which we live, commanding his hearers to give to each realm what properly belongs to it. This is actually the easy part of life. The deepest divide to which we must attend is between disingenuous hearts living a lie and transparent hearts living "in accordance with the truth." This deepest divide is what Jesus came to heal—for those who wish to be healed.*

> • *I repay to Caesar what belongs to Caesar and to God what belongs to God, when I . . .*

—*Living Liturgy*™, *Twenty-ninth Sunday in Ordinary Time 2017*

**ENTRANCE ANTIPHON** (Cf. Psalm 17[16]:6, 8)

To you I call; for you will surely heed me, O God;
turn your ear to me; hear my words.
Guard me as the apple of your eye;
in the shadow of your wings protect me.

COLLECT

Almighty ever-living God,
grant that we may always conform our will to yours
and serve your majesty in sincerity of heart.
Through our Lord Jesus Christ, your Son,
who lives and reigns with you in the unity of the Holy Spirit,
one God, for ever and ever. All: **Amen.**

## READING I (L 145-A) (Isaiah 45:1, 4-6)

### A reading from the Book of the Prophet Isaiah

*I have grasped the right hand of Cyrus to subdue the nations before him.*

> **Thus says the LORD to his anointed, Cyrus,**
> > **whose right hand I grasp,**
> **subduing nations before him,**
> > **and making kings run in his service,**
> **opening doors before him**
> > **and leaving the gates unbarred:**
> **For the sake of Jacob, my servant,**
> > **of Israel, my chosen one,**
> **I have called you by your name,**
> > **giving you a title, though you knew me not.**
> **I am the LORD and there is no other,**
> > **there is no God besides me.**
> **It is I who arm you, though you know me not,**
> > **so that toward the rising and the setting of the sun**
> > **people may know that there is none besides me.**
> **I am the LORD, there is no other.**

The word of the Lord. All: **Thanks be to God.**

## RESPONSORIAL PSALM 96

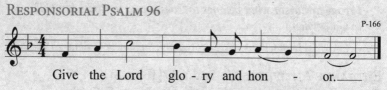

P-166

Give the Lord glo - ry and hon - or.___

Psalm 96:1, 3, 4-5, 7-8, 9-10

R℣. (7b) **Give the Lord glory and honor.**

Sing to the LORD a new song;
    sing to the LORD, all you lands.
Tell his glory among the nations;
    among all peoples, his wondrous deeds. R℣.

For great is the LORD and highly to be praised;
    awesome is he, beyond all gods.
For all the gods of the nations are things of nought,
    but the LORD made the heavens. R℣.

Give to the LORD, you families of nations,
    give to the LORD glory and praise;
    give to the LORD the glory due his name!
Bring gifts, and enter his courts. R℣.

Worship the LORD, in holy attire;
    tremble before him, all the earth;
say among the nations: The LORD is king,
    he governs the peoples with equity. R℣.

READING II (1 Thessalonians 1:1-5b)

**A reading from the beginning of the first Letter of Saint Paul to the Thessalonians**

*Calling to mind faith, love, and hope.*

**Paul, Silvanus, and Timothy to the church of the Thessalonians
in God the Father and the Lord Jesus Christ:
grace to you and peace.
We give thanks to God always for all of you,
remembering you in our prayers,
unceasingly calling to mind your work of faith and labor of love
and endurance in hope of our Lord Jesus Christ,
before our God and Father,
knowing, brothers and sisters loved by God,
how you were chosen.**

For our gospel did not come to you in word alone,
> but also in power and in the Holy Spirit and with
>> much conviction.

The word of the Lord. All: Thanks be to God.

GOSPEL (Matthew 22:15-21)
ALLELUIA (Philippians 2:15d, 16a)

℣. Alleluia, alleluia. ℟. **Alleluia, alleluia.**
℣. Shine like lights in the world
> as you hold on to the word of life. ℟.

✠ A reading from the holy Gospel according to Matthew

All: **Glory to you, O Lord.**

*Repay to Caesar what belongs to Caesar and to God what belongs to God.*

The Pharisees went off
> and plotted how they might entrap Jesus in speech.

They sent their disciples to him, with the Herodians,
> saying,
>> "Teacher, we know that you are a truthful man
>> and that you teach the way of God in accordance with
>>> the truth.

And you are not concerned with anyone's opinion,
> for you do not regard a person's status.

Tell us, then, what is your opinion:
> Is it lawful to pay the census tax to Caesar or not?"

Knowing their malice, Jesus said,
> "Why are you testing me, you hypocrites?

Show me the coin that pays the census tax."

Then they handed him the Roman coin.

He said to them, "Whose image is this and whose
> inscription?"

They replied, "Caesar's."

At that he said to them,
> "Then repay to Caesar what belongs to Caesar
> and to God what belongs to God."

The Gospel of the Lord. All: **Praise to you, Lord Jesus Christ.**

PRAYER OVER THE OFFERINGS

Grant us, Lord, we pray,
a sincere respect for your gifts,
that, through the purifying action of your grace,
we may be cleansed by the very mysteries we serve.
Through Christ our Lord. All: **Amen.**

COMMUNION ANTIPHON (Cf. Psalm 33[32]:18-19)

Behold, the eyes of the Lord
are on those who fear him,
who hope in his merciful love,
to rescue their souls from death,
to keep them alive in famine.

Or:

(Mark 10:45)

The Son of Man has come
to give his life as a ranson for many.

PRAYER AFTER COMMUNION

Grant, O Lord, we pray,
that, benefiting from participation in heavenly things,
we may be helped by what you give in this present age
and prepared for the gifts that are eternal.
Through Christ our Lord. All: **Amen.**

# Thirtieth Sunday in Ordinary Time

### October 29, 2017

---

*Reflection on the Gospel*

*To test Jesus the Pharisees in this gospel questioned him about "which commandment in the law is the greatest." Each Pharisee, no doubt, had some commandment governing religious practice he judged to be the most important. Jesus' answer to the Pharisees takes his hearers beyond any individual commandment or practice to the foundation of them all: loving God with one's whole being and loving neighbor as oneself. Jesus passed the "test" not only with his words but also with how he lived this double law of love.*

> • *I love God with my whole being and my neighbor as myself when I . . .*

*—Living Liturgy™, Thirtieth Sunday in Ordinary Time 2017*

## Entrance Antiphon (Cf. Psalm 105[104]:3-4)

Let the hearts that seek the Lord rejoice;
turn to the Lord and his strength;
constantly seek his face.

## Collect

Almighty ever-living God,
increase our faith, hope and charity,
and make us love what you command,
so that we may merit what you promise.
Through our Lord Jesus Christ, your Son,
who lives and reigns with you in the unity of the Holy Spirit,
one God, for ever and ever. All: **Amen.**

## Reading I (L 148-A) (Exodus 22:20-26)

### A reading from the Book of Exodus

*If you wrong the widow and the orphan, my wrath will flare up against you.*

Thus says the LORD:
"You shall not molest or oppress an alien,
   for you were once aliens yourselves in the land of Egypt.
You shall not wrong any widow or orphan.
If ever you wrong them and they cry out to me,
   I will surely hear their cry.
My wrath will flare up, and I will kill you with the sword;
   then your own wives will be widows, and your
      children orphans.

"If you lend money to one of your poor neighbors
      among my people,
   you shall not act like an extortioner toward him
   by demanding interest from him.
If you take your neighbor's cloak as a pledge,
   you shall return it to him before sunset;
      for this cloak of his is the only covering he has for his
         body.
What else has he to sleep in?
If he cries out to me, I will hear him; for I am
   compassionate."

The word of the Lord. All: Thanks be to God.

RESPONSORIAL PSALM 18

P-167

I love you, Lord,_____ my strength.

Psalm 18:2-3, 3-4, 47, 51

R̶. (2) **I love you, Lord, my strength.**

I love you, O LORD, my strength,
   O LORD, my rock, my fortress, my deliverer. R̶.

My God, my rock of refuge,
   my shield, the horn of my salvation, my stronghold!
Praised be the LORD, I exclaim,
   and I am safe from my enemies. R̶.

*(continued)*

The LORD lives and blessed be my rock!
Extolled be God my savior.
You who gave great victories to your king
and showed kindness to your anointed. R℣.

**A reading from the first Letter of Saint Paul to the Thessalonians**

*You turned from idols to serve the living and true God and to await his Son from heaven.*

**Brothers and sisters:**
**You know what sort of people we were among you for**
**your sake.**
**And you became imitators of us and of the Lord,**
**receiving the word in great affliction, with joy from**
**the Holy Spirit,**
**so that you became a model for all the believers**
**in Macedonia and in Achaia.**
**For from you the word of the Lord has sounded forth**
**not only in Macedonia and in Achaia,**
**but in every place your faith in God has gone forth,**
**so that we have no need to say anything.**
**For they themselves openly declare about us**
**what sort of reception we had among you,**
**and how you turned to God from idols**
**to serve the living and true God**
**and to await his Son from heaven,**
**whom he raised from the dead,**
**Jesus, who delivers us from the coming wrath.**

**The word of the Lord.** All: **Thanks be to God.**

℣. Alleluia, alleluia. R℣. **Alleluia, alleluia.**
℣. Whoever loves me will keep my word, says the Lord,
and my Father will love him and we will come to him. R℣.

☩ **A reading from the holy Gospel according to Matthew**

**All: Glory to you, O Lord.**

*You shall love the Lord your God and your neighbor as yourself.*

**When the Pharisees heard that Jesus had silenced the
    Sadducees,**
  **they gathered together, and one of them,**
  **a scholar of the law, tested him by asking,**
  **"Teacher, which commandment in the law is the
     greatest?"**
**He said to him,**
  **"You shall love the Lord, your God,**
  **with all your heart,**
  **with all your soul,**
  **and with all your mind.**
**This is the greatest and the first commandment.**
**The second is like it:**
  **You shall love your neighbor as yourself.**
**The whole law and the prophets depend on these two
    commandments."**

**The Gospel of the Lord.** All: **Praise to you, Lord Jesus Christ.**

PRAYER OVER THE OFFERINGS
Look, we pray, O Lord,
on the offerings we make to your majesty,
that whatever is done by us in your service
may be directed above all to your glory.
Through Christ our Lord. All: **Amen.**

COMMUNION ANTIPHON (Cf. Psalm 20[19]:6)
We will ring out our joy at your saving help
and exult in the name of our God.

Or:

(Ephesians 5:2)
Christ loved us and gave himself up for us,
as a fragrant offering to God.

PRAYER AFTER COMMUNION
May your Sacraments, O Lord, we pray,
perfect in us what lies within them,
that what we now celebrate in signs
we may one day possess in truth.
Through Christ our Lord. All: **Amen.**

# All Saints

## *November 1, 2017*

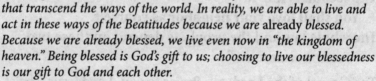

*Reflection on the Gospel*

*The Beatitudes seem to say that blessedness is a*
*reward given to those who live and act in ways*
*that transcend the ways of the world. In reality, we are able to live and*
*act in these ways of the Beatitudes because we are* already *blessed.*
*Because we are already blessed, we live even now in "the kingdom of*
*heaven." Being blessed is God's gift to us; choosing to live our blessedness*
*is our gift to God and each other.*

> • *I rejoice and am glad, because my reward will be great in heaven*
> *because . . .*

—Living Liturgy™, *All Saints 2017*

ENTRANCE ANTIPHON
Let us all rejoice in the Lord,
as we celebrate the feast day in honor of all the Saints,
at whose festival the Angels rejoice
and praise the Son of God.

COLLECT
Almighty ever-living God,
by whose gift we venerate in one celebration
the merits of all the Saints,
bestow on us, we pray,
through the prayers of so many intercessors,
an abundance of the reconciliation with you
for which we earnestly long.

Through our Lord Jesus Christ, your Son,
who lives and reigns with you in the unity of the Holy Spirit,
one God, for ever and ever. All: **Amen.**

READING I (L 667) (Revelation 7:2-4, 9-14)

## A reading from the Book of Revelation

*I had a vision of a great multitude, which no one could count,*
*from every nation, race, people and tongue.*

**I, John, saw another angel come up from the East,**
**holding the seal of the living God.**
**He cried out in a loud voice to the four angels**
**who were given power to damage the land and the sea,**
**"Do not damage the land or the sea or the trees**
**until we put the seal on the foreheads of the servants**
**of our God."**
**I heard the number of those who had been marked with**
**the seal,**
**one hundred and forty-four thousand marked**
**from every tribe of the children of Israel.**

**After this I had a vision of a great multitude,**
**which no one could count,**
**from every nation, race, people, and tongue.**
**They stood before the throne and before the Lamb,**
**wearing white robes and holding palm branches in**
**their hands.**
**They cried out in a loud voice:**

**"Salvation comes from our God, who is seated on the**
**throne,**
**and from the Lamb."**

**All the angels stood around the throne**
**and around the elders and the four living creatures.**
**They prostrated themselves before the throne,**
**worshiped God, and exclaimed:**

**"Amen. Blessing and glory, wisdom and thanksgiving,**
**honor, power, and might**
**be to our God forever and ever. Amen."**

Then one of the elders spoke up and said to me,
"Who are these wearing white robes, and where did
they come from?"
I said to him, "My lord, you are the one who knows."
He said to me,
"These are the ones who have survived the time of
great distress;
they have washed their robes
and made them white in the Blood of the Lamb."

**The word of the Lord.** All: **Thanks be to God.**

RESPONSORIAL PSALM 24

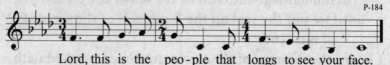

P-184

Lord, this is the peo-ple that longs to see your face.

Music: Jay F. Hunstiger, © 1990, administered by Liturgical Press. All rights reserved.

Psalm 24:1bc-2, 3-4ab, 5-6

R︶. (*See 6*) **Lord, this is the people that longs to see your
face.**

The LORD's are the earth and its fullness;
the world and those who dwell in it.
For he founded it upon the seas
and established it upon the rivers. R︶.

Who can ascend the mountain of the LORD?
or who may stand in his holy place?
One whose hands are sinless, whose heart is clean,
who desires not what is vain. R︶.

He shall receive a blessing from the LORD,
a reward from God his savior.
Such is the race that seeks him,
that seeks the face of the God of Jacob. R︶.

READING II (1 John 3:1-3)

**A reading from the first Letter of Saint John**

*We shall see God as he is.*

**Beloved:**
**See what love the Father has bestowed on us**
    **that we may be called the children of God.**
**Yet so we are.**
**The reason the world does not know us**
    **is that it did not know him.**
**Beloved, we are God's children now;**
    **what we shall be has not yet been revealed.**
**We do know that when it is revealed we shall be like him,**
    **for we shall see him as he is.**
**Everyone who has this hope based on him makes himself**
      **pure,**
    **as he is pure.**

**The word of the Lord.** All: **Thanks be to God.**

GOSPEL (Matthew 5:1-12a)
ALLELUIA (Matthew 11:28)
℣. Alleluia, alleluia. ℟. **Alleluia, alleluia.**
℣. Come to me, all you who labor and are burdened,
    and I will give you rest, says the Lord. ℟.

✛ **A reading from the holy Gospel according to Matthew**

All: **Glory to you, O Lord.**

*Rejoice and be glad, for your reward will be great in heaven.*

**When Jesus saw the crowds, he went up the mountain,**
    **and after he had sat down, his disciples came to him.**
**He began to teach them, saying:**

    **"Blessed are the poor in spirit,**
      **for theirs is the Kingdom of heaven.**
    **Blessed are they who mourn,**
      **for they will be comforted.**
    **Blessed are the meek,**
      **for they will inherit the land.**
    **Blessed are they who hunger and thirst for**
      **righteousness,**
      **for they will be satisfied.**

**Blessed are the merciful,**
    **for they will be shown mercy.**
**Blessed are the clean of heart,**
    **for they will see God.**
**Blessed are the peacemakers,**
    **for they will be called children of God.**
**Blessed are they who are persecuted for the sake of**
      **righteousness,**
    **for theirs is the Kingdom of heaven.**
**Blessed are you when they insult you and persecute you**
    **and utter every kind of evil against you falsely**
      **because of me.**
**Rejoice and be glad,**
    **for your reward will be great in heaven.”**

**The Gospel of the Lord.** All: **Praise to you, Lord Jesus Christ.**

PRAYER OVER THE OFFERINGS

May these offerings we bring in honor of all the Saints
be pleasing to you, O Lord,
and grant that, just as we believe the Saints
to be already assured of immortality,
so we may experience their concern for our salvation.
Through Christ our Lord. All: **Amen.**

COMMUNION ANTIPHON (Matthew 5:8-10)

Blessed are the clean of heart, for they shall see God.
Blessed are the peacemakers,
for they shall be called children of God.
Blessed are they who are persecuted for the sake of
    righteousness,
for theirs is the Kingdom of Heaven.

PRAYER AFTER COMMUNION

As we adore you, O God, who alone are holy
and wonderful in all your Saints,
we implore your grace,
so that, coming to perfect holiness in the fullness of your love,
we may pass from this pilgrim table
to the banquet of our heavenly homeland.
Through Christ our Lord. All: **Amen.**

# The Commemoration of All the Faithful Departed

## ALL SOULS' DAY

*November 2, 2017*

---

*Reflection on the Gospel*

*This gospel instills hope because God does not reject anyone who is faithful to Jesus. This gospel assures belonging because no one given to Jesus will be lost. This gospel promises salvation because those who believe in Jesus will be raised to new Life. The one stipulation is that, like Jesus, his followers do the will of the Father. Those faithful departed whom we remember this day are not lost—they have believed in Jesus, they have done the will of God, they have gained eternal Life.*

• *I do the will of the Father when I . . .*

—*Living Liturgy*™, *All Souls 2017*

## FIRST MASS

### Entrance Antiphon
(Cf. 1 Thessalonians 4:14; 1 Corinthians 15:22)
Just as Jesus died and has risen again,
so through Jesus God will bring with him
those who have fallen asleep;
and as in Adam all die,
so also in Christ will all be brought to life.

### Collect
Listen kindly to our prayers, O Lord,
and, as our faith in your Son,
raised from the dead, is deepened,
so may our hope of resurrection for your departed servants
also find new strength.
Through our Lord Jesus Christ, your Son,

who lives and reigns with you in the unity of the Holy Spirit, one God, for ever and ever. All: **Amen.**

*The following readings or those given in the Masses for the Dead, nos. 1011–1016, may be used.*

## Reading I (L 668) (Wisdom 3:1-9)

### A reading from the Book of Wisdom

*As sacrificial offerings he took them to himself.*

The souls of the just are in the hand of God,
  and no torment shall touch them.
They seemed, in the view of the foolish, to be dead;
  and their passing away was thought an affliction
  and their going forth from us, utter destruction.
But they are in peace.
For if before men, indeed they be punished,
  yet is their hope full of immortality;
Chastised a little, they shall be greatly blessed,
  because God tried them
  and found them worthy of himself.
As gold in the furnace, he proved them,
  and as sacrificial offerings he took them to himself.
In the time of their visitation they shall shine,
  and shall dart about as sparks through stubble;
They shall judge nations and rule over peoples,
  and the LORD shall be their King forever.
Those who trust in him shall understand truth,
  and the faithful shall abide with him in love:
Because grace and mercy are with his holy ones,
  and his care is with his elect.

The word of the Lord. All: Thanks be to God.

## Responsorial Psalm 23 (L 1013.1)

The Lord is my shep - herd; there is noth-ing I shall want.

Psalm 23:1-3, 4, 5, 6

R℣. (1) **The Lord is my shepherd; there is nothing I shall
    want.** *or:* R℣. (4ab) **Though I walk in the valley of
    darkness, I fear no evil, for you are with me.**

The LORD is my shepherd; I shall not want.
    In verdant pastures he gives me repose;
beside restful waters he leads me;
    he refreshes my soul. R℣.

He guides me in right paths
    for his name's sake.
Even though I walk in the dark valley
    I fear no evil; for you are at my side
with your rod and your staff
    that give me courage. R℣.

You spread the table before me
    in the sight of my foes;
You anoint my head with oil;
    my cup overflows. R℣.

Only goodness and kindness follow me
    all the days of my life;
And I shall dwell in the house of the LORD
    for years to come. R℣.

READING II (L 1014.3) (Romans 6:3-9)

**A reading from the Letter of Saint Paul to the Romans**

*We too might live in newness of life.*

**Brothers and sisters:**
**Are you unaware that we who were baptized into**
    **Christ Jesus**
    **were baptized into his death?**
**We were indeed buried with him through baptism into**
    **death,**
    **so that, just as Christ was raised from the dead**
    **by the glory of the Father,**
    **we too might live in newness of life.**

For if we have grown into union with him through a
    death like his,
  we shall also be united with him in the resurrection.
We know that our old self was crucified with him,
  so that our sinful body might be done away with,
  that we might no longer be in slavery to sin.
For a dead person has been absolved from sin.
If, then, we have died with Christ,
  we believe that we shall also live with him.
We know that Christ, raised from the dead, dies no more;
  death no longer has power over him.

The word of the Lord. All: Thanks be to God.

GOSPEL (L 1016.12) (John 6:37-40)
ALLELUIA (L 1015.5) (John 6:40)

℣. Alleluia, alleluia. ℞. **Alleluia, alleluia.**
℣. This is the will of my Father, says the Lord,
  that everyone who sees the Son and believes in him
    may have eternal life,
  and I shall raise him on the last day. ℞.

✠ A reading from the holy Gospel according to John

All: **Glory to you, O Lord.**

*Everyone who sees the Son and believes in him may have eternal
life and I shall raise him on the last day.*

Jesus said to the crowds:
"Everything that the Father gives me will come to me,
  and I will not reject anyone who comes to me,
  because I came down from heaven not to do my own will
  but the will of the one who sent me.
And this is the will of the one who sent me,
  that I should not lose anything of what he gave me,
  but that I should raise it on the last day.
For this is the will of my Father,
  that everyone who sees the Son and believes in him
  may have eternal life,
  and I shall raise him on the last day."

The Gospel of the Lord. All: **Praise to you, Lord Jesus Christ.**

## Prayer over the Offerings

Look favorably on our offerings, O Lord,
so that your departed servants
may be taken up into glory with your Son,
in whose great mystery of love we are all united.
Who lives and reigns for ever and ever. All: **Amen.**

## Communion Antiphon (Cf. John 11:25-26)

I am the Resurrection and the Life, says the Lord.
Whoever believes in me, even though he dies, will live,
and everyone who lives and believes in me will not die for
 ever.

## Prayer after Communion

Grant we pray, O Lord, that your departed servants,
for whom we have celebrated this paschal Sacrament,
may pass over to a dwelling place of light and peace.
Through Christ our Lord. All: **Amen.**

## SECOND MASS

## Entrance Antiphon (Cf. 4 Esdras 2:34-35)

Eternal rest grant unto them, O Lord,
and let perpetual light shine upon them.

## Collect

O God, glory of the faithful and life of the just,
by the Death and Resurrection of whose Son
we have been redeemed,
look mercifully on your departed servants,
that, just as they professed the mystery of our resurrection,
so they may merit to receive the joys of eternal happiness.
Through our Lord Jesus Christ, your Son,
who lives and reigns with you in the unity of the Holy Spirit,
one God, for ever and ever. All: **Amen.**

[*These are the traditional* Celebrating the Eucharist *selections taken from the Masses for the Dead.*]

## Reading I (L 1011.2) (Job 19:1, 23-27a)

### A reading from the Book of Job

*I know that my Vindicator lives.*

Job answered Bildad the Shuhite and said:
Oh, would that my words were written down!
    Would that they were inscribed in a record:
That with an iron chisel and with lead
    they were cut in the rock forever!
But as for me, I know that my Vindicator lives,
    and that he will at last stand forth upon the dust;
Whom I myself shall see:
    my own eyes, not another's, shall behold him;
And from my flesh I shall see God;
    my inmost being is consumed with longing.

**The word of the Lord.** All: **Thanks be to God.**

RESPONSORIAL PSALM 25 (L 1013.2)

P-186

To you, O    Lord,    I___ lift    my    soul.

Psalm 25:6 and 7b, 17-18, 20-21

℟. (1a) **To you, O Lord, I lift my soul.** *or:* ℟. (3a) **No one
    who waits for you, O Lord, will ever be put to shame.**

Remember that your compassion, O LORD,
    and your kindness are from of old.
In your kindness remember me,
    because of your goodness, O LORD. ℟.

Relieve the troubles of my heart;
    and bring me out of my distress.
Put an end to my affliction and my suffering;
    and take away all my sins. ℟.

Preserve my life and rescue me;
    let me not be put to shame, for I take refuge in you.
Let integrity and uprightness preserve me,
    because I wait for you, O LORD. ℟.

READING II (L 1014.5) (Romans 8:31b-35, 37-39)

**A reading from the Letter of Saint Paul to the Romans**

*What will separate us from the love of Christ?*

**Brothers and sisters:**
**If God is for us, who can be against us?**
**He did not spare his own Son**
  **but handed him over for us all,**
  **will he not also give us everything else along with him?**
**Who will bring a charge against God's chosen ones?**
**It is God who acquits us.**
**Who will condemn?**
**It is Christ Jesus who died, rather, was raised,**
  **who also is at the right hand of God,**
  **who indeed intercedes for us.**
**What will separate us from the love of Christ?**
**Will anguish, or distress or persecution, or famine,**
  **or nakedness, or peril, or the sword?**

**No, in all these things, we conquer overwhelmingly**
  **through him who loved us.**
**For I am convinced that neither death, nor life,**
  **nor angels, nor principalities,**
  **nor present things, nor future things,**
  **nor powers, nor height, nor depth,**
  **nor any other creature will be able to separate us**
  **from the love of God in Christ Jesus our Lord.**

**The word of the Lord.** All: **Thanks be to God.**

GOSPEL (L 1016.18) (John 17:24-26)
ALLELUIA (L 1015.3) (John 3:16)
℣. Alleluia, alleluia. ℟. **Alleluia, alleluia.**
℣. God so loved the world that he gave his only-begotten
  Son,
  so that everyone who believes in him might have
    eternal life. ℟.

✠ **A reading from the holy Gospel according to John**

All: **Glory to you, O Lord.**

*I wish that where I am they also may be with me.*

**Jesus raised his eyes to heaven and said:**
**"Father, those whom you gave me are your gift to me.**
**I wish that where I am they also may be with me,**
    **that they may see my glory that you gave me,**
    **because you loved me before the foundation of the**
        **world.**
**Righteous Father, the world also does not know you,**
    **but I know you, and they know that you sent me.**
**I made known to them your name and I will make it**
    **known,**
    **that the love with which you loved me**
    **may be in them and I in them."**

**The Gospel of the Lord.** All: **Praise to you, Lord Jesus Christ.**

PRAYER OVER THE OFFERINGS
Almighty and merciful God,
by means of these sacrificial offerings
wash away, we pray, in the Blood of Christ,
the sins of your departed servants,
for you purify unceasingly by your merciful forgiveness
those you once cleansed in the waters of Baptism.
Through Christ our Lord. All: **Amen.**

COMMUNION ANTIPHON (Cf. 4 Esdras 2:35, 34)
Let perpetual light shine upon them, O Lord,
with your Saints for ever, for you are merciful.

PRAYER AFTER COMMUNION
Having received the Sacrament of your Only Begotten Son,
who was sacrificed for us and rose in glory,
we humbly implore you, O Lord,
for your departed servants,
that, cleansed by the paschal mysteries,
they may glory in the gift of the resurrection to come.
Through Christ our Lord. All: **Amen.**

THIRD MASS

ENTRANCE ANTIPHON (Cf. Romans 8:11)
God, who raised Jesus from the dead,
will give life also to your mortal bodies,
through his Spirit that dwells in you.

COLLECT
O God, who willed that your Only Begotten Son,
having conquered death,
should pass over into the realm of heaven,
grant, we pray, to your departed servants
that, with the mortality of this life overcome,
they may gaze eternally on you,
their Creator and Redeemer.
Through our Lord Jesus Christ, your Son,
who lives and reigns with you in the unity of the Holy Spirit,
one God, for ever and ever. All: **Amen.**

READING I (L 1011.6) (Lamentations 3:17-26)

**A reading from the Book of Lamentations**

*It is good to hope in silence for the saving help of the Lord.*

**My soul is deprived of peace,**
     **I have forgotten what happiness is;**
**I tell myself my future is lost,**
     **all that I hoped for from the LORD.**
**The thought of my homeless poverty**
     **is wormwood and gall;**
**Remembering it over and over**
     **leaves my soul downcast within me.**
**But I will call this to mind,**
     **as my reason to have hope:**

**The favors of the LORD are not exhausted,**
     **his mercies are not spent;**
**They are renewed each morning,**
     **so great is his faithfulness.**
**My portion is the LORD, says my soul;**
     **therefore will I hope in him.**

Good is the LORD to one who waits for him,
>  to the soul that seeks him;

It is good to hope in silence
>  for the saving help of the LORD.

**The word of the Lord.** All: **Thanks be to God.**

RESPONSORIAL PSALM 27 (L 1013.3)

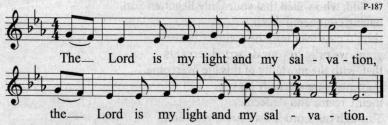

Music: Jay F. Hunstiger, © 1992, administered by Liturgical Press. All rights reserved.

Psalm 27:1, 4, 7 and 8b and 9a, 13-14

R̩. (1a) **The Lord is my light and my salvation.**
>  *or:* R̩. (13) **I believe that I shall see the good things**
>  **of the Lord in the land of the living.**

The LORD is my light and my salvation;
>  whom should I fear?

The LORD is my life's refuge;
>  of whom should I be afraid? R̩.

One thing I ask of the LORD;
>  this I seek:

To dwell in the house of the LORD
>  all the days of my life,

That I may gaze on the loveliness of the LORD
>  and contemplate his temple. R̩.

Hear, O LORD, the sound of my call;
>  have pity on me and answer me.

Your presence, O LORD, I seek!
>  Hide not your face from me. R̩.

I believe that I shall see the bounty of the LORD
>  in the land of the living.

Wait for the LORD with courage;
>  be stouthearted, and wait for the LORD! R̩.

## READING II (L 1014.14) (1 John 3:1-2)

**A reading from the first Letter of Saint John**

*We shall see him as he is.*

**Beloved:**
**See what love the Father has bestowed on us**
    **that we may be called the children of God.**
**Yet so we are.**
**The reason the world does not know us**
    **is that it did not know him.**
**Beloved, we are God's children now;**
    **what we shall be has not yet been revealed.**
**We do know that when it is revealed we shall be like him,**
    **for we shall see him as he is.**

**The word of the Lord.** All: **Thanks be to God.**

## GOSPEL (L 1016.16) (John 12:23-28) *or* Shorter Form [ ]
(John 12:23-26)
ALLELUIA (L 1015.7) (John 11:25a, 26)

℣. Alleluia, alleluia. ℟. **Alleluia, alleluia.**
℣. I am the resurrection and the life, says the Lord;
    whoever believes in me will never die. ℟.

✠ **A reading from the holy Gospel according to John**

All: **Glory to you, O Lord.**

*If it dies, it produces much fruit.*

[**Jesus said to his disciples:**
**"The hour has come for the Son of Man to be glorified.**
**Amen, amen, I say to you,**
    **unless a grain of wheat falls to the ground and dies,**
    **it remains just a grain of wheat;**
    **but if it dies, it produces much fruit.**
**Whoever loves his life will lose it,**
    **and whoever hates his life in this world**
    **will preserve it for eternal life.**
**Whoever serves me must follow me,**
    **and where I am, there also will my servant be.**
**The Father will honor whoever serves me.**]

"I am troubled now. Yet what should I say?
'Father, save me from this hour'?
But it was for this purpose that I came to this hour.
Father, glorify your name."
Then a voice came from heaven,
    "I have glorified it and will glorify it again."

**The Gospel of the Lord.** All: **Praise to you, Lord Jesus Christ.**

PRAYER OVER THE OFFERINGS
Receive, Lord, in your kindness,
the sacrificial offering we make
for all your servants who sleep in Christ,
that, set free from the bonds of death
by this singular sacrifice,
they may merit eternal life.
Through Christ our Lord. All: **Amen.**

COMMUNION ANTIPHON (Cf. Philippians 3:20-21)
We await a savior, the Lord Jesus Christ,
who will change our mortal bodies,
to conform with his glorified body.

PRAYER AFTER COMMUNION
Through these sacrificial gifts
which we have received, O Lord,
bestow on your departed servants your great mercy
and, to those you have endowed with the grace of Baptism,
grant also the fullness of eternal joy.
Through Christ our Lord. All: **Amen.**

# Thirty-First Sunday in Ordinary Time

*November 5, 2017*

*Reflection on the Gospel*

*The scribes and Pharisees don't practice what they preach and they relish titles but do not live up to the demands these titles place upon them. Both these ways of acting reveal a corrupted disposition toward God and God's people. Jesus admonishes the crowd and the disciples to focus on him and him alone as the true teacher and master. He is true Teacher and Master in showing us how to be servant of all: he humbled himself.*

• *Practice what you preach and . . .*

—*Living Liturgy*™, *Thirty-First Sunday in Ordinary Time 2017*

ENTRANCE ANTIPHON (Cf. Psalm 38[37]:22-23)

Forsake me not, O Lord, my God;
be not far from me!
Make haste and come to my help,
O Lord, my strong salvation!

COLLECT

Almighty and merciful God,
by whose gift your faithful offer you
right and praiseworthy service,
grant, we pray,
that we may hasten without stumbling
to receive the things you have promised.
Through our Lord Jesus Christ, your Son,
who lives and reigns with you in the unity of the Holy Spirit,
one God, for ever and ever. All: **Amen.**

READING I (L 151-A) (Malachi 1:14b—2:2b, 8-10)

## A reading from the Book of the Prophet Malachi

*You have turned aside from the way, and have caused many to falter by your instruction.*

A great King am I, says the LORD of hosts,
    and my name will be feared among the nations.
And now, O priests, this commandment is for you:
    If you do not listen,
if you do not lay it to heart,
    to give glory to my name, says the LORD of hosts,
I will send a curse upon you
    and of your blessing I will make a curse.
You have turned aside from the way,
    and have caused many to falter by your instruction;
you have made void the covenant of Levi,
    says the LORD of hosts.
I, therefore, have made you contemptible
    and base before all the people,
since you do not keep my ways,
    but show partiality in your decisions.
Have we not all the one father?
    Has not the one God created us?
Why then do we break faith with one another,
    violating the covenant of our fathers?

The word of the Lord. All: Thanks be to God.

## RESPONSORIAL PSALM 131

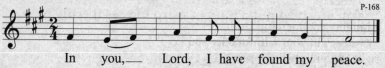

Music: Jay F. Hunstiger, © 1993, administered by Liturgical Press. All rights reserved.

Psalm 131:1, 2, 3

R̷. **In you, Lord, I have found my peace.**

O LORD, my heart is not proud,
    nor are my eyes haughty;
I busy not myself with great things,
    nor with things too sublime for me. R̷.

Nay rather, I have stilled and quieted
    my soul like a weaned child.

Like a weaned child on its mother's lap,
　　so is my soul within me. ℟.

O Israel, hope in the LORD,
　　both now and forever. ℟.

**A reading from the first Letter of Saint Paul to the Thessalonians**

*We were determined to share with you not only the Gospel of God, but our very selves as well.*

**Brothers and sisters:**
**We were gentle among you, as a nursing mother cares**
**　　for her children.**
**With such affection for you, we were determined to**
**　　share with you**
**　　not only the gospel of God, but our very selves as well,**
**　　so dearly beloved had you become to us.**
**You recall, brothers and sisters, our toil and drudgery.**
**Working night and day in order not to burden any of you,**
**　　we proclaimed to you the gospel of God.**

**And for this reason we too give thanks to God**
**　　unceasingly,**
**　　that, in receiving the word of God from hearing us,**
**　　you received not a human word but, as it truly is,**
**　　　　the word of God,**
**　　which is now at work in you who believe.**

**The word of the Lord.** All: **Thanks be to God.**

℣. Alleluia, alleluia. ℟. **Alleluia, alleluia.**
℣. You have but one Father in heaven
　　and one master, the Christ. ℟.

✠ **A reading from the holy Gospel according to Matthew**

All: **Glory to you, O Lord.**

*They preach but they do not practice.*

Jesus spoke to the crowds and to his disciples, saying,
  "The scribes and the Pharisees
    have taken their seat on the chair of Moses.
Therefore, do and observe all things whatsoever they tell
      you,
    but do not follow their example.
For they preach but they do not practice.
They tie up heavy burdens hard to carry
    and lay them on people's shoulders,
    but they will not lift a finger to move them.
All their works are performed to be seen.
They widen their phylacteries and lengthen their tassels.
They love places of honor at banquets, seats of honor in
      synagogues,
    greetings in marketplaces, and the salutation 'Rabbi.'
As for you, do not be called 'Rabbi.'
You have but one teacher, and you are all brothers.
Call no one on earth your father;
    you have but one Father in heaven.
Do not be called 'Master';
    you have but one master, the Christ.
The greatest among you must be your servant.
Whoever exalts himself will be humbled;
    but whoever humbles himself will be exalted."

**The Gospel of the Lord.** All: **Praise to you, Lord Jesus Christ.**

PRAYER OVER THE OFFERINGS
May these sacrificial offerings, O Lord,
become for you a pure oblation,
and for us a holy outpouring of your mercy.
Through Christ our Lord. All: **Amen.**

COMMUNION ANTIPHON (Cf. Psalm 16[15]:11)
You will show me the path of life,
the fullness of joy in your presence, O Lord.

Or:

(John 6:58)

Just as the living Father sent me
and I have life because of the Father,
so whoever feeds on me
shall have life because of me, says the Lord.

PRAYER AFTER COMMUNION

May the working of your power, O Lord,
increase in us, we pray,
so that, renewed by these heavenly Sacraments,
we may be prepared by your gift
for receiving what they promise.
Through Christ our Lord. All: **Amen.**

# Thirty-Second Sunday in Ordinary Time

*November 12, 2017*

*Reflection on the Gospel*

*This parable is fraught with symbolic images that turn our attention to the Second Coming of Christ, our own waiting in this in-between time of living in both light and darkness, the reality that some will be admitted to the heavenly banquet and some will not, the necessity of being known by Christ and being prepared for his coming. Wait we must, but this waiting is not inactive or empty. How we spend this waiting time determines how we will spend the rest of time.*

• *I prepare for the Second Coming of Christ by . . .*

—Living Liturgy™, *Thirty-Second Sunday in Ordinary Time 2017*

ENTRANCE ANTIPHON (Cf. Psalm 88[87]:3)

Let my prayer come into your presence.
Incline your ear to my cry for help, O Lord.

Collect

Almighty and merciful God,
graciously keep from us all adversity,
so that, unhindered in mind and body alike,
we may pursue in freedom of heart
the things that are yours.
Through our Lord Jesus Christ, your Son,
who lives and reigns with you in the unity of the Holy Spirit,
one God, for ever and ever. All: **Amen.**

Reading I (L 154-A) (Wisdom 6:12-16)

## A reading from the Book of Wisdom

*Wisdom is found by those who seek her.*

**Resplendent and unfading is wisdom,**
   **and she is readily perceived by those who love her,**
   **and found by those who seek her.**
**She hastens to make herself known in anticipation of**
      **their desire;**
   **whoever watches for her at dawn shall not be**
         **disappointed,**
   **for he shall find her sitting by his gate.**
**For taking thought of wisdom is the perfection of**
      **prudence,**
   **and whoever for her sake keeps vigil**
   **shall quickly be free from care;**
**because she makes her own rounds, seeking those**
      **worthy of her,**
   **and graciously appears to them in the ways,**
   **and meets them with all solicitude.**

**The word of the Lord.** All: **Thanks be to God.**

Responsorial Psalm 63

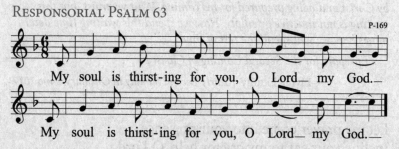

P-169

My soul is thirst-ing for you, O Lord__ my God.__

My soul is thirst-ing for you, O Lord__ my God.__

Psalm 63:2, 3-4, 5-6, 7-8

℟. (2b) **My soul is thirsting for you, O Lord my God.**

O God, you are my God whom I seek;
    for you my flesh pines and my soul thirsts
    like the earth, parched, lifeless and without water. ℟.

Thus have I gazed toward you in the sanctuary
    to see your power and your glory,
for your kindness is a greater good than life;
    my lips shall glorify you. ℟.

Thus will I bless you while I live;
    lifting up my hands, I will call upon your name.
As with the riches of a banquet shall my soul be satisfied,
    and with exultant lips my mouth shall praise you. ℟.

I will remember you upon my couch,
    and through the night-watches I will meditate on you:
you are my help,
    and in the shadow of your wings I shout for joy. ℟.

READING II (1 Thessalonians 4:13-18) *or* Shorter Form
(1 Thessalonians 4:13-14)

**A reading from the first Letter of Saint Paul to the
Thessalonians**

*God, through Jesus, will bring with him those who have fallen
asleep.*

[**We do not want you to be unaware, brothers and sisters,
    about those who have fallen asleep,
    so that you may not grieve like the rest, who have no
        hope.
For if we believe that Jesus died and rose,
    so too will God, through Jesus,
    bring with him those who have fallen asleep.**]
**Indeed, we tell you this, on the word of the Lord,
    that we who are alive,
    who are left until the coming of the Lord,
    will surely not precede those who have fallen asleep.**

For the Lord himself, with a word of command,
   with the voice of an archangel and with the trumpet
      of God,
   will come down from heaven,
   and the dead in Christ will rise first.
Then we who are alive, who are left,
   will be caught up together with them in the clouds
   to meet the Lord in the air.
Thus we shall always be with the Lord.
Therefore, console one another with these words.

The word of the Lord. All: Thanks be to God.

GOSPEL (Matthew 25:1-13)
ALLELUIA (Matthew 24:42a, 44)
℣. Alleluia, alleluia. ℟. **Alleluia, alleluia.**
℣. Stay awake and be ready!
   For you do not know on what day your Lord will
      come. ℟.

✢ **A reading from the holy Gospel according to Matthew**

All: **Glory to you, O Lord.**

*Behold, the bridegroom! Come out to meet him!*

Jesus told his disciples this parable:
   "The kingdom of heaven will be like ten virgins
   who took their lamps and went out to meet the
      bridegroom.
Five of them were foolish and five were wise.
The foolish ones, when taking their lamps,
   brought no oil with them,
   but the wise brought flasks of oil with their lamps.
Since the bridegroom was long delayed,
   they all became drowsy and fell asleep.
At midnight, there was a cry,
   'Behold, the bridegroom! Come out to meet him!'
Then all those virgins got up and trimmed their lamps.

The foolish ones said to the wise,
'Give us some of your oil,
for our lamps are going out.'
But the wise ones replied,
'No, for there may not be enough for us and you.
Go instead to the merchants and buy some for yourselves.'
While they went off to buy it,
the bridegroom came
and those who were ready went into the wedding feast
with him.
Then the door was locked.
Afterwards the other virgins came and said,
'Lord, Lord, open the door for us!'
But he said in reply,
'Amen, I say to you, I do not know you.'
Therefore, stay awake,
for you know neither the day nor the hour."

**The Gospel of the Lord.** All: **Praise to you, Lord Jesus Christ.**

PRAYER OVER THE OFFERINGS
Look with favor, we pray, O Lord,
upon the sacrificial gifts offered here,
that, celebrating in mystery the Passion of your Son,
we may honor it with loving devotion.
Through Christ our Lord. All: **Amen.**

COMMUNION ANTIPHON (Cf. Psalm 23[22]:1-2)
The Lord is my shepherd; there is nothing I shall want.
Fresh and green are the pastures where he gives me repose,
near restful waters he leads me.

Or:

(Cf. Luke 24:35)
The disciples recognized the Lord Jesus in the breaking of
bread.

PRAYER AFTER COMMUNION
Nourished by this sacred gift, O Lord,
we give you thanks and beseech your mercy,

that, by the pouring forth of your Spirit,
the grace of integrity may endure
in those your heavenly power has entered.
Through Christ our Lord. All: **Amen.**

# Thirty-Third Sunday in Ordinary Time

### *November 19, 2017*

### *Reflection on the Gospel*

*We are judged by the choices we make to use to the fullest potential what Jesus has "invested" in us. The most important choice we make in life is fidelity to whatever we are called to do—even in what seems to be small matters. The continuation of Jesus' saving work depends upon this fidelity. If we are faithful, Jesus will judge us worthy beneficiaries of the greatest return on any investment: a share in the riches of the "master's joy"—eternal Life.*

- *Since you were faithful in small matters, come, share your master's joy.*

—Living Liturgy™, *Thirty-third Sunday in Ordinary Time 2017*

ENTRANCE ANTIPHON (Jeremiah 29:11, 12, 14)
The Lord said: I think thoughts of peace and not of
   affliction.
You will call upon me, and I will answer you,
and I will lead back your captives from every place.

COLLECT
Grant us, we pray, O Lord our God,
the constant gladness of being devoted to you,
for it is full and lasting happiness
to serve with constancy
the author of all that is good.

Through our Lord Jesus Christ, your Son,
who lives and reigns with you in the unity of the Holy Spirit,
one God, for ever and ever. All: **Amen.**

READING I (L 157-A) (Proverbs 31:10-13, 19-20, 30-31)

**A reading from the Book of Proverbs**

*She works with loving hands.*

> **When one finds a worthy wife,**
> > **her value is far beyond pearls.**
>
> **Her husband, entrusting his heart to her,**
> > **has an unfailing prize.**
>
> **She brings him good, and not evil,**
> > **all the days of her life.**
>
> **She obtains wool and flax**
> > **and works with loving hands.**
>
> **She puts her hands to the distaff,**
> > **and her fingers ply the spindle.**
>
> **She reaches out her hands to the poor,**
> > **and extends her arms to the needy.**
>
> **Charm is deceptive and beauty fleeting;**
> > **the woman who fears the LORD is to be praised.**
>
> **Give her a reward for her labors,**
> > **and let her works praise her at the city gates.**

**The word of the Lord.** All: **Thanks be to God.**

RESPONSORIAL PSALM 128

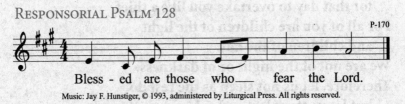

P-170

Bless - ed are those who— fear the Lord.

Psalm 128:1-2, 3, 4-5

℟. (*See* 1a) **Blessed are those who fear the Lord.**

> Blessed are you who fear the LORD,
> > who walk in his ways!
> For you shall eat the fruit of your handiwork;
> > blessed shall you be, and favored. ℟.

*(continued)*

Your wife shall be like a fruitful vine
in the recesses of your home;
your children like olive plants
around your table. R̸.

Behold, thus is the man blessed
who fears the LORD.
The LORD bless you from Zion:
may you see the prosperity of Jerusalem
all the days of your life. R̸.

## READING II (1 Thessalonians 5:1-6)

### A reading from the first Letter of Saint Paul to the Thessalonians

*Let the day of the Lord not overtake you like a thief.*

**Concerning times and seasons, brothers and sisters,
you have no need for anything to be written to you.
For you yourselves know very well that the day of the
Lord will come
like a thief at night.
When people are saying, "Peace and security,"
then sudden disaster comes upon them,
like labor pains upon a pregnant woman,
and they will not escape.**

**But you, brothers and sisters, are not in darkness,
for that day to overtake you like a thief.
For all of you are children of the light
and children of the day.
We are not of the night or of darkness.
Therefore, let us not sleep as the rest do,
but let us stay alert and sober.**

The word of the Lord. All: **Thanks be to God.**

GOSPEL (Matthew 25:14-30) *or* Shorter Form [ ] (Matthew 25:14-15, 19-21)

ALLELUIA (John 15:4a, 5b)

℣. Alleluia, alleluia. ℟. **Alleluia, alleluia.**

℣. Remain in me as I remain in you, says the Lord.
Whoever remains in me bears much fruit. ℟.

✠ **A reading from the holy Gospel according to Matthew**

All: **Glory to you, O Lord.**

*Since you were faithful in small matters, come, share your master's joy.*

[**Jesus told his disciples this parable:**
   **"A man going on a journey**
   **called in his servants and entrusted his possessions to**
         **them.**
**To one he gave five talents; to another, two; to a third,**
      **one—**
   **to each according to his ability.**
**Then he went away.]**
**Immediately the one who received five talents went and**
         **traded with them,**
   **and made another five.**
**Likewise, the one who received two made another two.**
**But the man who received one went off and dug a hole in**
      **the ground**
   **and buried his master's money.**

[**"After a long time**
   **the master of those servants came back**
   **and settled accounts with them.**
**The one who had received five talents came forward**
   **bringing the additional five.**
**He said, 'Master, you gave me five talents.**
**See, I have made five more.'**
**His master said to him, 'Well done, my good and faithful**
      **servant.**

Since you were faithful in small matters,
  I will give you great responsibilities.
Come, share your master's joy.']
Then the one who had received two talents also came
    forward and said,
  'Master, you gave me two talents.
See, I have made two more.'
His master said to him, 'Well done, my good and faithful
    servant.
Since you were faithful in small matters,
  I will give you great responsibilities.
Come, share your master's joy.'
Then the one who had received the one talent came
    forward and said,
  'Master, I knew you were a demanding person,
  harvesting where you did not plant
  and gathering where you did not scatter;
  so out of fear I went off and buried your talent in the
      ground.
Here it is back.'
His master said to him in reply, 'You wicked, lazy servant!
So you knew that I harvest where I did not plant
  and gather where I did not scatter?
Should you not then have put my money in the bank
  so that I could have got it back with interest on my
      return?
Now then! Take the talent from him and give it to the
    one with ten.
For to everyone who has,
  more will be given and he will grow rich;
  but from the one who has not,
  even what he has will be taken away.
And throw this useless servant into the darkness outside,
  where there will be wailing and grinding of teeth.'"

The Gospel of the Lord. All: **Praise to you, Lord Jesus Christ.**

PRAYER OVER THE OFFERINGS
Grant, O Lord, we pray,
that what we offer in the sight of your majesty
may obtain for us the grace of being devoted to you
and gain us the prize of everlasting happiness.
Through Christ our Lord. All: **Amen.**

COMMUNION ANTIPHON (Psalm 73[72]:28).
To be near God is my happiness,
to place my hope in God the Lord.

Or:

(Mark 11:23-24)
Amen, I say to you: Whatever you ask in prayer,
believe that you will receive,
and it shall be given to you, says the Lord.

PRAYER AFTER COMMUNION
We have partaken of the gifts of this sacred mystery,
humbly imploring, O Lord,
that what your Son commanded us to do
in memory of him
may bring us growth in charity.
Through Christ our Lord. All: **Amen.**

# Our Lord Jesus Christ, King of the Universe

*November 26, 2017*

---

*Reflection on the Gospel*

*Christ the King* will *come "in his glory." It is not "if" he will come, but "when." There is an imperative in the immediacy of this "when." The gospel claim is clear: Christ the King, arrayed in all his glory, is present now in the other. His throne is the person of the other. The "when" is now. The kingdom of God is now. The judgment is now. In our care for others here and now, Christ the King reigns.*

- *Christ will hand over the kingdom to his God and Father so that God may be all in all.*

—Living Liturgy™, *Christ the King 2017*

ENTRANCE ANTIPHON (Revelation 5:12; 1:6)
How worthy is the Lamb who was slain,
to receive power and divinity,
and wisdom and strength and honor.
To him belong glory and power for ever and ever.

COLLECT
Almighty ever-living God,
whose will is to restore all things
in your beloved Son, the King of the universe,
grant, we pray,
that the whole creation, set free from slavery,
may render your majesty service
and ceaselessly proclaim your praise.
Through our Lord Jesus Christ, your Son,
who lives and reigns with you in the unity of the Holy Spirit,
one God, for ever and ever. All: **Amen.**

READING I (L 160-A) (Ezekiel 34:11-12, 15-17)
**A reading from the Book of the Prophet Ezekiel**

*As for you, my flock, I will judge between one sheep and another.*

Thus says the Lord GOD:
> I myself will look after and tend my sheep.

As a shepherd tends his flock
> when he finds himself among his scattered sheep,
> so will I tend my sheep.

I will rescue them from every place where they were
> scattered
> when it was cloudy and dark.

I myself will pasture my sheep;
> I myself will give them rest, says the Lord GOD.

The lost I will seek out,
> the strayed I will bring back,
> the injured I will bind up,
> the sick I will heal,
> but the sleek and the strong I will destroy,
> shepherding them rightly.

As for you, my sheep, says the Lord GOD,
> I will judge between one sheep and another,
> between rams and goats.

The word of the Lord. All: Thanks be to God.

RESPONSORIAL PSALM 23

P-171

The Lord is my shep - herd; there is noth-ing I shall want.

Music: Jay F. Hunstiger, © 1990, administered by Liturgical Press. All rights reserved.

Psalm 23:1-2, 2-3, 5-6

R︎. (1) **The Lord is my shepherd; there is nothing I shall
want.**

> The LORD is my shepherd; I shall not want.
> > In verdant pastures he gives me repose. R︎.

> Beside restful waters he leads me;
> > he refreshes my soul.
> He guides me in right paths
> > for his name's sake. R︎.

*(continued)*

You spread the table before me
in the sight of my foes;
you anoint my head with oil;
my cup overflows. R℣.

Only goodness and kindness follow me
all the days of my life;
and I shall dwell in the house of the Lord
for years to come. R℣.

## READING II (1 Corinthians 15:20-26, 28)

**A reading from the first Letter of Saint Paul to the Corinthians**

*Christ will hand over the kingdom to his God and Father so that God may be all in all.*

**Brothers and sisters:**
**Christ has been raised from the dead,**
**the firstfruits of those who have fallen asleep.**
**For since death came through man,**
**the resurrection of the dead came also through man.**
**For just as in Adam all die,**
**so too in Christ shall all be brought to life,**
**but each one in proper order:**
**Christ the firstfruits;**
**then, at his coming, those who belong to Christ;**
**then comes the end,**
**when he hands over the kingdom to his God and**
**Father,**
**when he has destroyed every sovereignty**
**and every authority and power.**
**For he must reign until he has put all his enemies under**
**his feet.**
**The last enemy to be destroyed is death.**
**When everything is subjected to him,**
**then the Son himself will also be subjected**
**to the one who subjected everything to him,**
**so that God may be all in all.**

**The word of the Lord.** All: **Thanks be to God.**

GOSPEL (Matthew 25:31-46)
ALLELUIA (Mark 11:9, 10)

℣. Alleluia, alleluia.  ℟. **Alleluia, alleluia.**

℣. Blessed is he who comes in the name of the Lord!
Blessed is the kingdom of our father David that is to
come! ℟.

✝ **A reading from the holy Gospel according to Matthew**

All: **Glory to you, O Lord.**

*The Son of Man will sit upon his glorious throne and he will
separate them one from another.*

**Jesus said to his disciples:**
**"When the Son of Man comes in his glory,**
**and all the angels with him,**
**he will sit upon his glorious throne,**
**and all the nations will be assembled before him.**
**And he will separate them one from another,**
**as a shepherd separates the sheep from the goats.**
**He will place the sheep on his right and the goats on**
**his left.**
**Then the king will say to those on his right,**
**'Come, you who are blessed by my Father.**
**Inherit the kingdom prepared for you from the**
**foundation of the world.**
**For I was hungry and you gave me food,**
**I was thirsty and you gave me drink,**
**a stranger and you welcomed me,**
**naked and you clothed me,**
**ill and you cared for me,**
**in prison and you visited me.'**
**Then the righteous will answer him and say,**
**'Lord, when did we see you hungry and feed you,**
**or thirsty and give you drink?**
**When did we see you a stranger and welcome you,**
**or naked and clothe you?**
**When did we see you ill or in prison, and visit you?'**

And the king will say to them in reply,
'Amen, I say to you, whatever you did
for one of the least brothers of mine, you did for me.'
Then he will say to those on his left,
'Depart from me, you accursed,
into the eternal fire prepared for the devil and his
angels.
For I was hungry and you gave me no food,
I was thirsty and you gave me no drink,
a stranger and you gave me no welcome,
naked and you gave me no clothing,
ill and in prison, and you did not care for me.'
Then they will answer and say,
'Lord, when did we see you hungry or thirsty
or a stranger or naked or ill or in prison,
and not minister to your needs?'
He will answer them, 'Amen, I say to you,
what you did not do for one of these least ones,
you did not do for me.'
And these will go off to eternal punishment,
but the righteous to eternal life."

**The Gospel of the Lord.** All: **Praise to you, Lord Jesus Christ.**

PRAYER OVER THE OFFERINGS
As we offer you, O Lord, the sacrifice
by which the human race is reconciled to you,
we humbly pray
that your Son himself may bestow on all nations
the gifts of unity and peace.
Through Christ our Lord. All: **Amen.**

COMMUNION ANTIPHON (Psalm 29[28]:10-11)
The Lord sits as King for ever.
The Lord will bless his people with peace.

PRAYER AFTER COMMUNION

Having received the food of immortality,
we ask, O Lord,
that, glorying in obedience
to the commands of Christ, the King of the universe,
we may live with him eternally in his heavenly Kingdom.
Who lives and reigns for ever and ever. All: **Amen.**

# EUCHARISTIC PRAYER FOR RECONCILIATION I

Preface

It is truly right and just
that we should always give you thanks,
Lord, holy Father, almighty and eternal God.

For you do not cease to spur us on
to possess a more abundant life
and, being rich in mercy,
you constantly offer pardon
and call on sinners
to trust in your forgiveness alone.

Never did you turn away from us,
and, though time and again we have broken your covenant,
you have bound the human family to yourself
through Jesus your Son, our Redeemer,
with a new bond of love so tight
that it can never be undone.

Even now you set before your people
a time of grace and reconciliation,
and, as they turn back to you in spirit,
you grant them hope in Christ Jesus
and a desire to be of service to all,
while they entrust themselves
more fully to the Holy Spirit.

And so, filled with wonder,
we extol the power of your love,
and, proclaiming our joy

at the salvation that comes from you,
we join in the heavenly hymn of countless hosts,
as without end we acclaim:

**Holy, Holy, Holy Lord God of hosts.**
**Heaven and earth are full of your glory.**
**Hosanna in the highest.**
**Blessed is he who comes in the name of the Lord.**
**Hosanna in the highest.**

Priest:

You are indeed Holy, O Lord,
and from the world's beginning
are ceaselessly at work,
so that the human race may become holy,
just as you yourself are holy.
Look, we pray, upon your people's offerings
and pour out on them the power of your Spirit,
that they may become the Body and ✛ Blood
of your beloved Son, Jesus Christ,
in whom we, too, are your sons and daughters.

Indeed, though we once were lost
and could not approach you,
you loved us with the greatest love:
for your Son, who alone is just,
handed himself over to death,
and did not disdain to be nailed for our sake
to the wood of the Cross.

But before his arms were outstretched between heaven and earth,
to become the lasting sign of your covenant,
he desired to celebrate the Passover with his disciples.

As he ate with them,
he took bread
and, giving you thanks, he said the blessing,
broke the bread and gave it to them, saying:

Take this, all of you, and eat of it,
for this is my Body,
which will be given up for you.

In a similar way, when supper was ended,
knowing that he was about to reconcile all things in himself
through his Blood to be shed on the Cross,
he took the chalice, filled with the fruit of the vine,
and once more giving you thanks,
handed the chalice to his disciples, saying:

Take this, all of you, and drink from it,
for this is the chalice of my Blood,
the Blood of the new and eternal covenant,
which will be poured out for you and for many
for the forgiveness of sins.

Do this in memory of me.

The mystery of faith.

People:

**A**    **We proclaim your Death, O Lord,
and profess your Resurrection
until you come again.**

**B**    **When we eat this Bread and drink this Cup,
we proclaim your Death, O Lord,
until you come again.**

**C**    **Save us, Savior of the world,
for by your Cross and Resurrection
you have set us free.**

Priest:

Therefore, as we celebrate
the memorial of your Son Jesus Christ,
who is our Passover and our surest peace,
we celebrate his Death and Resurrection from the dead,
and looking forward to his blessed Coming,
we offer you, who are our faithful and merciful God,
this sacrificial Victim
who reconciles to you the human race.

Look kindly, most compassionate Father,
on those you unite to yourself
by the Sacrifice of your Son,
and grant that, by the power of the Holy Spirit,
as they partake of this one Bread and one Chalice,
they may be gathered into one Body in Christ,
who heals every division.

Be pleased to keep us always
in communion of mind and heart,
together with N. our Pope and N. our Bishop.*
Help us to work together

---

\* Mention may be made here of the Coadjutor Bishop, or Auxiliary Bishops,
as noted in the *General Instruction of the Roman Missal*, no. 149.

for the coming of your Kingdom,
until the hour when we stand before you,
Saints among the Saints in the halls of heaven,
with the Blessed Virgin Mary, Mother of God,
the blessed Apostles and all the Saints,
and with our deceased brothers and sisters,
whom we humbly commend to your mercy.

Then, freed at last from the wound of corruption
and made fully into a new creation,
we shall sing to you with gladness
the thanksgiving of Christ,
who lives for all eternity.

Through him, and with him, and in him,
O God, almighty Father,
in the unity of the Holy Spirit,
all glory and honor is yours,
for ever and ever.

People: **Amen.**

Then follows the Communion Rite, p. 23.

## EUCHARISTIC PRAYER FOR RECONCILIATION II

Preface
It is truly right and just
that we should give you thanks and praise,
O God, almighty Father,
for all you do in this world,
through our Lord Jesus Christ.

For though the human race
is divided by dissension and discord,
yet we know that by testing us
you change our hearts
to prepare them for reconciliation.

Even more, by your Spirit you move human hearts
that enemies may speak to each other again,
adversaries may join hands,
and peoples seek to meet together.

By the working of your power
it comes about, O Lord,
that hatred is overcome by love,
revenge gives way to forgiveness,
and discord is changed to mutual respect.

Therefore, as we give you ceaseless thanks
with the choirs of heaven,
we cry out to your majesty on earth,
and without end we acclaim:

**Holy, Holy, Holy Lord God of hosts.**
**Heaven and earth are full of your glory.**
**Hosanna in the highest.**
**Blessed is he who comes in the name of the Lord.**
**Hosanna in the highest.**

Priest:

You, therefore, almighty Father,
we bless through Jesus Christ your Son,
who comes in your name.
He himself is the Word that brings salvation,
the hand you extend to sinners,
the way by which your peace is offered to us.
When we ourselves had turned away from you
on account of our sins,
you brought us back to be reconciled, O Lord,
so that, converted at last to you,
we might love one another
through your Son,
whom for our sake you handed over to death.
And now, celebrating the reconciliation
Christ has brought us,
we entreat you:
sanctify these gifts by the outpouring of your Spirit,
that they may become the Body and ✠ Blood of your Son,
whose command we fulfill when we celebrate these mysteries.

For when about to give his life to set us free,
as he reclined at supper,
he himself took bread into his hands,
and, giving you thanks, he said the blessing,
broke the bread and gave it to his disciples, saying:

**Take this, all of you, and eat of it,**
**for this is my Body,**
**which will be given up for you.**

In a similar way, on that same evening,
he took the chalice of blessing in his hands,
confessing your mercy,
and gave the chalice to his disciples, saying:

TAKE THIS, ALL OF YOU, AND DRINK FROM IT,
FOR THIS IS THE CHALICE OF MY BLOOD,
THE BLOOD OF THE NEW AND ETERNAL COVENANT,
WHICH WILL BE POURED OUT FOR YOU AND FOR MANY
FOR THE FORGIVENESS OF SINS.

DO THIS IN MEMORY OF ME.

The mystery of faith.

People:

**A**   **We proclaim your Death, O Lord,
and profess your Resurrection
until you come again.**

**B**   **When we eat this Bread and drink this Cup,
we proclaim your Death, O Lord,
until you come again.**

**C**   **Save us, Savior of the world,
for by your Cross and Resurrection
you have set us free.**

Priest:

Celebrating, therefore, the memorial
of the Death and Resurrection of your Son,
who left us this pledge of his love,
we offer you what you have bestowed on us,
the Sacrifice of perfect reconciliation.

Holy Father, we humbly beseech you
to accept us also, together with your Son,
and in this saving banquet
graciously to endow us with his very Spirit,
who takes away everything
that estranges us from one another.

May he make your Church a sign of unity
and an instrument of your peace among all people
and may he keep us in communion
with N. our Pope and N. our Bishop*
and all the Bishops
and your entire people.

Just as you have gathered us now at the table of your Son,
so also bring us together,

---

* Mention may be made here of the Coadjutor Bishop, or Auxiliary Bishops,
as noted in the *General Instruction of the Roman Missal*, no. 149.

with the glorious Virgin Mary, Mother of God,
with your blessed Apostles and all the Saints,
with our brothers and sisters
and those of every race and tongue
who have died in your friendship.
Bring us to share with them the unending banquet of unity
in a new heaven and a new earth,
where the fullness of your peace will shine forth
in Christ Jesus our Lord.

Through him, and with him, and in him,
O God, almighty Father,
in the unity of the Holy Spirit,
all glory and honor is yours,
for ever and ever.

People: **Amen.**

Then follows the Communion Rite, p. 23.